Sibylle Heilbrunn, Muki Tsur
The Kibbutz Between Dialogue and Dilemma

Culture and Social Practice

Sibylle Heilbrunn is affiliated with the Fritz Bauer Forum in Bochum, a space for democracy, diversity and human rights, where she organizes a project fostering German-Israeli dialogue on political responsibility and democratic resilience. She also serves as a visiting professor at Touro University Berlin. She earned her PhD in organizational sociology from the University of Haifa in 1999. From 2014 to 2024, she was dean of the School of Social Sciences and Humanities at Kinneret College on the Sea of Galilee. In 2026, she leads the MA in Innovation and Entrepreneurship Management there. Her research explores entrepreneurship through critical theory and intersectionality, focusing on inequality, marginalization, and social positioning, with particular attention to refugee, migrant, and women entrepreneurs.

Muki Tsur is a member of Kibbutz Ein Gev and lectures in pre-military preparatory programs and in frameworks for lifelong learning and senior education. The historian, writer, and educator is an honorary doctorate recipient of the Open University of Israel and has held public positions in his kibbutz, Ein Gev, and within the kibbutz movement. He has authored and edited numerous books and studies on the history of practical Zionism, the kibbutz movement, and Hebrew culture. His research focuses on collective memory, social and kibbutz identity, and key figures in the history of settlement and Israeli society.

Sibylle Heilbrunn, Muki Tsur

The Kibbutz Between Dialogue and Dilemma

Community, Conflict, and Collective Thinking as Lived Practice

[transcript]

The writing and publication of this book were made possible by the generous support of the University of Haifa and the Friends of Yad Tabenkin-United Kibbutz Movement Archives.

Bibliographic information published by the Deutsche Nationalbibliothek
The Deutsche Nationalbibliothek lists this publication in the Deutsche Nationalbibliografie; detailed bibliographic data are available online at https://dnb.dnb.de

Hermannstraße 26 | D-33602 Bielefeld | live@transcript-verlag.de

Cover design: Kordula Röckenhaus
Printing: Elanders Waiblingen GmbH, Waiblingen
https://doi.org/10.14361/9783839477588
Print-ISBN: 978-3-8376-7857-4 | PDF-ISBN: 978-3-8394-7758-8
ISSN of series: 2703-0024 | eISSN of series: 2703-0032

Printed on permanent acid-free text paper.

We dedicate this book to Avishai Grossman (1937–2023)
and to our families and friends

Contents

Foreword 9

Acknowledgements 13

1. **Why This Conversation, and Why Now?**
   Setting the Stage 15

2. **Where Did the Kibbutz Idea Come From?**
   Founding Motives, Biographies, and Ideological Crossroads 29

3. **Who Gets to Belong?**
   Bounded Equality in the Kibbutz 45

4. **Who Gets to Make the Soup?**
   Gender, Labor, and the Paradoxes of Equality 61

5. **Who Raises the Children?**
   Transmission, Rebellion, and Renewal 75

6. **Will the Lazy and the Diligent Balance Out?**
   Work, Motivation, and Evolving Contributions 97

7. **Can the Artist Be a Worker?**
   Art, Culture, and the Question of Productivity 113

8. **Whose Factory Is It?**
Enterprise, Industry, and Innovation 131

9. **What Do We Know and Refuse to Know?**
Land and the Kibbutz 147

10. **Can Solidarity Be Initiated?**
The Kibbutz Movement after October 7 165

11. **Can the Kibbutz Carry Its Unresolved Questions?**
A Retrospective Synthesis 183

12. **Is the Room Still Open?**
For Avishai Grossman 207

Appendix: A Six-panel Visual Timeline of the Kibbutz Movement, 1880–2026 221

References 229

Glossary 235

Foreword

In this book, Sibylle Heilbrunn and Muki Tsur attempt a historical and praxeological reconstruction of a history spanning over a century, one that is closely linked to Jewish history in the late ninetheenth and, in particular, the twentieth century. In doing so, they interweave their respective biographies and personal, at times quite divergent, interpretations of concepts and practices with philosophical and social-scientific perspectives. As the reader progresses through the text, it becomes clear that their approaches could hardly be more different.

At first glance, it seems rather unlikely that such a contrasting pair of authors could develop a shared perspective. Yet it is precisely from this diversity and contrast that a bifocal view of extraordinary depth emerges. This is probably only possible because both have been familiar with building bridges for decades and are committed – in different ways – to understanding and dialogue. Not least, mutual deep respect and personal affinity also help to create a solid foundation for the necessary discourse, beyond theoretical positions and possible ideological differences.

In doing so, Sibylle Heilbrunn and Muki Tsur do not shy away from difficult and, in some cases, personally painful topics. They lay bare misconceptions and dashed hopes and acknowledge assessments that clearly could not stand up to subsequent reality. Where speaking for themselves is no longer possible, eyewitnesses are given a voice to explore the respective topic from their perspective.

The presented reconstruction of the theory and practice of the kibbutz should not be read episodically in the sense of mere individual stories. Rather, the developments of the Israeli kibbutzim are embedded in what one would today call a systemic context of social, economic and political developments in Palestine and later in Israel. The stylistic device of the episode serves here to give concrete form to the general; the stories told are not chosen at random, but represent ideal-typical, constitutive moments in the history of the kibbutz. In this respect, the reconstructive approach is reminiscent of Anthony Giddens' theory of structuration (Giddens, 1984), which focuses on the interplay between individual action and social structures. It is all the more commendable that the authors do not merely recount a success story of the kibbutz, but engage critically – and self-critically – with the sometimes tragic translations of 'good' ideas into a practice that often proved contradictory.

In this context, it is worth mentioning an insight from Muki Tsur, which he articulated during a conversation and which is freely reproduced here: an organization that no longer adequately meets the needs of its members loses its raison d'être. Ideology alone is not sufficient in the long run; its implementation must serve life (cf. Zirkler 2019: 60 ff.). The remarks by Sibylle Heilbrunn and Muki Tsur make it clear how guiding principles must continually be revitalized and rematerialized in order to endure. Accordingly, the book – at least on second glance – offers a surplus of meaning: on the one hand, it can be read as a reconstruction of the development of the kibbutzim, but on the other hand also as a history of the transformation of social systems. At the same time, it becomes apparent that every social system generates its own contradictions and dilemmas from which it cannot escape. To this day, however, the kibbutzim in Israel have managed, in very different ways, to find answers that have so far ensured their survival.

Against this backdrop, the fundamental idea of the kibbutz does not appear in any way outdated – on the contrary. Sociological literature from recent years attests to a serious risk of collapse in (at least Western-oriented) societies, rooted in a belief in unlimited possibilities and a performance-oriented mindset (Sennett 1998; Bröckling 2007; Han 2010). While the participants enjoy the material benefits of the capitalist system – insofar as they actually benefit from them – and its meritocratic promises (Sandel 2021), they are increasingly becoming exhausted by its performance-driven demands and all the associated consequences. Communitarian 'alternative models' seem to offer possible ways out here. Today, various like-minded working and living communities can be found in the form of cooperatives, collectives or social enterprise organizations, each of which addresses the longing for cohesion, belonging and solidarity beyond the private sphere in its own, and significantly less radical, way.

The kibbutzim in Israel are also evolving. Today, new forms adapted to the available possibilities can be found, such as so-called 'vertical' kibbutzim in urban areas or 'educator kibbutzim', which are dedicated to training in various fields. These forms seek to preserve the original ideas while reinterpreting their practical implementation. The power that this fundamental idea of the kibbutz can unleash is particularly evident in times of (exogenous) crises, and this too will be discussed.

Much of what is described in this text is based on my own experiences during numerous visits and conversations in Israel. Around ten years before this book was published, we began offering study trips to students on our Bachelor's program in Applied Psychology in Zurich, which Sibylle Heilbrunn and I had planned together and led on site. The group of students from Zurich had the special opportunity to live at Kibbutz En Gev on the Sea of Galilee for just under a week at a time and to experience the daily life of the kibbutz in depth. We invited guests to give lectures and lead workshops on various topics and undertook excursions into the surrounding area to familiarize ourselves – as far as this is at all possible – directly with local conditions. Muki Tsur introduced us to the history of the kibbutzim and, during his guided tours of En Gev, explained important events and key turning points. In the small museum documenting the history of En Gev, we were able to marvel at the achievements of the pioneers and learn essential facts about the ideological basis of the kibbutz movement as well as daily life on the kibbutz. During my repeated visits to En Gev, I also had a series of in-depth conversations with Muki Tsur, most recently one on leadership, which was deeply inspiring and which I incorporated in parts into my lectures. Although we never spoke explicitly about it, I gained the impression that, with regard to the kibbutzim, Muki espouses an ethic that prioritizes goodwill, kindness and forbearance, an attitude that Nicolas Rescher has described as a genuine and serious concern for people's interests (Rescher 1989).

Conversely, during those years, Arab and Palestinian as well as Jewish and Israeli students, albeit in significantly smaller numbers, also had the opportunity to undertake study trips to Switzerland. These trips were organized by Sibylle Heilbrunn and accompanied by colleagues from the Kinneret Academic College on the Sea of Galilee, where Sibylle was working at the time. Among others, Muki's daughter Zohar Tsur was part of this group.

Many of our students, including quite a few Germans studying in Switzerland, were deeply impressed by their experiences in and around En Gev. For many, these were their first 'real' encounters with Jewish life in general and with a communitarian way of life in particular. Above all, the idea of prioritizing community over (capitalist) self-interest and profit maximization met with widespread approval. At the same time, quite a few felt that such an approach would be difficult to implement in Switzerland. And yet the critique of consumerism and capitalism inherent in the kibbutz proved to strike a strong chord, just as Erich Fromm had already succinctly formulated it in his well-known book *To Have or To Be* (Fromm 1976). The psychologically well-documented tension between community, belonging and cohesion on the one hand, and individuality, personally attributable success and career on the other, as elaborated, for instance, in the psychology of Fritz Riemann (2021) is also clearly observable in this country. In this respect, En Gev was always a kind of real-world laboratory for us as teachers and students: a place where we could study, in a concrete way, how people in Israel, and specifically in the kibbutz, deal with the challenges arising from the tension between community, the individual and economic viability. It also became apparent that the kibbutzim repeatedly faced existential questions and, in some cases, paid a high price by having to make do with very little for extended periods.

This book by Sibylle Heilbrunn and Muki Tsur offers fundamental insights into the fundamental questions of human life, which are presumably inherent to the *human condition* (Arendt 1958/2020). It is to be hoped that this book will find a wide readership and give new impetus to the discourse on the role of communities based on solidarity.

Basel and Zurich, May 2026
Prof. Dr. Michael Zirkler

Acknowledgements

Sibylle Heilbrunn: This book grew out of conversation, and so any list of thanks must begin with my partner in that conversation. To Muki Tsur, for the inspiring talks and exchanges that became this book, for a true intellectual discourse, and for a true friendship that ran through all of it. To Zohar Tsur, Muki's daughter, who kept us going: organizing our meetings, sustaining the rhythm of our work, and becoming part of the dialogue herself.

To Ori Idan, who transcribed every interview, and who was far more than a transcriber, an inspiring partner in thinking through what we had said and what it meant. To Michael Zirkler, who wrote the foreword and who listened patiently to my lamentations about how to proceed when the way forward was not yet clear. To Chen Boyer, who took the time to make photographs of Muki and myself.

I am grateful to Shuli Dichter, who educated us about the questions discussed in Chapter 9. I learned a great deal from him, and I believe in his perspective on the Palestinian–Jewish/Israeli question. Thanks also to Avital and Atar Geva of Kibbutz Ein Shemer, who gave their time to be interviewed for the chapter on the arts, and to our son Ran Heilbrunn, who helped shape that chapter into its final form. His partner Keith Whitson is my technological pillar, and thank you Keith for designing the appendix for our book.

To my dearest friends in Germany, Ingeborg and Wolf Schroedter, and Claudia and Friedemann Heck, a very special thanks. Inge was the first reader of the English chapter drafts, commenting on both content and style from the perspective of a German audience rather unfamiliar with the kibbutz, its history and its present. Friedemann then received the AI-translated German chapters and carried out the German-language editing, engaging closely with both content and style. To both of you, my deep gratitude.

Over the year and a half of writing, I spoke about kibbutz dilemmas with everyone in my environment, whether they welcomed it or not. Our bicycle group, most of them kibbutz members themselves, were drawn into the conversation every Saturday morning, and they added valuable insights week after week, so that this book grew by one fact, one perspective, at a time. Conversations with our close friends, Avital Nadler, Gidi Maestro, Ales and Avner Shomroni, Noah Michaeli and Nimrod Bessor, Yoav and Revital Ben Naftali kept circling the book's questions and dilemmas. My thanks to all of you for the patience and the perspectives you added.

And finally, to my partner Alex, who had to listen to my dilemma of the day, again and again, and never lost his patience.

In these very difficult times in Israel, it is good to be surrounded by friends.

Muki Tsur: I wish to thank the Institute for Kibbutz Studies at the University of Haifa for many years of trust and shared inquiry.

I wish to thank my students, members of the urban kibbutzim, instructors of the youth movements, students of the pre-military academies (*mechinot*), and adult learners from kibbutzim across the country, who have given me, over the years, both inspiration and information of real value.

I wish to thank my daughter Zohar Tsur, who carried the organizational side of the conversations between Sibylle and myself, and whose own work leading the community of Kibbutz Ein Gev brought into our dialogue the very questions that community is now living with.

And I wish to thank my family, who have accompanied me and my work, from my youth into old age, with love and with humor.

1. Why This Conversation, and Why Now?
Setting the Stage

Kibbutz Ein Gev in 1950

Source: Archives Ein Gev, photographer unknown

The kibbutz is inevitably and deeply entangled in both our biographies, though in different ways and to different extents. Muki Tsur, my friend and the main narrator of this book, lives with his family at Kibbutz Ein Gev, his house on the very shores of the Sea of Galilee. I myself came to Israel in the late 1970s as a volunteer at Kibbutz Barkai, to investigate the communal idea. I was then a young student of empirical cultural sciences at the University of Tübingen, and found the communal experiment extremely intriguing.

The communitarian ethos has resurfaced at pivotal moments throughout human history, often as an alternative to prevailing social and economic systems unable to address fundamental human problems. It has frequently emerged as a response to the alienation, competition, and inequality associated with capitalist developments. The impulse to create communal aspiration and vision is particularly evident in moments of social upheaval, rapid change, and crisis.

Looking back across the sweep of human history, communal life has emerged time and again as a compelling response to the tensions between spiritual ideals, economic justice, and the longing for belonging. Rooted in religious devotion, shaped by evolving social contracts, and adapted to changing material and societal realities, the historical waves of communalism reveal both a persistent human urge for something different, a different form of society, and the diverse forms that urge has taken.

The earliest waves of communal life were grounded in religious foundations, where shared rituals and collective organization served both spiritual and practical ends. In ancient Jerusalem, the Temple community exemplified how sacred space could anchor not only worship but an integrated social and economic life. Priestly orders and lay participants maintained a communal rhythm of work, charity, and celebration, fostering solidarity rooted in covenant and tradition. Early Christianity, too, particularly as recorded in the Acts of the Apostles, adopted models of radical sharing and resource distribution. These communities challenged the prevailing individualism and hierarchy of Roman society, pioneering ideals of compassion and mutual care that would echo through the centuries. The early Islamic Ummah recapitulated these themes: under the Constitution of Medina, Muslims, local tribes, and allies forged a collective identity grounded in cooperation, mutual protection, and economic sharing, enacting in practice the values of zakat and social responsibility. In the East, the Buddhist Sangha established by the Buddha in the fifth century BCE provided yet another dimension: a spiritual community structured by codes of discipline and ethics, sustaining itself on charity and united by shared aspiration. In the American context, the first historical wave of communalism was catalyzed by religious migration. German Protestant pietists such as the Ephrata Cloister in Pennsylvania (1730s) and the Shakers, led by Ann Lee (1770s), created enduring models of group living grounded in faith, discipline, and mutual aid. The Shakers, in particular, became the most robust utopian movement in American history, establishing eighteen communities over more than two centuries.

The advent of industrial capitalism, with its profound disruptions and developing inequalities, provoked a "golden age" of intentional community. This second wave included Owenite, Fourierist, Oneida Perfectionist, Mormon, and Amana communities, at least 119 experiments between 1800 and 1859, as documented by historian Sterling F. Delano (2004). Secular socialism was realized in such places as Robert Owen's New Harmony and the Fourierist phalansteries, which envisioned pleasure and fulfillment through communal labor and social planning. Religious experiments thrived alongside: the Shakers added innovation and gender equality to the ethos of celibacy and collective ownership; the Oneida Community reimagined marriage, child-rearing, and economic production. Across the Atlantic, experiments like the Familistère in France and John Ruskin's Guild of St. George blended nostalgia for pre-industrial values with critiques of modernity, pioneering cooperative principles that would later inform broader movements. While these nineteenth-century endeavors left a mixed legacy, the enduring desire for alternatives provided fertile ground for new approaches in the rapidly changing context of the twentieth century. This wave was characterized by smaller, more targeted communities, early forms of cohousing in Scandinavia, cooperative housing projects, and the influence of the German *Lebensreform* and *Wandervogel* movements, which sought to recover a sense of harmony with nature and community in the face of deepening urbanization and alienation.

Each historical wave of communalism has combined critique of contemporary realities with creativity in suggesting alternatives. Whether emerging from religious ideals, social crisis, or ideological vision, communal experiments have offered a laboratory for negotiating the contradictions of human society between individual and collective, tradition and innovation, production and compassion. Most faded or were transformed, challenged by internal tensions or changing circumstances, yet their recurrent emergence points to a fundamental human desire for a life rich in connection, meaning, and shared destiny.

Against this backdrop of recurring communal experimentation, with its cycles of hope, innovation, and transformation, a new chapter was about to unfold. It was in this tradition that, at the start of the twentieth century, a new and more enduring experiment in communal living took shape, the subject of our book: the kibbutz in Palestine/Israel. Emerging in a context of both socialist ideals and Zionist aspirations, the kibbutz was intended by its founders as a unique model for building a new society.

The early kibbutz movement was deeply influenced by socialist and anarchist ideals prevalent in Europe at the time. The writings of Karl Marx, with his critique of capitalist alienation, and Gustav Landauer (Landauer, 1919), with his vision of decentralized, self-governing communities, offered a powerful framework for imagining alternative social orders. These ideas found fertile ground among the pioneers of the kibbutzim, who sought to create a society based on equality, cooperation, and collective ownership. Unlike its utopian predecessors, which tended to remain marginal or dissolve under external and internal pressures, the kibbutz successfully enacted principles of collective ownership, democratic participation, and radical economic equality on a remarkable scale for an extended period. Emerging from socialist and Zionist currents in Palestine, it became not only a strategy for agricultural and national development, but also a vehicle for personal and collective transformation. Its members strove to transcend division by class, gender, and origin, forging a society centered on shared responsibility, trust, and hope. Over the decades, kibbutzim would become sites of ongoing innovation in education, gender equality, and moral philosophy, illustrating both the flexibility and the challenges of communal life.

The kibbutz's journey exposes the enduring dilemmas and creative potential inherent in the communal idea. Our book circles around these dilemmas, negotiating the contradictions of human society between individual and collective, tradition and innovation, production and compassion. As we enter the twenty-first century, characterized by unprecedented economic volatility from the 2008 financial crisis to housing unaffordability driving young people toward co-housing experiments, by rapid technological transformation that increases social isolation, and by social fragmentation evidenced in political polarization from Brexit to rising authoritarianism globally, the long history of communal experimentation urges us to reconsider the possibilities of collective life and shared purpose. Nowhere is this more relevant than in Israel, where contemporary crises, political polarization, the decline of liberal democracy, security threats, and socioeconomic instability, underscore both the risks of isolation and the promise of solidarity. The kibbutz, uniquely Israeli yet globally resonant, stands not merely as a relic of the past but as a dynamic reference point for understanding the material, ethical, and creative foundations upon which communal living can be rebuilt and reimagined.

The Continuing Relevance of the Kibbutz Experiment

The kibbutz story has drawn considerable scholarly attention over the decades, generating extensive academic research, articles, and publications across multiple languages. Yet we believe our contribution offers something distinctive, particularly given how the resilience and enduring relevance of the kibbutz ideal received dramatic confirmation during two pivotal moments of the last decade.

The first confirmation emerged during the COVID-19 pandemic and the societal upheaval it unleashed. This crisis prompted a surprising wave of Israelis to reconsider kibbutz life, a rural way of living that many had dismissed as a relic of Israel's socialist past. The pandemic revealed the kibbutz's structural advantages: quality of life remained notably high, especially for children and elderly members, while established patterns of shared leadership and communal solidarity enabled kibbutz communities to navigate this unprecedented period with remarkable resilience. Where individual households struggled in isolation, kibbutz members found strength in collective response and mutual support.

The second, more profound confirmation came in the aftermath of the October 7, 2023 attack on Israel's southern border communities. This unprecedented crisis forced the evacuation of over 143,000 people from kibbutzim and neighboring settlements, yet it also catalyzed an extraordinary demonstration of solidarity that illuminated the enduring vitality of communal values. The kibbutz movement's response encompassed immediate shelter provision, sophisticated coordination networks, and a remarkable transformation from spontaneous aid into sustained reciprocal relationships. This crisis response effectively reactivated foundational principles of mutual aid and collective responsibility, values that had appeared dormant during decades of economic privatization and ideological retreat.

These events demonstrated that the kibbutz idea remains far more than a historical curiosity; it constitutes a vital force capable of generating innovative responses to contemporary challenges. The movement's capacity to mobilize resources, coordinate complex logistics, and sustain community bonds under extreme pressure provides compelling evidence for renewed examination of communal experiments in our era of global uncertainty and social fragmentation.

Our book emerges from this recognition. We seek to understand not only what the kibbutz has been, but what it continues to offer, both to Israeli society grappling with internal divisions and external threats, and to a world increasingly aware of the limitations of purely individualistic responses to collective challenges. Through dialogue and careful attention to persistent dilemmas, we explore how communal experiments adapt, endure, and renew themselves across generations of change.

As Europe also faces growing social inequality, with housing costs forcing creative alternatives such as the co-housing boom in Scandinavia, and contends with the upheavals of globalization that have sparked everything from Brexit to the rise of intentional communities seeking local resilience, the kibbutz presents a powerful case study in alternative economic arrangements, where equality, cooperation, and solidarity challenge the dominance of individualistic capitalism. By analyzing its triumphs and shortcomings, we glean vital lessons about the potential for crafting more just, sustainable, and equitable societies in times of uncertainty, both within Israel and beyond.

Who We Are

Our analysis is not conducted from a position of detached scholarship. The kibbutz is deeply entangled in both our biographies, though in different ways and to different extents. My own path led me from Germany to Israel in the late 1970s, as a volunteer at Kibbutz Barkai, driven by a desire to investigate the communal idea firsthand. As a young student of empirical cultural sciences at the University of Tübingen, I found the communal experiment not only intellectually intriguing but transformative for my evolving professional identity.

Muki Tsur stands as one of the most influential intellectuals of Israeli society and the kibbutz movement. Born in Jerusalem in March 1938, at the time of the *Anschluss*, he spent his early childhood in South America, where his father represented the State of Israel between 1949 and 1953. There, as he recalls, "I joined a youth movement, and at age eleven I decided to live on a kibbutz, even though I didn't know what that meant." When his father became ambassador to Paris, Tsur refused "the diplomatic life of our parents in Paris and Moscow" and instead helped found a youth commune in Jerusalem. At eighteen, he arrived with the Amirim core group at Kibbutz Ein Gev, a border community on the eastern shore of the Sea of Galilee, and enlisted in the *Nahal*. He has served as kibbutz secretary three times.

After the Six-Day War, the historian in him emerged strongly: he co-edited *The Seventh Day*, the influential collection of soldiers' reflections published in

1967, and *Conversations Between Young People*. He has taught the history of the Land of Israel at Oranim College of Education and at Jordan Valley College, to Jewish and Arab students alike. From 1989 to 1993 he served as secretary of the United Kibbutz Movement during its years of crisis. Across his writings and his life, he has consistently treated the kibbutz, in his own phrase, as "a story of indispensable hope", a movement continually inventing itself, and Israeli society, through dialogue and pluralism.

My own path to this collaboration followed a very different trajectory. I was born in Germany, where my family still lives, and my first experience in Israel began in 1977 as a volunteer at Kibbutz Barkai. It was there that I met my partner, and together we built our life in Pardes Hanna, raising three children. The two boys now live in Germany; our daughter lives with her partner and our four grandchildren right next door. For ten years I served as Dean of the School of Social Sciences and Humanities at Kinneret Academic College, a position that allowed me to bridge worlds, both academically and personally.

After my initial kibbutz stay, I returned to Germany to continue my studies at the University of Tübingen. Soon after, I came back to Israel in the early 1980s and shifted my academic path to sociology and the humanities at Tel Aviv University. I remember my many conversations with Avraham Shomroni, who was then secretary at Barkai, about making the right choices at the university and in the kibbutz. As a German non-Jewish woman living in Israel, I often ask myself why I chose this path, why I have become, in some ways, a "representative" of the German people facing its Jewish history and victims. In 2012, I decided to address this question explicitly in my research, embarking on a journey with Anita Haviv-Horiner to study the national belonging of second-generation Holocaust survivors in Germany and Israel. The resulting interviews formed the core of our book 'Heimat-Vielleicht' (*Perhaps – Homeland*), which reveals how belonging is woven from both collective and intensely personal threads.

Reflecting on my personal journey, I cannot separate my work from my lived experience. Living in Israel, a challenging task in itself, was always predicated on the possibility of regular travel abroad. COVID shook the foundations of that "deal" for the first time, and the aftermath of October 7, 2023 challenged my willingness to stay, forcing me to reconsider repeatedly.

Throughout my career, I have sought to expose the structural forces that shape opportunity and exclusion. In my research on entrepreneurs across Israel's diverse social spaces, I have emphasized the unique challenges faced by particular groups against the backdrop of the universal phenomenon of entrepreneurship, exposing the structural inequalities that disadvantage them. Underlying all my research is the conviction that stories of belonging and exclusion, privilege and disadvantage, tell us how society itself can be repaired.

And so I find my personal story deeply entwined with the questions at the heart of this book: Who belongs, and on what terms? What does it mean to build a new life, to redefine home, to challenge inherited boundaries of nationality, class, and culture? For me, these are not merely academic questions but the foundation of my life story, and of my continuing journey as both scholar and participant in the ongoing work of social creation.

How We Started Working Together

These parallel yet intersecting journeys, Muki's lifelong commitment to kibbutz life and my scholarly fascination with the communal experiment, might never have converged into collaborative work without a specific catalyst.

The genesis of our collaboration is inseparable from Kinneret's setting on the shores of the Sea of Galilee, and from the student body I came to know there. It is a mosaic of Israeli society: Jews from nearby cities such as Beit Shean and Tiberias, Palestinian Israelis from towns such as Nazareth, Druze, Circassians, Christians both religious and secular, young women and men from the Golan Heights and from local kibbutzim. For many, entering academia represented their first real encounter with peers outside their own communities, a meeting not without tension, given the complex and often fraught realities of Israeli society.

üIn 2017, three years into my tenure, I was fortunate to meet my esteemed colleague Prof. Dr. Michael Zirkler from the *Zürcher Hochschule für Angewandte Wissenschaften* in Switzerland. Our meeting led to a joint initiative: an educational journey for Swiss students to Israel. It was only natural to welcome them to Kibbutz Ein Gev, both Muki's home and a living embodiment of the themes of this book. For the next six years Muki served as guide for these Swiss visitors, illuminating the kibbutz ethos through stories and walking tours of Ein Gev and its people.

Our intention extended beyond simply introducing Swiss students to the kibbutz or to the Israeli academic environment. Together with Michael Zirkler, who had by then become our dear friend, we aimed to offer a nuanced window into the complexities and conflicts defining both Israeli and Palestinian realities. To this end, we regularly invited Vivian Silver, a close friend of Muki's and a tireless peace activist, to speak about the NGO she had founded together with her Palestinian partner from Gaza. Their testimony, and the dialogue they modeled, left a deep impression on the participants, embodying the possibility of cooperation and hope amid division and violence. For three years, Vivian and her partner captivated Swiss and Israeli students with their personal stories, shared vision, and accounts of concrete peace-building efforts. Tragically, Vivian Silver was murdered in her home at Kibbutz Be'eri during the Hamas attack on October 7, 2023, a devastating loss for all who knew her, and for our hopes for peace. We remain profoundly grateful that our students were able to witness the inspiring exchange that Vivian and her partner brought to life, a testament to the enduring human capacity for dialogue and reconciliation. Their example stands as a quiet sign of hope for better days for all in the region.

Over the course of eight years, encounters between Swiss and Israeli students became a recurring site of dialogue around dilemmas and around evolving understandings of different worlds. In many ways, these exchanges became highlights of my work at Kinneret, and they deepened the bond and shared purpose between Muki and myself.

The second dimension of our collaboration traces back to a course I co-developed at Kinneret College from 2018 to 2020, together with our adopted daughter Maria Gretzky and Zohar Tsur, Muki's daughter. The project extended far beyond traditional academics; it invited students to articulate the contours of their own transitions into adulthood, opening a space for expressing aspirations, grappling with uncertainties, and composing an autobiography not of retrospect but of emergence. Our challenge to the students was both simple and ambitious: "Write the opening chapter of your adult life. Capture not its conclusion but its point of departure. Offer us an autobiography that is vibrant, raw, and unresolved, not a chronicle of a journey completed, but of childhood and youth at the threshold of transformation."

Within these narratives, students explored questions of belonging, the complexities of inherited tradition, and the pursuit of future dreams. Each account revealed the search for anchors that provide a sense of security, as well as the yearning for sails to carry them toward uncharted horizons.

This first book we produced together, titled *Kaleidoscope of the Others*, was, above all, an attempt to amplify the voices of Israel's periphery. All too often the formative experiences of young people at the margins are neglected, omitted from the dominant narratives that construct our collective identity. Our aim was to address this gap and to create space for those whose lived realities and perspectives are rarely brought to the fore. In our work, we were determined not just to collect stories but to foster a sense of agency and visibility for those living outside the centers of cultural and social power. The book became a testament to the diversity, vulnerability, and hopefulness of young Israelis from a variety of communities whose journeys remain underrepresented.

The partnership that grew out of this project was rooted in mutual respect and shared purpose. We did not simply edit texts together; we learned to listen together, to listen truly to how the periphery speaks, dreams, and contends with adversity. With each new voice and narrative, we reinforced our commitment to documenting Israel's social mosaic in all its complexity.

Looking back, I see our collaboration as more than an academic endeavor; it is an act of civic responsibility. The stories we collected and shaped then are not just about individuals; they are about Israeli society's readiness to listen to itself, to repair itself, and to discover hope in previously unrecognized places. Through this process we strove to be both witnesses and facilitators of a wider, more inclusive conversation; anchored in the conviction that every story deserves to be heard.

Muki framed the spirit of our conversations in a passage he titled "A Kind of Opening", written to me in the difficult months of 2024:

A Kind of Opening

The conversations were very important to me, both in terms of the questions that were raised and in terms of the familiarity between us, especially given the difficult hours during which they took place. The conversation published in this book is a conversation between a sociological researcher and a kibbutz member involved in his historical story. The researcher (Sibylle), who spent extended time in the kibbutz and was part of its education system, had already been involved for many years in the affairs and leadership of the kibbutz movement. The emotional involvement of both authors in the subject obligates the reader to be critical.

Let me tell you a story. During a visit I made to one of the radical communes established in the United States in the late 1960s, I discovered that all its members insisted on smiling all the time. I asked them about this custom. They replied that smiling creates a necessary connection between people, and that they need to live every moment of the encounter. I remembered that this did not happen in the kibbutz; sometimes people meet each other with sour faces. I told this to the commune people. They answered me: "For you, adaptation is important; for us, intensity. If we do not feel the intensity of the shared experience, we leave the commune. You settle for generations." And yes, I knew that there are people who leave the kibbutz. The departures are part of being a kibbutz society, a voluntary society, but the kibbutz defines itself in terms of generations.

Once I met a group of Chinese visitors who asked me how the kibbutz had survived so many years while the Chinese commune disappeared, despite its enormous human scope. I answered them that the difference lay in the fact that one can leave the kibbutz: it is based on choice. And despite this, the kibbutz does not seek only moments of partnership; it aims for generations.

It is also important for me to preface our conversation with another event from the late 1960s. A student from the United States came to the kibbutz, equipped with a small writing machine; she recorded her impressions during work breaks throughout the day. It was important for her to record every moment in utopia, but she discovered that this was not utopia, and she came to me with a proposal: let us establish a commune of intellectuals. "A commune of intellectuals, that is meaningless," I answered her. "It is of the utmost importance to me that my neighbor is a dairyman, that another is a builder, that another is a dietitian, and that I am a teacher. The real challenge is partnership among ordinary people."

The tension between people and ideas is an inseparable part of kibbutz life, as one of the kibbutz teachers once said: "I am looking for simple people who will rise up, not special people. That is the test." The founding generation felt the great gap between people and ideas, and the pain it creates, but believed this situation was temporary. Many of the founders thought that the second generation, growing up in the kibbutz, would not experience the tension in which they themselves lived; they would see something natural in the kibbutz completely. Those who came from another society had to deal with the memory of the forms of life in which they had lived before, and with the way they had been educated, but this, they believed, was a temporary situation. A new generation would be born whose natural environment was the kibbutz, and that generation would not bear the constraints and pains of adaptation to the new order.

This was the deep error of the founding generation. The second generation born in the place was not less tormented than the first, though not with the same torments. It had no problem doing agricultural work, but dealing with the idea was harder for them. Despite the variety of opinions and currents that operated in the kibbutz and influenced its path, the kibbutz was not built as a religious sanctuary that believes in eternity. It saw itself as belonging to history, obligated to it and active in its development. Unlike places of worship, it has no sacred objects except the faithful deed. Its members held human repair and a just society as guiding ideals, but ideals enacted in daily life: in work, in social orders, and in politics.

Dialogue and Dilemmas: The Spirit and Structure of Our Kibbutz Book

In writing this book we were guided not by the search for answers but by a commitment to dialogue, both as a method and as an ethos. From the outset, the kibbutz seemed to us less a subject than a dynamic field of ongoing conversation, an unending "thinking together" in which ideas, ideals, and identities continually encounter, contest, and reshape each other. Our dialogical approach mirrors the ethos of the kibbutz itself: a community forged not through rigid consensus but through continual negotiation, plurality, and respectful disagreement.

This method draws on a long tradition of dialogical scholarship in the social sciences, work that uncovers marginalized experiences, democratizes inquiry, and bridges the apparent gap between theory and lived reality (Fetzer & Ghorashi, 2025). In our practice it meant listening to each other, to our interlocutors, and to the multitude of voices our research touched; it meant asking difficult questions and reflecting on experience in real time. Our differences as authors became not obstacles but resources for complex insight. The book that has emerged refuses to offer the comfort of "truth delivered from above"; it invites readers instead into a conversation, sometimes messy and uncomfortable, through which both individuals and communities grow.

Dilemmas as the Organizing Thread

If dialogue is the process, dilemmas are the substance. In the kibbutz, dilemmas are not abstract puzzles but lived intersections where ideals confront reality, where old values must be weighed against new conditions, and where easy answers do not present themselves. The chapters that follow are organized around such dilemmas, about belonging, family, education, work, art and culture, enterprise, land, the kibbutz's place in Israeli society, and the questions that have surfaced in the aftermath of October 7. The titles of those chapters are themselves questions, posed in the spirit of this method. We do not seek to resolve the dilemmas they name. We seek to illuminate their depth and their dynamism, and to make audible the dialogue circling around them, which is itself an act of community. It is in the dialogue about dilemmas, rather than in their resolution, that genuine insight and creativity emerge.

The Book as a Participatory Journey

We invite readers not only to absorb information but to join the dialogue, as insiders, outsiders, critics, or dreamers. Each chapter offers stories, voices, and arguments that reflect the diversity of Israel's peripheral and central spaces; our aim, here as in our earlier collaborations, is to give voice to those living outside the dominant narratives and to recognize the dilemmas that define all attempts at building community.

The kibbutz remains, for us, a living experiment in pluralism, democracy, and peace, and a reminder that meaning and justice arise not from singular truths but from ongoing negotiation. Through this work we hope the book becomes a space where dilemmas invite reflection rather than threaten it, where dialogue is a bridge rather than an obstacle, and where every reader finds a voice in the ongoing story of communal life.

2. Where Did the Kibbutz Idea Come From?

Founding Motives, Biographies, and Ideological Crossroads

Sibylle Heilbrunn and Muki Tsur, Beit Gabriel 2026

Source: Chen Boyer, photographer

The Shop Without Prices: Summer 1977

It was the summer of 1977 when I first walked into the kibbutz shop at Barkai. I had arrived as a volunteer, a young student from Tübingen, drawn by curiosity about this communal experiment I had read about in my studies of empirical cultural sciences. But nothing in my academic preparation had equipped me for the moment I stepped through that door. The shelves were stocked like any other store: toiletries, notebooks, work clothes, small household items. But something was profoundly, unsettlingly absent. There were no price tags. Nowhere. I stood there, disoriented, searching for the familiar markers of value, the numbers that would tell me what things cost, what I could afford, what exchange would be required. There was nothing. I could simply take what I needed. Coming from my upper-middle-class German bourgeois family background, where every transaction was calculated, every purchase weighed against scarcity and budget, this absence felt like stepping into an alternate reality. This wasn't just a different economic system; it was the materialization of a completely different philosophy about human relationships, need, and value. The shop without prices became, for me, the threshold moment, the instant when the abstract ideals I had studied became concrete, tactile, real. That moment crystallized a question that would shape not only my years at Barkai but my entire relationship with the kibbutz idea: What drives individuals to join such a radically different way of life? How do universal visions and personal quests collide or coalesce in the decision to become part of a communal experiment? These questions are not merely historical curiosities but living inquiries that continue to illuminate broader conversations about human motivation, social belonging, and the possibility of alternative forms of community in an era dominated by individualism and market logic.

Jerusalem 1949

As Chapter 1 described, Muki's path to Ein Gev began in childhood, in the wake of catastrophe in his family's European past. For him, that path was inseparable from Jewish history, identity, and the search for collective renewal. The kibbutz represented not just a social experiment but a Jewish answer to Jewish questions, questions of survival, identity, belonging, and the possibility of creating a new form of Jewish life freed from the constraints and traumas of diaspora existence.

The ideological formation that shaped Muki's generation was inseparable from the trauma of European Jewish experience. As he explains: "You have to take into account that in *Hashomer Hatzair*, secularism is sometimes a religion… in our kibbutz, for example, there was a list on *Yom Kippur* of those who eat because of their conscience... you have to take into account that many of us experienced the fall of Vienna to the Nazis." Muki maintains that the experience of catastrophe was not abstract history but lived memory that demanded response. The fall of Vienna, the Holocaust, the centuries of persecution and alienation formed the backdrop against which the kibbutz took on its deepest meaning for many of his generation. The kibbutz offered a way to rebuild Jewish life on entirely new foundations, to reconnect with the land and with productive labor, to forge a new Jewish identity that was simultaneously rooted in tradition and radically modern.

For Muki's generation, this took the form of a stark dilemma between Hanita and Madrid: should young Hashomer Hatzair members build a new kibbutz in northern Palestine (Hanita, founded in 1938 on the Lebanese border) or sail to Spain to fight for the Republic against fascism? The compromise "We establish Hanita, but remember Madrid" captured the synthesis of Zionist and socialist identity that defined Hashomer Hatzair. But notably, the priority was clear: the Jewish project came first. Madrid was to be remembered, but Hanita was to be built.

Two Paths, One Question

What emerges from these two threshold moments, my disorientation in a shop without prices and Muki's childhood commitment at age eleven, is a fundamental question that would shape not only our individual journeys but our understanding of the entire kibbutz experiment: What propels individuals to join such a radically different way of life? How do universal visions and personal quests collide or coalesce in the decision to become part of a communal experiment? The tensions we explore in this chapter concern the intersection of ideology and biography, the negotiation between universal socialist vision and particular Jewish identity, the transformation of abstract philosophy into lived practice, and the ongoing dialogue between individual authenticity and collective commitment. These dilemmas remain urgent today as communities worldwide grapple with questions of how to balance personal autonomy with social solidarity, how to create meaningful alternatives to atomized individualism, and how to sustain collective purpose across generations.

The Ideas That Answered the Call

The kibbutz movement did not arise from a vacuum but from the confluence of multiple intellectual and spiritual currents coursing through early twentieth-century Jewish life. These currents converged most powerfully among the pioneers of the *Second Aliyah*, who arrived in Palestine between 1904 and 1914. These young idealists carried with them a distinctive synthesis of socialist theory, Zionist aspiration, and a profound yearning for personal and collective regeneration, a synthesis that would fundamentally shape the communal experiments they established.

The Question Gordon Answered: Labor as Renewal

At the heart of kibbutz ideology stood the radical philosophy of Aaron David Gordon (1856–1922), whose "religion of labor" transformed work from economic necessity into spiritual practice (Perlmutter, 1971). Unlike many Zionist pioneers who arrived in Palestine as young revolutionaries, Gordon immigrated in 1904 at the age of forty-eight, having spent decades as an estate manager in Russia. Despite possessing no previous experience with manual labor, Gordon threw himself into the pioneer lifestyle, working first in Petah Tikva and ultimately settling at one of the first communal settlements. Gordon's central philosophical claim posited that manual labor, particularly agricultural work, constituted not merely productive activity but the very path to human regeneration and authentic connection with nature and community. For Gordon, the Jewish people had been alienated from productive labor through centuries of diaspora existence, forced into commerce and intellectual pursuits yet severed from the fundamental human experience of working the land. As he argued, diaspora existence had compelled Jews to survive through what he characterized as "the dried-up resources of history and religion" (My Jewish Learning 2017). The revival of the Jewish people, in Gordon's vision, demanded nothing less than the reestablishment of the bond between Jews and their land through physical labor. Drawing on influences as diverse as Kabbalistic and Hasidic mysticism, Nietzschean existentialism, and Tolstoyan agrarian anarchism, Gordon maintained that manual labor was essential not only for the regeneration of the Jewish people but also possessed a more holistic spiritual value. As he articulated, "it is through labour that a people becomes rooted in its soil and culture." This philosophy of labor became a "surrogate moral code" for the early kibbutzniks, creating a secular religiosity akin to Tolstoy's notion of seeking "the Kingdom of God not without, but within ourselves" (Gordon, n.d.). The kibbutz pioneers embraced Gordon's vision with fierce devotion. Labor became sacred, not in a metaphorical sense but as lived practice. The early kibbutzniks understood themselves as forging new Jewish identities through their bodies, through sweat and soil, through the physical transformation of both the land and themselves. This was no escapist utopianism but rather what might be termed pragmatic idealism: a conviction that changing material conditions and daily practices could fundamentally reshape human character and social relations. Gordon's philosophy resonated powerfully precisely because it offered a response to both Jewish alienation and capitalist exploitation. It promised personal transformation through productive labor while simultaneously building the material foundation for Jewish national renewal. Work became the meeting point of individual spiritual quest and collective political project.

For Muki and his generation, Gordon's "religion of labor" resonated precisely because it offered a path to Jewish renewal through physical reconnection with the land. The centuries of diaspora had alienated Jews from productive labor, forcing them into commerce and intellectual pursuits but severing them from the fundamental human experience of working the soil. The kibbutz promised to heal this alienation, to create "new Jews" who would be farmers and builders, who would renew their people through the transformation of both land and self.

Buber's Dialogue: Building Community Through Encounter

Martin Buber's philosophy of dialogue and community provided another crucial foundation for kibbutz thought, particularly for movements such as Hashomer Hatzair (Near, 1986). Buber's concept of the "I-Thou" relationship, a genuine encounter between whole persons, stood in stark contrast to the "I-It" relations that characterized modern capitalist society, where individuals treated one another as objects or means to ends. The "I-Thou" relation, for Buber, constituted the very foundation of authentic existence and community. It is mutual, transformative, and characterized by genuine encounter, openness, and reciprocity. Modern society, according to Buber, is dominated by "I-It" relations, thereby causing alienation, loneliness, and a loss of meaning (Doubrawa, 1998). The kibbutz, as Buber envisioned it, would be a society structured around "I-Thou" relations, where people encountered one another as whole persons, not as means to ends (Potok, 2015). Buber emphasized the importance of small communities where immediate relationships remained possible between members. From these living communities, he argued, the "communal spirit" would emerge "in the form of strong and realistically fulfilled communal cells," with humanity ultimately becoming "an association of such communities." At the basis of society, Buber maintained, there must be many small communal cells where people may say "Thou" and "We" (Doubrawa, 1998). For Buber, true community could not be legislated or engineered from above. It emerged only through authentic dialogue, through the willingness of individuals to meet one another in their full humanity. The kibbutz, as he conceptualized it, would be a "full cooperative", not merely an economic arrangement but an embrace of whole life, where work, family, education, culture, and politics were integrated into a comprehensive vision of human flourishing (Mendes-Flohr 2019). Buber was explicit that a kibbutz deserved this name only "if the number of its members does not exceed that of the circle of people any one person may know personally," emphasizing that "the vital question is, whether direct contact from one person to another exists and whether in turning towards another we really mean him, in his being-in-the-world and how he has become" (Doubrawa 1998). This dialogical understanding carried profound implications reflected throughout the chapters of this book. It meant that the kibbutz could never be a static utopia, a perfect society achieved once and for all. Instead, it would remain an ongoing experiment, continually negotiated and renegotiated through conversation and encounter. The tension between individual authenticity and collective commitment, far from being a problem to be solved, became the creative engine of communal life.

The Synthesis: Zionism, Socialism, and Jewish Renewal

The kibbutz represented a unique and historically significant synthesis of Zionist nationalism and socialist internationalism, a combination that was far from self-evident and often internally contradictory, posing many dilemmas addressed in this book. The fundamental question confronting the movement was how one could be simultaneously committed to building a Jewish national home and to universal principles of equality and social justice. How could particularistic Jewish identity coexist with the universalist aspirations of socialism?

Different kibbutz movements answered these questions differently, yet all grappled with the fundamental challenge of reconciling Jewish renewal with social revolution (Shafir & Peled, 2002). Some emphasized the national dimension, positioning the kibbutz as the vanguard of Zionist settlement and state-building. Others stressed the universal socialist vision, presenting the kibbutz as a model of egalitarian society that transcended national boundaries. The movement represented what scholars have characterized as "utopian socialism," with the first kibbutzim established in the early 1900s as communes based on economic, social, and political equality among members. Yet in practice, these streams often flowed together in complex and mutually reinforcing ways. The ethical identification with nature that Gordon preached drew upon Jewish sources even as it spoke to universal human needs. The commitment to social justice that animated kibbutz socialism was rooted in prophetic Jewish tradition even as it allied with international labor movements. The very act of settling the land was simultaneously a nationalist project and a socialist experiment in collective ownership and democratic self-governance. Labor Zionism, which provided the ideological framework for the kibbutz movement, emerged during the Second Aliyah as a synthesis of socialist and nationalist principles. The pioneers believed that a Jewish state could be created only through the efforts of the Jewish working class making *aliyah* to the Land of Israel and building a country through the creation of a Labor Jewish society with rural kibbutzim and *moshavim*, alongside an urban Jewish proletariat. Influenced by Marxist ideologies spreading throughout Russia, these immigrants sought to implement socialist values through the exclusive use of Hebrew language and Jewish labor, along with the creation of defense organizations to work toward independence. Yet the deeper paradox lay elsewhere. Labor Zionism's revolutionary promise, to leave behind the diaspora past and forge a "new Jew" reconnected to land and productive labor, contained within it the seeds of a profound irony. As Nir Tsuk observes, the very communities established to break with traditional Jewish existence and create an egalitarian socialist alternative would become foundational building blocks of Israeli Jewish nationalism (Tsuk. 2005). The kibbutz, conceived as a universal experiment in communal living that happened to be Jewish, gradually transformed into a distinctively national institution, one that both embodied and reproduced the ethnic boundaries and power structures it had initially sought to transcend. This transformation was not accidental but embedded in Labor Zionism's internal contradictions. The movement sought to be simultaneously particular and universal: to create a new form of Jewish life while demonstrating principles applicable to all humanity, to build a Jewish national home while practicing international socialist solidarity, to escape the constraints of diaspora identity while remaining fundamentally defined by Jewishness. These tensions could not be permanently resolved but instead generated ongoing contradictions that would shape kibbutz development across generations. The kibbutz did create a uniquely powerful vision capable of mobilizing diverse individuals around a common project promising both personal transformation and collective redemption. It offered an alternative socialist model that sought to reconcile communal ideals with the practical demands of nation-building. But this reconciliation came at a cost: the universal socialist vision became increasingly subordinated to nationalist imperatives, the egalitarian experiment increasingly served the project of ethnic state formation, and the communities that had rejected diaspora hierarchy reproduced new forms of exclusion based on national belonging. The kibbutz thus answered multiple Jewish needs simultaneously, but it did so in ways that revealed the movement's fundamental ambivalence. It offered refuge and security in the aftermath of catastrophe, yet this security was built on land claimed from others and defended through ethnic exclusivity. It provided a framework for creating new forms of Jewish identity and practice, yet these "new" forms often reproduced hierarchies between Ashkenazi and *Mizrahi* Jews, between veterans and newcomers, between Jews and Arabs. It reconnected Jews with the land of Israel, yet this reconnection required severing or subordinating the connections of those who had continuously inhabited that land. It demonstrated that Jews could build a just society that honored both particular Jewish values and universal socialist principles, but the justice remained bounded, the universalism compromised by the particularism it could never fully escape.

For Muki, raised within this ideological framework and shaped by historical trauma that made collective solidarity seem not just desirable but necessary for survival, the kibbutz represented the only coherent response to the crisis of Jewish existence in the modern world. This conviction was genuine and, given the historical circumstances, understandable. Yet it also illustrates how even the most idealistic visions, when embedded within nationalist projects, risk reproducing the very structures of domination they seek to overcome. The kibbutz's trajectory from revolutionary commune to national institution reveals not the failure of individual commitment but the difficulty of maintaining universal ideals within particularist frameworks, a difficulty that continues to challenge communities seeking to balance solidarity with justice, belonging with openness, in our own time.

The Critical Lens: Marx, the Frankfurt School, and the Critique I Brought

My own path to the kibbutz followed a fundamentally different trajectory, rooted not in Jewish particularity but in the universal critique of inequality and capitalism. Coming from Germany, from a capitalist family background, I arrived at Barkai as a volunteer in 1977, driven by intellectual curiosity about communal experiments but more fundamentally by a growing awareness of the systemic injustices built into the economic order I had grown up within. The shop without prices captured the essence of what drew me to the kibbutz. Standing there, disoriented by the absence of the price tags that structure all economic transactions in capitalist society, I confronted the material reality of an alternative system. This wasn't about Jewish renewal or national rebirth; it was about the possibility of organizing human economic life according to principles of equality and mutual aid rather than competition and accumulation. My family background had taught me the logic of capitalism intimately: every transaction calculated, every purchase weighed against scarcity and budget, every relationship mediated by considerations of economic advantage. This was presented not as one possible way of organizing society but as natural, inevitable, the only rational system. Yet my studies in empirical cultural sciences had exposed me to critiques of this supposedly natural order, particularly through engagement with Marx and the Frankfurt School.

Understanding What We Rejected: The Origins of Inequality

To understand what drew people to the kibbutz, we must first understand what they were rejecting. The kibbutz emerged as a radical response to fundamental questions about the nature and origins of human inequality, questions that have preoccupied social thinkers for centuries. Yanis Varoufakis, in *Talking to My Daughter About the Economy* (2017), offers one influential account, tracing the roots of inequality back to the agricultural revolution, when humans first learned to produce more food than they immediately needed. This surplus, the extra grain stored in granaries, the additional livestock in pens, became the foundation for all subsequent inequality. Before agriculture, hunter-gatherer societies were relatively egalitarian because there was little to accumulate and hoard. But once surplus existed, everything changed. According to his analysis, the surplus needed to be stored, protected, and distributed, which meant someone had to control it. Those who gained control over the granaries and storehouses suddenly held power over others. This wasn't a natural or inevitable development; it required most people to accept, whether willingly or through coercion, that a few would control resources the entire community had helped produce. To manage this surplus, early civilizations developed writing, not for literature or philosophy but as accounting ledgers to track who owed what to whom. This created a class of scribes and administrators who became essential to maintaining the system. The surplus also generated debt relationships: when your harvest failed, you borrowed from the stores, creating obligations that bound you to those in control. Debt became a powerful tool for maintaining hierarchy. Protecting the surplus from outsiders and enforcing internal control required organized violence. Warrior classes emerged, then armies, then states. The state itself arose partly to protect the hierarchy that surplus had created. But force alone couldn't sustain such systems indefinitely. Religious and cultural narratives developed to legitimize inequality, stories of divine right, natural order, or superior virtue that made hierarchy seem inevitable rather than constructed. Finally, once established, inequality became self-reinforcing. Those with power extracted more surplus, invested in better tools and weapons, and further consolidated their position.

Varoufakis emphasizes that this entire structure wasn't natural or inevitable; it required specific historical conditions and, crucially, the acceptance of the majority. However, this account, while illuminating certain dynamics, risks oversimplification. Varoufakis's framework helps us understand how surplus *can* lead to hierarchy and domination, but it presents this as if it were the only possible outcome. Recent archaeological and anthropological research challenges such deterministic narratives: as Graeber and Wengrow argue in *The Dawn of Everything* (2021), the relationship between agricultural surplus and social hierarchy was far more variable and contingent than linear accounts suggest, with numerous examples of societies that maintained egalitarian structures despite surplus production. What Varoufakis's analysis underemphasizes is that surplus production was also the precondition for virtually all human advancement, for cities, specialized crafts, scientific inquiry, art, literature, and complex social organization. The challenge, then, is not surplus itself but rather the specific social arrangements through which it has historically been controlled and distributed. A romanticized return to subsistence economies would mean abandoning not just hierarchy but also the material foundations for cultural and technological development. The kibbutz, in this light, was not an attempt to eliminate surplus but to reorganize it, to demonstrate that communities could generate and manage surplus without recreating the ancient patterns of domination.

This perspective reveals that inequality isn't fixed or unchangeable. It is a human creation, built on the control of surplus resources, and like any human creation, it can be challenged and transformed. For me, the kibbutz represented precisely such a challenge: an attempt to organize surplus production and distribution according to radically different principles, to break the ancient connection between surplus and hierarchy, to demonstrate that communities could function without the mechanisms of price, private accumulation, and debt that had structured human societies for millennia. Marx's analysis revealed how capitalism systematically produces and reproduces inequality, how the control of surplus resources, returning to Varoufakis's framework, creates hierarchies that then appear natural or inevitable. The surplus that some accumulate comes from the labor of others, creating relationships of exploitation disguised as voluntary exchange. Private property, wage labor, market competition: these mechanisms ensure that those who control resources can extract value from those who do not, perpetuating cycles of inequality across generations.

The Frankfurt School deepened this critique by showing how capitalism colonizes not just economic life but consciousness itself. Adorno and Horkheimer's (1944/2002) analysis of the "culture industry" in *Dialectic of Enlightenment* demonstrated how even leisure, art, and personal relationships become commodified, how instrumental reason reduces all human activity to calculation of advantage, how the possibility of genuine alternatives becomes increasingly difficult to imagine from within the system itself.

I found in the kibbutz a living refutation of capitalism's claim to inevitability. Here was a community that had abolished private property, eliminated the wage relation, socialized the means of production, and organized distribution according to need rather than market mechanisms. The shop without prices was the most visceral demonstration of this alternative logic: goods were available not to those who could pay but to those who needed them, trust replaced surveillance, mutual responsibility replaced individual calculation.

What I found so compelling was that this wasn't merely an economic arrangement but a comprehensive challenge to the assumptions that structure capitalist society. The collective dining hall meant that domestic labor was socialized rather than privatized, that women were freed from the private servitude that capitalism relegates to the "reproductive sphere." The rotation of work assignments meant that the division between mental and manual labor, between prestigious and degraded work, could be challenged and potentially overcome. The democratic general assembly meant that those who did the work controlled the enterprise, that economic decisions were made collectively rather than imposed by capital. Thus, for me, the kibbutz offered proof that the critiques of capitalism I had encountered theoretically could be realized practically. It demonstrated that human beings were capable of organizing themselves according to principles of solidarity and equality, that the competitive individualism capitalism assumes and enforces is not the only possibility, that communities could function on bases other than private accumulation and market exchange.

Yet I also approached the kibbutz with the critical tools provided by my theoretical formation. The Frankfurt School's pessimism about the totalizing power of modern rationalization raised questions: Could small-scale communities really resist the pressures of the larger capitalist system? How long could alternative forms of organization survive when embedded within a capitalist state and global economy? Would the kibbutz movement ultimately be incorporated, its radical potential domesticated, its alternative logic gradually eroded by the surrounding market society? These questions were not merely academic but reflected genuine uncertainty about whether the alternatives the kibbutz embodied could be sustained. The shop without prices demonstrated that another world was possible, but could it endure? Could it expand? What would happen when the founding generation's ideological commitment gave way to subsequent generations raised without the experience of capitalist alienation that had driven the founders' search for alternatives?

My journey to the kibbutz was thus driven not by connection to Jewish history or identity but by engagement with the critique of inequality and capitalism. I came seeking to understand how communities could organize themselves according to non-capitalist principles, whether Marx's vision of a society beyond exploitation could be realized, whether the Frankfurt School's diagnosis of capitalism's totalizing power was complete or whether spaces of genuine resistance remained possible.

Biography Meets Philosophy: Competing Frameworks

The philosophical currents that shaped the kibbutz movement found expression in the concrete decisions of individuals. Each person who joined a kibbutz brought their own biography, their own mixture of conviction and circumstance, ideology and personal need. Yet beneath this diversity, two fundamental motivations emerge: the Jewish quest for renewal and collective redemption, and the universal critique of inequality and capitalism. Muki's and my own paths to kibbutz life illustrate these distinct yet complementary drives.

For Muki, understanding the kibbutz has always begun with Martin Buber's philosophy of dialogue. The distinction between "I-It" and "I-Thou" relations provided the fundamental framework for evaluating kibbutz practice. The kibbutz, as Muki experienced it, was an attempt to create a society structured around "I-Thou" relations, where people encountered each other as whole persons, not as means to ends. This wasn't abstract theory. In the kibbutz, it was lived daily. When decisions were made in the general assembly, when members worked together in the fields or the dining hall, when they struggled through conflicts about education or economics, these were exercises in dialogue. The kibbutz was a laboratory for experimenting with authentic encounter as the basis of social organization. Herbert Marcuse's critique of advanced industrial society complemented this Buberian framework. Marcuse's analysis of how capitalism creates "false needs," and his call for a society organized around human fulfillment rather than production for profit, echoed the kibbutz rejection of consumerism and individual accumulation. For Marcuse, genuine freedom required not just political rights but liberation from the alienation and repression inherent in capitalist work relations. The kibbutz experiment, with its emphasis on meaningful labor, democratic participation, and the integration of work with other dimensions of life, represented precisely the kind of alternative Marcuse theorized: a social formation that refused the separation of economic life from ethical life, that rejected the reduction of human beings to productive units. For Muki, these philosophical frameworks provided both justification for the kibbutz experiment and criteria for evaluating its success. The question was always: Did kibbutz practice enable genuine encounter? Did it create conditions for meaningful, creative work? Did it resist the instrumentalization of human relationships?

As set out earlier, my own intellectual formation in Marx and the Frankfurt School led me to approach the kibbutz through different lenses, attentive to material conditions and structural contradictions, and to the questions about whether small-scale alternatives could resist incorporation into the broader capitalist order. Where Muki saw the kibbutz primarily through the lens of dialogue and encounter, I was more focused on material conditions and structural contradictions. Where he emphasized the possibility of authentic relationships, I was attentive to the ways broader economic and political forces constrained those possibilities. These different emphases sometimes led to different interpretations of the same phenomena, creating productive tensions in our conversations about what the kibbutz represented and what it could teach.

The Shop Without Prices Revisited: Two Interpretations

Standing in that shop at Barkai, we each would have seen something different. For Muki, the absence of price tags would have represented Buber's dialogical community made tangible, a space where relationships were not mediated by exchange value, where members encountered one another as persons rather than as parties to transactions. For me, the same shop represented the concrete negation of capitalism's fundamental logic, Marx's vision in practice, a space organized by need rather than exchange, where surplus was socialized rather than appropriated. Both interpretations were valid; both captured something essential. The intersection, Jewish renewal and the critique of capitalism answered simultaneously by the same simple absence of price tags, reveals something profound about the kibbutz's power to mobilize diverse motivations toward a common experiment.

What emerges from these philosophical frameworks and personal stories is a complex picture of motivation and commitment, and an interplay of vision and biography. People joined the kibbutz for many reasons: ideological conviction, personal search, circumstantial opportunity, family connection. Some came as true believers in socialist Zionism; others were drawn by the promise of community and belonging; still others sought escape from conventional paths or personal transformation. The kibbutz demanded total commitment, not just adherence to economic arrangements but participation in a comprehensive way of life. This "full cooperative," as Buber called it, meant that joining the kibbutz was never purely an economic decision or even a political one. It was an existential choice, a decision about how to live, about what kind of person to become, about what values to embody in daily practice.

Yet this totality also created profound tensions. What happened when personal desires conflicted with communal needs? How did individual creativity find expression within collective frameworks? Could the kibbutz truly reconcile the universal socialist vision with the particularist demands of Zionist settlement? Could it balance the ethical imperatives inherited from Jewish tradition with the secular rationalism of socialist ideology? These were not abstract philosophical problems but lived dilemmas that every kibbutz member confronted in daily decisions about work, family, education, and community. The founding generation believed, perhaps naively, that these tensions would diminish in subsequent generations. As Muki put it in the opening reflection given in Chapter 1, the second generation born in the place "was not less tormented than the first generation, though not with the same torments." The dilemmas proved permanent precisely because they arose from the fundamental structure of the kibbutz experiment: the attempt to reconcile individual authenticity with collective commitment, universal vision with particular identity, ideological purity with pragmatic adaptation. These tensions were not bugs in the system but features of any serious attempt to build alternative forms of social life.

So why did people join the kibbutz?

The question admits no single answer because the kibbutz itself was never a single thing. It was simultaneously a Zionist settlement strategy and a socialist experiment, a community of spiritual regeneration and a pragmatic agricultural enterprise, a refuge from conventional society and an attempt to transform it. For someone like Muki, steeped in the kibbutz ideology and shaped by the trauma of European Jewish history, the kibbutz represented the synthesis of Jewish renewal and social justice, the materialization of a vision carried from Vienna through Jerusalem to the shores of the Galilee. For someone like me, coming from outside as a young volunteer, approaching from the universalist critique of capitalism and inequality, the kibbutz offered both a glimpse of alternative possibilities and proof that those alternatives were real: a lived critique of capitalist assumptions, embodied in something as simple and profound as a shop without prices; an answer, however partial, to the Frankfurt School's pessimism about whether human beings could ever organize themselves according to principles of solidarity rather than competition. Yet I also brought the critical tools that demanded scrutiny of whether these alternatives could be sustained, whether they truly escaped the logic of domination they sought to transcend. The philosophical foundations, Gordon's religion of labor, Buber's dialogical community, the synthesis of Zionism and socialism, Marcuse's vision of non-repressive civilization, Marx's materialist analysis, provided frameworks for understanding and justifying the kibbutz experiment. But the lived reality always exceeded these frameworks, generated new questions, revealed contradictions that theory alone could not resolve. What motivated individuals to join, and how do personal hopes and communal demands interact? These questions remain alive precisely because the kibbutz understood itself not as a completed utopia but as an ongoing experiment, a conversation that each generation must continue in its own terms. The shop without prices that surprised me in 1977 materialized a set of assumptions about human nature and social possibility. Whether those assumptions could be sustained, how they would be tested and transformed, and what they might offer to wider society, these questions would unfold in the decades to come, through the daily negotiations of thousands of individuals trying to live according to principles that the world declared impossible.

As we explore in the following chapters, this tension between hope and realism, between vision and biography, between universal ideals and particular lives, would define every dimension of kibbutz experience, from family life to economic organization, from education to culture, from internal governance to external relations. The question of why people joined the kibbutz opens onto the larger question of how they tried to live there, what they created, what they struggled with, and what their experiment might still teach us about the enduring human quest for more just, meaningful, and solidaristic forms of community. The shop without prices, where this inquiry began, thus becomes a fitting symbol for the entire kibbutz project. It represented a space where multiple visions, Jewish renewal, socialist transformation, dialogical community, liberation from capitalism, could converge in concrete practice. That convergence was never seamless, never free from tension and contradiction. But it was real. And in being real, it posed questions that remain urgent: How do we build communities of genuine solidarity? How do we balance individual authenticity with collective commitment? How do we create alternatives to the atomized individualism and market logic that dominate contemporary life? These questions cannot be answered in the abstract. They require the kind of biographical commitment and philosophical reflection that brought both Muki and me to the kibbutz, along different paths, toward a shared experiment in living otherwise.

3. Who Gets to Belong?

Bounded Equality in the Kibbutz

The entrance gate of Kibbutz Ein Gev, 2026

Source: Zohar Tsur, daughter of Muki Tsur

A Personal Entry Point

It was a winter evening in 1983 when I first encountered the admission committee at Kibbutz Barkai. I had arrived at Barkai in 1977 as a volunteer and partner of a kibbutz member; in the years that followed I completed my BA at Tel

Aviv University, and only then did I return to contemplate something that felt both thrilling and startling: staying permanently, becoming a member, crossing the threshold from temporary visitor to committed participant in this communal experiment. The process would require appearing before the admission committee, a group of veteran members who would evaluate my suitability for membership. This committee would then recommend or not to the general assembly, in which all members had a vote.

I remember sitting outside the meeting room, nervous, aware that I was about to be judged not on my professional qualifications or economic potential but on something far more nebulous and profound: my capacity and willingness to become part of this particular community. Would I fit in? Could I contribute? Did I share the values? Would I remain committed? These unspoken questions crystallized a fundamental tension at the heart of kibbutz life. The admission committee embodied a paradox. On one hand, it represented democratic participation, members collectively deciding who would join their community. On the other hand, it concentrated gatekeeping power, the ability to exclude those deemed unsuitable. This tension between openness and closure, between welcome and boundary-drawing, defines one of the kibbutz's most persistent dilemmas.

A Conceptual Framework

This chapter explores how kibbutzim manage one of the most challenging questions any community faces: Who gets to belong? To answer this question, I introduce two interrelated concepts that will guide the analysis throughout. **Gatekeeping** refers to the formal, institutional processes through which kibbutzim determine membership: the admission committee interviews, the general assembly votes, the official criteria for approval. These are the visible, procedural mechanisms of inclusion and exclusion. **Boundaries of belonging** encompass something broader and often subtler: the informal cultural, social, and ethnic lines that shape who feels comfortable seeking entry, who is welcomed once inside, and who can participate as an equal. These boundaries operate through shared cultural references, language patterns, and unspoken social hierarchies rather than explicit rules. Through their interplay, dilemmas evolve: formal gatekeeping procedures can reinforce informal cultural boundaries, and informal hierarchies can contaminate ostensibly democratic processes. This distinction parallels Lamont and Fournier's (1992) framework of "symbolic boundaries", the conceptual and cultural attitudes that separate groups, and Brubaker's (1992) analysis of the gap between formal citizenship and substantive belonging.

At the deepest level, this chapter examines what I call *bounded equality*: the kibbutz's simultaneous commitment to radical internal equality among members while maintaining exclusive external boundaries determining who can access that equality. This is my own framing, inspired by Tsuk's (2005) analysis of the kibbutz as a community whose flourishing has depended on the relationship between state, market, and local solidarity. The shop without prices, the iconic symbol of kibbutz egalitarianism, exemplifies this paradox perfectly. Within the community, distribution operates on need and trust, without market mechanisms or surveillance. But one must first be accepted into the community to access that shop. The equality is real but not universal; it applies within defined boundaries.

Understanding bounded equality is crucial because it reveals a fundamental tension: the kibbutz abolished class distinctions among members yet reproduced various ethnic, national, and ideological hierarchies determining who could even enter. An uncomfortable question arises: Can a community practice radical internal equality while maintaining exclusionary external boundaries without contradicting its own egalitarian principles? The dilemmas I explore concern the evolution from a partnership of similarity to a community of diversity, the challenge of maintaining shared identity while embracing pluralism, the role of voluntariness in creating authentic belonging, and the ongoing negotiation between cohesion and inclusivity. These questions remain urgent today as societies worldwide grapple with immigration, citizenship, and the boundaries of belonging.

The Institution of Gatekeeping

The admission committee embodied the kibbutz's approach to managing membership boundaries. Unlike residential communities where economic criteria typically determine entry, or political communities where citizenship laws establish rules, the kibbutz relied on social evaluation. The committee assessed prospective members on compatibility with existing members, commitment to community values, and likely contribution to collective life, then recommended candidates to the general assembly for final approval (Gavron, 2000).

This process had genuine advantages. It allowed communities to maintain social cohesion and select members truly committed to communal living rather than merely seeking economic advantage. It created space for evaluating whether individuals could thrive in collective life's demanding environment, where privacy was limited, personal conflicts inescapable, and economic security came with social obligations. But the admission committee also concentrated significant power. Even as a recommending body, it shaped who would be presented for consideration. It created opportunities for maintaining homogeneity, for excluding the different, for reproducing existing hierarchies. The criteria of fitting in, commitment to values, social compatibility were inherently subjective, open to bias even when members believed they applied principled standards. Muki has reflected on this in our conversations, and his comment reveals the tension between necessary particularity and ostensible objectivity:

> "The admission committee asked questions about values, about willingness to accept community decisions, about equality and work. But of course, they also evaluated whether the person seemed comfortable, whether they spoke the right way, whether they shared our cultural references. We believed we were selecting for ideological commitment, but we were also selecting for social similarity."

Gatekeeping's Historical Evolution

The Founding Era (1909–1948): When Ideology Was Everything

In the kibbutz movement's early decades, membership meant joining a revolutionary experiment (Near, 1992). Entry pathways were narrow and demanding. Most members arrived through youth movements where they spent years absorbing socialist and Zionist ideals before reaching a kibbutz. The youth movement wasn't simply a stepping stone; it was a total experience forming identity, values, and life trajectory. By the time of application, candidates had undergone extensive socialization, they knew the songs, shared the language, understood the values. The admission committee's role was less conversion than confirmation, verifying that candidates had internalized membership's commitments. This entry mode created remarkable homogeneity and intense solidarity. Members shared not just economic arrangements but fundamental beliefs about society and meaning. Entry requirements were explicitly selective: ideological commitment came first, collective agricultural labor was essential, and candidates relinquished personal property.

After Statehood (1949–1970s): Institutionalization and Its Tensions

Following Israeli independence in 1949, kibbutz admission became more formalized (Near, 1997). The youth movement connection continued, supplemented by military service in units like Palmach and Nahal, which combined combat training with settlement work. The classic pathway emerged: initial contact through youth movements or military, a six-month to one-year trial, rigorous evaluation by the admission committee, and final approval by the general assembly.

As the process systematized, new tensions emerged. The second generation, children born in kibbutzim, created a fundamental challenge. They hadn't chosen kibbutz life through years of ideological preparation; they had simply been born there. Their path to membership was fundamentally different: inherited rather than earned through demonstrated commitment. This raised uncomfortable questions: Were members' children automatically entitled to membership? Should they face the same scrutiny as outsiders? How could communities maintain ideological intensity across generations when the founders' forging conditions no longer existed? During this same period international volunteerism began. Starting in the 1960s, thousands of young Europeans and Americans came as volunteers. Most stayed briefly, but some, like me, considered permanent membership. Volunteers demonstrated communal values' universal appeal while raising questions about maintaining distinctive Jewish character while incorporating non-Jewish members.

The Crisis Years (1980s–2000s): Pragmatism Replaces Purity

The 1980s economic crisis fundamentally altered everything (Balberg, 2024; Near, 1997; Palgi & Reinharz, 2011). Many kibbutzim accumulated crushing debt and faced demographic decline as youth left for cities. Communities that had been highly selective now struggled to attract enough members for economic viability. The membership calculus shifted dramatically. Some kibbutzim began accepting previously rejected candidates, relaxing ideological requirements for practical contributions. Economic skills became more valuable than ideological commitment. The admission committee's power remained, but the context had changed completely.

This period saw new membership categories emerge. As kibbutzim privatized economic aspects and introduced salary differentials, they created tiered belonging: full membership with complete rights and responsibilities, permanent residency with partial participation, and renters living in the community without full membership. These reflected economic necessities and loosening ideological boundaries.

Contemporary Pluralism: Multiple Pathways In

By the twenty-first century, kibbutzim had developed varied entry pathways reflecting diverse motivations (Palgi & Reinharz, 2011). The unified ideological pathway had splintered into multiple options: full membership with more flexible criteria, partial membership and residency options allowing participation without total commitment, and preferential consideration for returning children and relatives.

The trajectory from ideological purity to pragmatic pluralism reveals fundamental tensions in balancing identity with openness. The founding generation could be highly selective because they were creating something new. Later generations inherited established communities but faced economic pressures, demographic decline, and eroding ideological certainty. Entry pathway diversification represents both achievement and loss. It demonstrates kibbutzim's adaptability, those maintaining rigid criteria often declined or disappeared, while adaptive ones survived. Yet adaptation required compromises. Can communities accepting members for pragmatic rather than ideological reasons maintain the solidarity that made the original experiment meaningful?

Boundaries of Belonging: Inherited, Ethnic, National

The Second Generation: Inheriting Without Choosing

The second generation revealed a profound challenge to communal ideology. Could communities require the same ideological commitment from those born into them as from those who chose to join? Should children of members undergo admission committee scrutiny? Treating children as automatic members risked diluting commitment. But subjecting them to evaluation violated the principle of community as extended family. Many children left kibbutzim as young adults. Yet surprisingly, many began returning with their own families, seeking quality of life, safety, nature, community, even while maintaining more individual autonomy (Balberg, 2024; Palgi & Reinharz, 2011). The second generation's experience revealed that community identity cannot simply be transmitted across generations. Each must find its own relationship to collective values, its own reasons for belonging or leaving.

Ethnic Boundaries: Palestinian Israelis

Nowhere was the tension between universal socialist principles and particular Jewish identity more acute than in relationships with Arab neighbors. Kibbutz Metzer, adjacent to the Arab village of Meiser developed close educational connections, with Arab teachers working in leadership roles in Metzer's kindergartens. Yet when I asked Muki whether a Palestinian family from Meiser could become members, his response revealed those boundaries: "I don't know... I assume not, in fact, I don't know about an Israeli Palestinian family becoming Kibbutz members." Palestinian Israelis might labor in kibbutz fields or factories, but could not apply for membership. This exclusion reflected the kibbutz's dual nature as both socialist experiment and Zionist project, seeking to create specifically Jewish communities. Muki acknowledges this directly: "The kibbutz saw, and sees, itself as a Jewish/Israeli creation where the entry ticket, in the end, sits on Judaism."

Mizrahi Jews: Internal Jewish Hierarchies

The kibbutz was predominantly Ashkenazi, traditionally shaped by European cultural norms (Balberg, 2024; Near, 1992, 1997). *Mizrahi* Jews faced significant barriers operating through cultural expectations rather than explicit policy[1]. As Muki observed, kibbutz members believed they were selecting for

1 The relationship between Ashkenazi and Mizrahi Jews in Israel is the subject of a large and contested historical, sociological, and cultural literature, and of a continuing public debate that reaches far beyond the kibbutz. This book does not enter or adjudicate that debate. Our concern here is narrower: how ethnic boundaries operated in the specific question of who could and could not become a kibbutz member. On the term itself, "Mizrahi" carries different valences in Hebrew and in English scholarly and political discourse, and in Hebrew is easily confused with "Mizrachi," the religious-Zionist party.

ideological commitment but were also selecting for social similarity, evaluating whether candidates spoke the right way and shared the right cultural references. Mizrahi immigration also created practical challenges. Unlike earlier self-selecting waves of young pioneers, Mizrahim came with families of varying sizes and compositions. Many preferred the *moshav*, where families maintained their own households and farms while sharing marketing, retaining, as Muki has put it, the family as the center of social life. This wasn't simply discrimination; many Mizrahi Jews genuinely preferred settlement forms preserving family autonomy.

For those who did join kibbutzim, hierarchies occasionally manifested in day-to-day interactions, in who sat with whom at the dining hall as well as in job assignments. By the 1980s, accumulated resentment between the groups fueled political alienation, crystallized in Begin's famous 1981 characterization of kibbutzim as "millionaires in swimming pools" (Balberg, 2024). The reality was multifaceted: Ashkenazi cultural hegemony created barriers through implicit bias; structural constraints around family composition created practical challenges; and genuine cultural differences meant many Mizrahi Jews preferred settlement forms preserving family autonomy. These factors reinforced each other, creating a system where exclusion resulted from both discrimination and divergent preferences. Even today, kibbutzim remain disproportionately Ashkenazi while moshavim became largely Mizrahi institutions.

National Boundaries: International Volunteers and Foreign Members

My own arrival at Barkai in 1977 came when international volunteerism had become common. From the 1960s onward, kibbutzim hosted thousands of young people attracted by communal living, Israeli socialism, or travel opportunities. Volunteers demonstrated that kibbutz principles could transcend national boundaries. Yet they raised questions about whether the kibbutz could remain distinctively Jewish while incorporating non-Jewish members. The conversion requirement embodied this tension. Religious kibbutzim required it explicitly; even secular kibbutzim struggled with non-Jewish members. Marriages between foreign volunteers and kibbutz members numbered over 1,100 in the 1970s alone (Balberg, 2024). Many kibbutzim worried that "the foreigner would eventually take their spouse to their home country", a

---

It is used here in its English-scholarly sense, as an identifier for Jews of Middle Eastern and North African origin.

fear not unfounded, though some volunteers chose to stay, converting and becoming members.

Muki has noted a striking pattern: "The hardest problem was with youth movement members from abroad, and especially those from Europe," who "expressed the strongest opposition" to accepting non-Jewish members. Those most shaped by traditional ideology proved most resistant to expanding boundaries. Volunteers participated in kibbutz life, working, eating communally, joining activities, but remained outside the membership structure, without voting rights or long-term security. They were strangers in the kibbutz: present but not fully integrated. For me, as a non-Jewish volunteer contemplating permanent membership, the path revealed boundaries with particular clarity. My commitment to socialist principles was insufficient without embracing Jewish identity, which I personally decided not to adopt versus conversion. For me, as an atheist, conversion to Judaism was never an option. Thus, the shop without prices embodied universal values, but access required crossing particular boundaries of identity and belonging.

Three Stories from the Threshold: Pathologies of Gatekeeping Failure

The abstract tensions explored above, between openness and identity, between principled gatekeeping and discriminatory exclusion, become painfully concrete in the lives of individuals who encountered the boundaries of belonging. The following three stories, spanning from the 1950s to the early 2000s and beyond, reveal how admission and membership decisions could fail in fundamentally different ways. Each illustrates a distinct mechanism of exclusion: ideological control that punished critical thinking, factional warfare that weaponized democratic processes, and prejudice masquerading as economic pragmatism.

The Polish Journey: When Ideology Demanded Silence

In the late 1950s, a young kibbutz member, himself from a family that had survived the Holocaust, traveled to Europe, including Poland. What he witnessed shook him profoundly: the communist regime's suppression of dissent, Soviet control over Eastern Europe, all contradicting everything he thought the left stood for. He returned to his kibbutz and began speaking openly about what he had seen, denouncing the Soviet Union as an antidemocratic dictatorship that betrayed socialist ideals. The response was swift and severe: he was expelled from the kibbutz. The official reason was ideological deviation. Many kibbutzim in the 1950s still maintained strong allegiances to the Soviet Union, viewing it as the leading force of international socialism despite mounting evidence of authoritarianism. To publicly criticize the USSR was seen not merely as political disagreement but as betrayal of the movement's foundational ideology. The young man's first-hand observations, informed by his own family's experience of totalitarianism, were deemed less important than loyalty to the party line.

The irony was devastating. Here was someone whose family had fled one totalitarian regime, now being punished for recognizing another. His crime was not lack of commitment to socialist values but rather holding those values seriously enough to apply them critically. For this, he lost his home and community. The expulsion revealed how ideology could become its own form of authoritarianism, demanding conformity rather than critical engagement.

The South American Family: When Power and Resentment Collided

In 2003, a kibbutz in southern Israel faced a crisis. A prominent family, originally from South America, had become central to kibbutz life. The parents of the kibbutz-member family were very wealthy and had made substantial financial donations to the community. The husband served as human resources coordinator, advocating for efficiency measures and outcome assessments that sparked significant controversy. When the family's son's wife began the standard process toward membership, she was widely perceived as unmotivated in her work assignments. When her candidacy came before the general assembly, she was denied membership. Within weeks, the entire extended family, more than twelve people, left the kibbutz.

The official reason for denying the young woman's membership was her perceived lack of work commitment. But the kibbutz narrative told a different story. Many believed the vote was less about the candidate herself than about accumulated resentment toward her family's wealth, influence, and push for organizational changes that threatened traditional ways of operating. The admission vote had become a proxy battle, a way for members to register their opposition to the family's dominance and attitudes. The irony was profound: the gatekeeping mechanism designed to protect community values had been weaponized to settle scores. A young woman paid the price for tensions that had nothing to do with her individual merit. And the kibbutz lost an entire family whose involvement and resources had been substantial. This case demonstrates how democratic gatekeeping mechanisms can become weaponized to settle factional conflicts, transforming admission votes into proxy battles over community direction and power.

The Transplant Recipient: When Medical History Trumped Belonging

Around 2020, in a kibbutz in central Israel, a couple seemed to embody successful integration across cultural boundaries. The husband was kibbutz-born, from a prominent founding family. His wife, originally a volunteer from Finland, had become a physiotherapist. Together they adopted two children and built a life deeply rooted in the community. One of their children required a kidney transplant during adolescence, a procedure that proved successful. The child struggled with substance use during this difficult period but completed rehabilitation, married, started a family. The young couple rented a house on the kibbutz, their children attending kibbutz schools, their lives intertwined with the community where one partner had grown up.

When they applied for membership, the kibbutz management person on the admission committee voted against acceptance. The stated reasons were two: first, the candidate's drug history, significantly exaggerated beyond the adolescent struggles that had been resolved years earlier; and second, concerns that the medical history of kidney transplantation meant the family might not be able to stand economically on their own feet, potentially becoming a burden on the collective. The parents were outraged. Both well-established, contributing members of the community, they saw the decision as fundamentally prejudiced and unjust. The young family continues to live on the kibbutz to this day: residents but not members, inside but perpetually outside. Their children grow up in a community that refuses to fully embrace one of their parents. The grandparents remain, their own membership now shadowed by the knowledge that the community they helped build rejected their child. This case exposes perhaps the most insidious failure: discrimination masquerading as neutral economic pragmatism.

Together, these three cases, spanning more than half a century, demonstrate that gatekeeping mechanisms can fail in fundamentally different ways. The Polish-journey expulsion shows ideological rigidity at its most extreme, when loyalty to international socialism trumped personal experience, family history, and direct observation of authoritarian practice. The South American case reveals the weaponization of democratic processes to settle factional conflicts: supposedly objective criteria, work commitment, contribution to community, became proxies for accumulated resentments about wealth and power. The transplant case exposes the most insidious failure of all: the permanence of a liminal status, living on the kibbutz but denied membership, creates an ongoing reminder of exclusion that affects not just the rejected individual but children and grandparents across three generations. In each case, supposedly principled boundaries became instruments of exclusion that contradicted the very values they purported to defend.

Contemporary Negotiations: Bounded Equality and Complex Pluralism

The contemporary kibbutz landscape reflects ongoing negotiation between openness and closure, between maintaining distinctive identity and embracing diversity. Different kibbutzim have navigated these tensions in different ways, creating a spectrum of approaches to membership and belonging. Bounded equality, radical equality within the community combined with clear boundaries determining who can access that equality, captures both the kibbutz's genuine commitment to egalitarianism among members and its simultaneous exclusivity in determining membership itself (cf. Tsuk, 2005). This bounded equality both enables and limits the kibbutz's egalitarian experiment. The boundaries create the social trust and shared commitment necessary for radical economic equality. As Muki has explained: "We can have the shop without prices because we know each other, because we've vetted each other. That's the condition for this kind of sharing." But these same boundaries also prevent the kibbutz from serving as a universal model, from demonstrating that equality is possible for all humanity regardless of ethnic, national, or religious identity. The question remains uncomfortable: Can a community practice radical internal equality while maintaining exclusionary external boundaries without contradicting its own egalitarian principles?

These dilemmas of bounded equality do not end once a person has crossed the threshold into membership; they also shape the conditions under which belonging is maintained over time. From this perspective, voluntariness becomes a crucial test of whether equality in the kibbutz is genuinely chosen or silently coerced. From the very beginning, the kibbutz has emphasized the voluntary nature of membership. No one is forced to join or remain; membership is a choice freely made and freely sustained. This voluntariness distinguishes the kibbutz from totalitarian experiments in collectivization and has deep ethical significance. Yet voluntariness intersects with questions of exit costs. Leaving a kibbutz means abandoning homes, relationships, identities built over lifetimes. For older members especially, the costs can be prohibitive, making continued membership more ambiguous than the principle suggests. As Muki has acknowledged: "When people have lived here for forty or fifty years, when all their friends are here, when they've built their whole lives around this place, can we really say it's still voluntary if they stay even when they're unhappy with the changes?" This question became particularly acute during the privatization debates of the 1990s and 2000s, when some members felt forced to accept changes they fundamentally opposed because leaving was not a realistic option. The principle of voluntariness, straightforward in the founding era, revealed its complexity when communities underwent transformation, a complexity I take up at length in Chapter 6.

Contemporary kibbutzim are significantly more diverse than their founders could ever have imagined. They include members from different ethnic backgrounds, levels of religious observance, political views, and relationships to work and community. Some have accepted non-Jewish members; others maintain the conversion requirement. Some have developed highly pluralistic cultures; others maintain more traditional homogeneity. The admission committee still exists in most kibbutzim, though its role and power have changed. In some communities it has become more formal and structured, with explicit criteria and transparent processes designed to prevent discrimination. In others it has weakened as economic pressures have made communities more willing to accept anyone willing to join and contribute. The questions asked have shifted from ideological purity to practical compatibility. As one current admission-committee member explained: "We don't ask about Marx anymore. We ask whether people can live with noise from neighbors, whether they'll accept majority decisions even when they disagree, whether they understand what communal life requires. The ideology has faded; the practical questions remain."

Fundamental dilemmas persist nonetheless. How much diversity can a community absorb while maintaining coherent identity? When does openness to new members threaten the bonds that make community meaningful? How can communities balance the genuine need for social cohesion with the ethical imperative to avoid exclusion and discrimination? These questions have no final answers but require ongoing negotiation, shifting with each generation and each new challenge. Some kibbutzim have experimented with more inclusive approaches. Urban kibbutzim, in particular, have often embraced greater diversity, defining community less through ethnic or ideological homogeneity and more through shared commitment to specific projects or values. These communities demonstrate that alternatives to the traditional model are possible, successfully integrating members from diverse backgrounds by focusing on common practices rather than common origins (Palgi & Reinharz, 2011). I return to the urban kibbutzim and the migration of the kibbutz idea to small urban margins in Chapter 11.

Reflexive Interlude: Two Positions on Belonging

What follows is a brief meta-reflection on our two positions in this world, mine as a scholar and former volunteer, Muki's as a kibbutz member of more than six decades, rather than new empirical material. It is an attempt to think through, rather than resolve, the tensions this chapter has explored. We have described the kibbutz as a community that practiced radical internal equality while maintaining exclusionary external boundaries. There is a certain irony in writing this, given that I myself was a beneficiary of those boundaries even while partially, and at times informally, remaining outside them. This liminal position, insider and outsider, member and stranger, taught me something crucial about bounded equality. The shop without prices was not simply a marketplace alternative; it was a statement about who belonged, whose needs mattered, whose claims on community resources were legitimate. Those who remained outside the membership structure were reminded daily of the boundaries that made the community possible.

Muki's position is different from mine. As kibbutz-born, as a founder of his own community at Ein Gev and later a long-standing member of Yad Tabenkin, as someone deeply committed to the kibbutz's ideals, he could fully participate in the shop without prices, could vote on all community decisions, could claim the kibbutz as unambiguously his. Yet in our conversations he has expressed profound unease about the boundaries his community maintains. "We created something remarkable," he often says, "but it cost us something too." What did it cost? The ability to claim that socialism could be universal, that human equality was possible not just among the chosen few but for all humanity. The shop without prices worked, but only because people had been vetted, selected, deemed compatible. Its very success as an egalitarian model depended on the exclusivity that prevented it from being universal.

Both of us, from our different positions, have grappled with this dilemma. Can you have genuine community without boundaries? Can you practice radical equality without selecting who gets to participate? Can the shop without prices exist without admission committees? The honest answer is that we don't know. What we do know is that the question itself matters. It forces communities to acknowledge the tension rather than pretend that openness and particularity can be seamlessly integrated. It demands honesty about what belonging costs, both for those included and those excluded. It insists that we cannot celebrate egalitarian achievements while ignoring the boundaries that make them possible. In a sense, then, the kibbutz is not a failure to be overcome but a teacher to be listened to. It shows that the challenge isn't whether to have boundaries but how to make them as just as possible while maintaining what makes community meaningful. It demonstrates that transparency about exclusion is more honest, and ultimately more ethical, than pretending that boundaries don't exist or don't matter.

Conclusion

The admission committee that I first encountered on a winter evening in 1983 continues operating in most kibbutzim today. What it evaluates and how it decides, however, has transformed as profoundly as the communities themselves. The evolution from ideological purity to pragmatic flexibility did not eliminate gatekeeping's fundamental dilemmas; it merely transformed them.

Kibbutzim today must navigate the same tensions their founders faced, but in a radically different context. They must decide how much diversity to embrace while maintaining coherent identity. They must balance the genuine need for social cohesion with the ethical imperative to avoid exclusion. They must figure out how to adapt to economic and demographic pressures without abandoning the values that make them distinctive. Different communities have made different choices. Some have opened their doors dramatically, accepting members from diverse backgrounds and creating new forms of belonging. Others have remained more closed, maintaining stricter criteria and more homogeneous membership. Most occupy some middle ground, making pragmatic compromises with their ideals.

What unites them is the persistence of the dilemma itself. Bounded equality remains the kibbutz's defining characteristic, and defining paradox. The shop without prices still exemplifies radical internal equality. But access to that shop still depends on passing through the admission committee's gates. Perhaps this is as it should be. The kibbutz may not have solved the problem of how to combine radical equality with legitimate community boundaries. But in grappling honestly with that problem, in acknowledging its difficulty rather than pretending it does not exist, the kibbutz offers valuable lessons for any community seeking to remain both distinctive and just, both particular and open to universal human values.

The question of who gets to belong remains urgently alive. The answer is no simpler today than it was on that winter evening in Barkai. But the communities that keep asking the question, that remain unsettled by their own boundaries, that refuse easy answers, these communities keep the ethical tension alive. And in doing so they remind us all that belonging is never a purely economic or ideological matter. It is always, fundamentally, a moral question.

4. Who Gets to Make the Soup?
Gender, Labor, and the Paradoxes of Equality

Children sleeping in a children's house with an adult present, 1950s

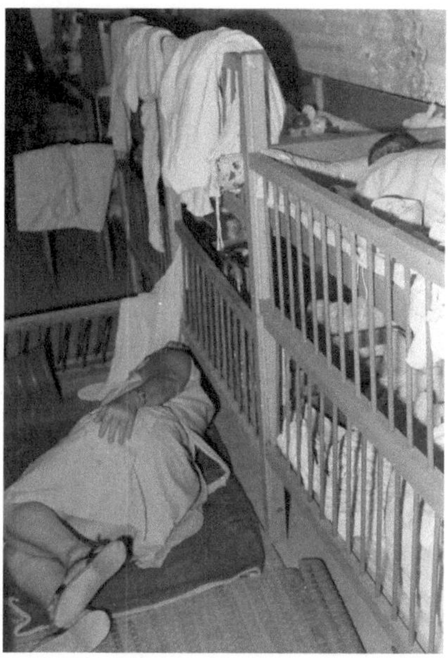

Source: Archives Ein Gev, photographer unknown

In 1914, at three in the morning, Miriam Baratz made her way through the darkness of Degania to the cowshed. She arrived hours before the official milking shift because she had discovered that if she wanted to work with the cows, the work she loved, the work that embodied the pioneering ideal of transforming oneself through labor, she had to arrive before the man formally assigned to that task. When he came and found the work already done, there was nothing left for him to do. The cowshed became her domain (Balberg, 2024, pp. 16–17).

This is not a story of women's liberation in any straightforward sense. It is a story of one woman's extraordinary determination to claim what, in a community committed to equality, should have been available to her as a matter of course. Sixty years later, in the early 1980s, a kibbutz member approached Muki Tsur during debates about family sleeping with a very different declaration: "I want my wife to work less and then, when I come back from work, she'll make me the soup." The sentence sounds almost caricatured in its traditionalism, jarringly at odds with a movement that had promised gender equality from its inception.

Yet the consequences of this trend were paradoxical. The shift from communal sleeping in the children's houses to family sleeping at home actually enabled a significant expansion of women's professional work. The closed system of childcare that had confined women's labor for decades opened up, ironically, because of the soup.

The story of gender, family, and kinship in the kibbutz evolves between Miriam getting up at three in the morning to claim the cowshed and women in the 1980s reclaiming their time and careers through family sleeping arrangements. It is a story in which intentions and outcomes repeatedly diverge. Some of the women's own decisions are later remembered as male conspiracies, and achieved equality generates new forms of inequality. Eventually, the reinvention of gender relations becomes both a vehicle of liberation and a source of new burdens.

This chapter examines two interconnected dilemmas that shape the kibbutz's attempt to reorganize gender relations. First, did family sleeping arrangements empower or burden women? The transition from communal to family-based sleeping arrangements[1] exposes the paradox at the heart of

1 Sleeping arrangements in the kibbutz refer to where children spent the night. Under communal sleeping, in place across most of the movement from the 1920s onward, children slept in dedicated children's houses (batei yeladim) with peer groups and rotating night-watch carers, returning to their parents' homes only for daytime visits. Un-

the kibbutz gender project: a change driven in part by conventional gender assumptions ("she'll make me the soup") nevertheless created unprecedented opportunities for women's professional advancement. Second, can equality coexist with the supposedly "natural" pull of gender difference? The founding promise of gender equality confronted a powerful ideological retreat in the 1980s and 1990s, when sociological research produced within the kibbutz movement itself insisted that women "are something else" and should not be "forced into the male image." The closely related question of how the kibbutz attempted to reorganize kinship itself, the children's houses, the place of biological and communal parenting, is the subject of Chapter 5.

The First Dilemma: Mothers' Guilt and the Dialectic of Collective Education

My discussion in this section leans closely on Mira Balberg's (2024) reconstruction of Degania's early years and the dilemmas around work, gender, and childrearing. When Miriam Ostrowsky (Baratz) married Yosef Baratz in June 1912, Balberg describes how the young bride spent her wedding day in the kitchen, cooking for the guests together with Sarah Malkin, and then, at two in the morning, left the celebrations to milk the cows. In Balberg's account, food preparation and cleaning were taken for granted as women's responsibility; even on this "national wedding," as Miriam later called it, she felt primarily "the weight of great responsibility" toward the collective rather than a claim to personal celebration.

A year later, when Gideon, Miriam's and Degania's first child, was born, Balberg notes Miriam's recollection that she "had no objection" when comrades woke the baby late at night to show him off. Yet the group soon discovered that it had given almost no thought to what children would mean for its communal ethos. Balberg uses this episode to highlight a fundamental contradiction in Degania's self-understanding: in a community where productive work for the collective was the decisive criterion of membership, childcare did not

der family sleeping, which spread gradually from the 1970s and was adopted by the last kibbutzim in 1999, children slept at home with their parents and used the children's houses only as daytime educational and care institutions. The shift is the central institutional change in the kibbutz reinvention of kinship, treated in detail in Chapter 5.

count as productive labor, and mothers found themselves structurally penalized. Miriam's response, as Balberg quotes her, was to try to "continue [her] life exactly as it had been before," rising at three in the morning, working until ten at night, and bringing Gideon to the cowshed, where she laid him on straw while she worked. Even this heroic effort did not resolve the contradiction; the group decided that because some of her time was spent caring for the baby, Miriam would receive only two-thirds of the standard members' allowance.

I use these early scenes as a lens on what later scholarship, particularly Spiro (1979) and Palgi and Reinharz (2011), will conceptualize as the "closed women's sector." Formally, women were equal members of the collective. In practice, Balberg shows how they were increasingly concentrated in caring and service roles such as education, kitchen, and laundry, while men dominated agriculture, industry, and political leadership. Communal childcare, which emerged as the dominant solution once more members married and had children, institutionalized this division by casting childcare as a "shared responsibility" that was in fact always allocated to women, according to seasonal and administrative considerations.

Balberg also attends to the emotional and subjective dimensions of this arrangement. On the one hand, communal childrearing loosened traditional parental control and enabled new affective constellations in which children often formed their deepest attachments to peers and caregivers rather than to parents. On the other hand, testimonies from later decades, such as the woman from Kibbutz Beit HaShita who retrospectively described twenty years in childcare as a "nightmare" that left her feeling intellectually atrophied and trapped by conscience, underscore the extent to which the women's sector functioned as a domain of confinement, even as it was framed ideologically as an arena of equality and social importance. Yosef Baratz's own retrospective judgment captures the bitter irony of this evolution: the female comrade who came to Palestine hoping to reinvent herself as a land worker "like her friends" found that "her fate here is as her fate was there." The early Degania vignettes thus crystallize a pattern that would endure for decades. The women's sector was structurally indispensable and symbolically celebrated, yet organized in ways that reinscribed gendered hierarchies under communalist and egalitarian rhetoric.

The Dialectic of Collective Education

Muki characterizes this history as "the dialectic of collective education": an arrangement initially devised to ease women's double burden that ultimately fixed them in the very caregiving roles they had hoped to leave behind. When I asked why the women's sector remained closed to outside labor while the men's sector gradually opened to non-member workers, his answer pointed to a subtle mechanism of control:

> "Collective education created a commitment to education that claims that whoever participates in the educational process must be a member of the kibbutz. And how do you convince people to comply? By mobilizing mothers' guilt, telling a mother: you're not a good mother if you don't participate in the educational process. So the mothers felt guilty. And you have to remember this was at a time when family values were returning in a very strong way. I think it was a result of World War II; the idea of starting a family and having children became so central that it completely closed off the women's sector."

The mechanism Muki describes is both elegant and cruel. Women were told that, as mothers, they bore a distinctive moral obligation to work in the children's houses, whereas agricultural and industrial labor could be delegated to hired workers. Precisely because childcare was framed as a privileged expression of maternal commitment, it could not be externalized in the same way. Mothers' guilt became the lock on a door that might otherwise have opened.

Against this background, the later debates over family sleeping arrangements gain their full significance. Muki recalls a conversation he held with a member of Ein Gev:

> "In my kibbutz, when the debates about sleeping arrangements began, a member who has just passed away recently, a member of my youth group, came to me and said: 'Listen, I want family sleeping. You know why? Because I want my wife to work less and when I come back from work she'll make me...' I completed his sentence: '...the soup.' And I heard that, and I really wanted family sleeping myself, really wanted it. But I said: Wait, but that's crazy. What is he saying? What is he saying here?"

Some of the men, in other words, wanted their wives to take care of them and serve the soup, an opinion that could not have been articulated in the formative years of the kibbutz movement. Muki then formulates the paradox at the heart of this process: “Now, the big paradox was that the move to family sleeping actually liberated the women.” When I asked him whether women were part of the discussions, he replied that they were very much in favor of the move, in part because educational researchers and others had been telling them for years that they were not good mothers, while no one was telling the men that they were not good fathers. The women’s sector remained closed precisely because women had been told they must work in the children’s houses because they were mothers. The men’s sector had opened up earlier, by bringing in nonmembers to work in agriculture and industry; only with the shift to family sleeping did the women’s sector begin to open in parallel.

What that shift brought, in Muki’s deliberately provocative formulation, was that women for the first time “got what liberated women get in many places, that other, non-liberated women work for them.” The point underscores a structural pattern that many feminist analyses of the kibbutz identify more broadly: women’s entry into professional and public life often rests on the labor of other, typically less privileged women who perform care work and domestic tasks. In the kibbutz, the transition to family sleeping, together with the gradual externalization of cleaning, laundry, and parts of childcare, enabled some women to be “liberated” because paid caregivers, cleaners, and migrant workers took over responsibilities that had once been borne collectively.

For me, this insight was not merely theoretical but deeply experiential. I myself experienced kibbutz childcare (irrespective of the sleeping arrangements) as one of the changes that made it seem feasible to combine career and family. Several of my German friends, of similar or slightly older generations, chose not to have children in order to pursue careers; by contrast, the kibbutz appeared to offer a different horizon, an arena in which both might be possible. Interestingly, many kibbutz-born women of my generation did not share my perspective. I remember comments when I started the MA at Tel Aviv University criticizing that I did not stay in the kibbutz to finally (I was then twenty-six years old) start a family. My generation of kibbutz-born women had, in the end, a rather conservative view on women’s role in the family. Planning and pursuing a career was usually not part of it.

In Barkai, the decisive turning point in sleeping arrangements came in 1999, the year in which the remaining kibbutzim that had not yet moved to family sleeping made the change. By then I was already working outside the kibbutz and my professional life was taking shape. The decision coalesced almost silently, without, as I recall, even a formal kibbutz meeting: children would not return to the children's houses at night, and the arrangement that had been provisional for so long became permanent.

The Women's Strike

While the move to family sleeping revealed the paradoxical liberation of some women, Muki's story of the women's strike in the early 1990s exposed the fractures within the women's community itself. One day in the early 1990s, Muki, then serving as general secretary of the entire kibbutz movement, received a call. The women in one kibbutz had refused to go to work in the children's houses. He describes the scene vividly:

> "I still remember, all the women sitting in the club house and there's a bookshelf, and behind the bookshelf sits the kibbutz secretary to listen to what is going on. And then a conversation starts and it turns out that in the women's community there was a fight between the women who said: we were left with the floor rag and you go to teach."

The conflict was not primarily between men and women, but between women. Over the years, some had managed to move into professional work (teaching, social work, external employment in other kibbutzim or nearby cities), while others remained in what they called the "dirty work": cleaning, childcare, kitchen labor. On both sides, a language of liberation was intertwined with a language of family. "It was within the women's community," Muki notes. "It exploded. It was an eye-opening conversation for me. I understood, first of all, the tension that exists within the women's community. On the one hand, they discovered women's liberation anew, and on the other hand, they wanted to continue the process of family life: making family life the central thing. The women who worked outside spoke in the name of women's liberation. The women who were inside spoke in the name of family. And I remember my position then: remember you're one community, one women's community. Remember how you stand against the men's community, not how you stand against each other in the women's community."

As a sociologist, I was struck by how quickly the women's debate slid into moral language about "good" mothers and "liberated" women, obscuring the material reorganization of work that made these identities possible. This was not only a struggle between competing feminist idioms, "women's liberation" versus "the family," but also a structural transformation in the political economy of kibbutz labor, shaped by wider shifts in state policy, resource allocation, and exposure to markets. In Tsuk's (2005) terms, even such an intentional community could not "ignore the structure": decisions about who remained in "dirty work" inside the kibbutz, and who accessed professional or external employment, were mediated by the changing triangle of state, market, and community rather than by gender ideology alone.

The underlying process was clear. As kibbutzim increasingly outsourced physically demanding or low-status work, members of both genders withdrew from manual labor and moved into managerial, professional, or external employment, consolidating what Tsuk calls a "governing class" within the cooperative framework. Yet women's work in childcare remained "inside" much longer than men's work in agriculture or industry, anchoring some women in what they themselves called the dirty work even as others exited into recognized professions and into denser networks with the state and the market. The women's strike thus exposed not only divisions among women, but also how class-like differentiations, gendered occupational hierarchies, and the shifting relationship between kibbutz and state intersected to reproduce inequality under the banner of equality.

Vivian Silver and the Two Kinds of Equality

A further turning point in Muki's understanding came from Vivian Silver, a kibbutz member working in architecture, who would later be killed in the Hamas attack of October 7, 2023. She walked into his office and stated without preamble: "Listen, there's no equality." Muki's initial response was disbelief. "As a historian," he later told me,

> "I remembered all the statements, and all the battles, and all the wonderful literature of liberated women, and I said: It can't be that this is happening. It's very interesting that I just didn't read reality correctly. She stood in the office, I remember even where in the office, and said: 'Listen, you don't understand what's going on,' and she convinced me."

The conversation led to the creation of a special department for women's equality within the kibbutz movement, headed by Vivian Silver. More importantly, it forced Muki to acknowledge a broader cognitive failure. "I see myself," he said, "as not reading reality correctly. This sometimes happens to us because we're educated in a certain way; we read the situation according to what's in our head and heart more than what's really happening." Ideology, in other words, had become a lens that filtered out inconvenient realities.

What Muki names here is a form of epistemic relativism: what counts as truth varies with the position from which one observes, and ideological commitment can function as a filter that admits only the evidence compatible with it. Vivian Silver was standing inside the same kibbutz movement Muki had served as general secretary, but from her position the equality claim that he had received as historical fact was not visible at all. The literature of liberated women he could quote, the public statements of equality, the formal mechanisms of equal distribution: none of these were what she meant when she said there was no equality. She meant something he had not been trained to see. Muki himself sketched the deeper logic of this blindness.

> "The perception in the kibbutz is that there's gender equality because there's equality in the kibbutz. That is, if there's equality in the kibbutz, then there must be gender equality, and therefore women don't have to do laundry and cook. This really hides deeper processes of inequality, even if we look, for example, at the distribution of assets, of money. In the economic distribution, there really was equality. You didn't get a smaller budget because you're a woman, you didn't get a smaller house because you're a woman. The equality in everything related to tangible goods, it really was perfect."

Perfect equality in the material realm concealed profound inequality in the realm of work, decision-making, and autonomy. Women and men received identical budgets, identical housing, identical work compensation. This was historically significant and genuinely transformative. Yet it also made it easier to deny or downplay the gendered allocation of tasks, the closing of the women's sector, and the pressures that funneled women toward certain forms of labor and not others.

In my own experience in Barkai, women were really drawn into family life after the move to family sleeping, and suddenly were happy. I never understood this, probably due to my own family history. For the kibbutz women, having a washing machine and not going to the dining room to eat was a kind of "liberation." In my view it was a misunderstanding of what "quality of life" is about. What can be better, after all, than having one's laundry and cooking done by others? Yet in this process having private domestic conveniences was interpreted as liberation, even when it coincided with increased domestic responsibility and reduced participation in public, political, or economic centers of power.

Summing up the first dilemma: liberation in the kibbutz context was never a simple linear process. Measures that were experienced as emancipatory in one domain (family sleeping, private washing machines, professional work outside the kibbutz) could simultaneously reinforce or create new inequalities in another. Equality in material distribution coexisted with inequality in labor, voice, and time.

The Second Dilemma: When Equality Becomes Sameness, and Back Again

If the first dilemma revealed the paradoxes of liberation, the second turns to the conceptual core of the gender question: does equality require sameness, or can genuine equality accommodate, even embrace, difference? Throughout its history, the kibbutz oscillated between two problematic poles. In its first decades, it pursued equality by erasing gender difference, expecting women to conform to "male" norms of work and public participation. When this model faltered, the movement swung toward biological essentialism, insisting that women were "something else entirely" and that respecting them meant affirming their distinct nature. Both positions contained important insights; both inflicted damage; neither produced a stable, egalitarian ordering of gender relations.

In the 1980s and 1990s, as family sleeping became widespread and women were increasingly concentrated in domestic and educational work, the kibbutz movement developed an internal intellectual rationale for retreating from earlier feminist aspirations.

> "All kinds of studies start to appear," Muki recalls, "proving femininity is something entirely different from masculinity, biologically. These studies came from within the kibbutz movement. People felt these gaps that existed. I remember the researcher who did this, and I just didn't know what to do with it. Because he did it with total honesty, but with a very clear messianic sense that women's liberation had to end."

The timing is crucial. These were not conservative religious texts or outside attacks on feminism, but works produced inside the socialist, ostensibly egalitarian kibbutz world, drawing authority from the prestige of social science. "The move to family sleeping was accompanied by a reaction that claimed: "The woman is something else," Muki explains. He recalls a sociological study by Tiger and Shepher (1975) "that talked about how women are something else and shouldn't be forced into the male image, and the whole women's liberation story was a mistake."

What made this particularly powerful, and in a sense dangerous, was the kibbutz's distinctive openness to sociological research. As Muki notes, "the kibbutz, unlike communes, was always open to sociological research. And the sociological research always influenced the kibbutz. That is, it wasn't research that just parked on a shelf. Rather, people read the research and behaved accordingly." Research claiming deep, biologically grounded differences between men and women did not merely describe existing patterns; it helped reshape them. The idea that women should not be "forced into the male image" was easily translated into arguments that they should not occupy certain roles, work certain hours, or shoulder specific responsibilities. What was framed as a humane correction to earlier "masculinizing" tendencies thus legitimated the re-closing of the women's sector.

Neumann (2024) shows how these developments undermined gender equality not only through material arrangements but through ideological realignments. Studies asserting that women "are something else" created an intellectual framework in which assigning women to domestic and caregiving roles could be presented as respect for their authentic nature rather than as exclusion. The argument had a certain intuitive appeal. Perhaps, it suggested, the kibbutz's mistake had not been insufficient commitment to equality but commitment to the wrong kind of equality, one that demanded women become like men. Perhaps genuine respect required recognizing fundamental differences and organizing social life around them.

Yet there is another way to read the same process. For decades, the kibbutz had constrained women's opportunities by closing the women's sector, channeling women into childcare and services, and externalizing men's work but not women's. When economic and demographic changes made family sleeping and expanded domestic labor inevitable, the movement needed a discourse to explain why women once again bore the primary responsibility. A biologized concept of difference supplied that discourse. The signs of this confusion were already visible in the late 1960s, when Kibbutz Artzi decided to allocate "one working hour a day for household chores, thus operating under the assumption that household tasks were the responsibility of women." What appeared as an attempt to recognize and compensate domestic labor in fact reinforced the idea that such work naturally belonged to women. The "improvement" confirmed rather than challenged the entrenched division of labor (Agassi, 1989).

Across these decades, then, the kibbutz moved between two untenable poles. In the early period, equality meant sameness: women were expected to work as men did, in the same sectors and at the same pace, with little recognition of embodiment, reproductive labor, or the double burden. This model generated exhaustion and disillusionment. In the later period, the movement embraced difference: women were understood as fundamentally distinct from men, and equality was redefined as the right to fulfill a gendered nature. This model stabilized inequality while presenting itself as care.

The kibbutz never fully articulated a third position: equality that takes difference seriously without turning it into destiny. It lacked a conceptual framework able to acknowledge that bodies, reproductive roles, and historical burdens are real, while insisting that they do not prescribe fixed social positions. Differences, in other words, do not have to transform into hierarchies. Perhaps this is the most honest assessment: the kibbutz did not resolve the problem of gender equality, not because it failed to try, but because the conceptual tools available to twentieth-century socialism were insufficient.

Acknowledging this limitation does not erase the significance of the experiment. The kibbutz shows that material equality, while necessary, is not sufficient; that formal freedom does not guarantee genuine choice when structural and cultural pressures persist; and that scientific discourse can legitimize domination as easily as liberation. The question of how to combine equality with difference therefore remains open. The dilemma persists.

Concluding Thoughts

The two dilemmas explored in this chapter, the paradox of liberation through traditional arrangements and the oscillation between equality-as-sameness and equality-as-difference, are not separate puzzles but facets of a single unresolved tension at the heart of the kibbutz experiment. Miriam Baratz rising at three in the morning to claim the cowshed and the member requesting that his wife make the soup are separated by six decades, yet they inhabit the same unfinished story. A community that genuinely aspired to remake the most intimate relations of human life discovered, again and again, that gender and care work resist ideological blueprints, without thereby proving that ideology was pointless.

What the kibbutz achieved, material equality between women and men, collective responsibility for children, a sustained willingness to question arrangements that most societies treat as natural, remains historically remarkable, even as its failures remind us that structural transformation without continuous critical reflection can reproduce the very hierarchies it set out to abolish. If there is a lesson here, it is not that the kibbutz "got it wrong," but that the reinvention of gender relations is never completed. Each generation inherits a set of arrangements it did not choose, and must decide anew what to preserve, what to discard, and what to reimagine. The dialogue between liberation and belonging, between the claims of community and the irreducible singularity of women's lives, continues. The closely related question of how the kibbutz attempted to reorganize kinship and the rearing of its children is taken up next, in Chapter 5.

5. Who Raises the Children?

Transmission, Rebellion, and Renewal

Children of Ein Gev with their kindergarten teacher, 1950s

Source: Archives Ein Gev, photographer unknown

The Junk Garden and the Deep Error

In the early years of the kibbutz, designing a children's yard was a matter of the highest seriousness. Parents formed committees, drew plans, and debated every detail of the physical and pedagogical environment in which their children would grow. Under the influence of Montessori and other progressive theories, arguments erupted over questions that might seem minor from the outside but were, within the kibbutz's self-understanding, foundational: should dolls be permitted, or were they instruments of bourgeois domesticity? What kind of space would best allow children to develop as creators rather than consumers of a world made by others?

For a time, the kibbutz became, as Muki puts it, an "ornamental garden," a meticulously planned environment of beauty and order. Then a counter-idea emerged: the "junk garden." Children, the argument went, needed not aesthetic perfection but raw material, disorder, things to take apart and reassemble, "because children need to be given the feeling that they create, not that they enter the world, but that they create in the world."

This oscillation between the ornamental garden and the junk garden captures something essential about the kibbutz's educational project. It was a community that placed the child at the center of its collective life, invested extraordinary thought and energy in the question of how the next generation should be raised, and was prepared to dismantle its own arrangements when they proved inadequate. "The kibbutz always was a special society whose center is in childhood," Muki observes, "in giving childhood, in granting childhood, in legitimizing childhood."

Yet this beautiful seriousness coexisted with what he calls "the deep error of the founding generation." The founders, who had experienced the wrenching gap between their ideals and their own capacities, believed the problem was temporary. Children raised inside the kibbutz, who would never know the shtetl, the bourgeois family, or the old hierarchies, would, they thought, grow up free from the tensions that plagued their parents. They were wrong. "The second generation born in the place was not less tormented than the first generation, though not with the same torments. It had no problem working agricultural work, but dealing with the idea was harder for them."

When a third generation arrived, and after them a fourth, many turned to their elders and said, in effect: "Stop with the weird ideas. Now we do everything sane. Everything needs to be normal." Normalcy here did not mean a return to some pre-kibbutz past, but alignment with a national middle-class

Israeliness of intact nuclear families, recognized credentials, and rising levels of private consumption. The demand for normalcy was itself a kind of wound, and the transition made many more. Kibbutz education is thus a story of repeated reinvention under pressure: pressure from within, as each generation discovered that inherited values could not simply be transmitted like agricultural techniques, and pressure from without, as the Israeli state, the university system, and an increasingly credentialist economy demanded conformity to standards the kibbutz had been designed to transcend.

As my later comparison with post-war Germany will suggest, the question of whether a society's values can survive across generations is not unique to the kibbutz. But the kibbutz confronted it with unusual intensity and self-awareness, because education was never peripheral to the project; it was the project. In this chapter, I approach the kibbutz as a generational project, asking how a revolutionary way of life tries to reproduce itself over time through education, and where and why that reproduction fails when it encounters new historical conditions, shifting aspirations, and changing social structures.

At stake is, first, the dilemma of whether revolutionary values can in fact be transmitted to generations that never lived through the revolution itself, and thus relate to its founding myths more as inherited memory than as formative experience. Closely linked is a second dilemma: whether education can remain a communal mission when the community that once defined itself through shared labor, equality, and collective responsibility is itself transforming under economic pressures, political disillusionment, and the individualization of life trajectories. A third dilemma emerges at the level of institutional practice: should kibbutz education preserve its pedagogical distinctiveness, its emphasis on collective responsibility, autonomy, and work as an educational principle, or should it conform to national standards that promise social mobility and recognition but risk diluting the movement's original ethos. Each of these dilemmas crystallizes a shared question: how can a revolutionary community educate its heirs when those heirs neither experienced the founding rupture nor necessarily share its horizon, yet must decide whether and how to carry its legacy forward.

The Origins of Communal Childrearing

Before I take up the dilemmas of transmission, communal mission, and political commitment, it is worth recalling how communal childrearing came into being in the first place. The system was not, as later memory would have it, a fully theorized pedagogical doctrine imposed from above. It was, in its founding moment, a practical and even desperate response to a stark problem: how could a community committed to equal participation in productive labor also ensure that its first children survived their infancy?

Contrary to the widespread belief that communal childrearing was imposed by male leadership, Muki locates its founding in a 1919 conference of about two hundred mothers and single women, with only four men present, who spent three days talking and crying as they tried to devise arrangements that would allow women to participate in collective labor while ensuring their children's survival. Before educational theories or pedagogical models, he emphasizes, stood a stark imperative: "First of all, that the children should live." Over the decades, this origin story largely disappeared. "I met many, many women," Muki recalls, "none of them believed me that the children's house was the result of the women's decision. They all thought it was a male plot. The male plot locked the children in the children's houses." A solution crafted by women under conditions of scarcity and danger came to be remembered as a patriarchal imposition. The gap between historical origins and later memory reveals how contested the question of who "owns" children remained, and how easily institutionalized care can be reinterpreted as an instrument of control.

Hashomer Hatzair and the Abolition of the Father

Some kibbutzim pushed this reimagining of family further than others. Hashomer Hatzair, the socialist-Zionist youth movement that combined Marxist and Freudian ideas, sought nothing less than to eliminate the Oedipal complex by abolishing paternal authority. Muki summarizes their logic succinctly: "Freud said Oedipus, so there's no Oedipus because there's no father. Together, without the father, we'll free the son, and the son without Oedipus will be healthy and a worker."

This was not merely theoretical. In Hashomer Hatzair kibbutzim, the parent-child tie was defined in "mechanical, biological terms," and children addressed their parents only by first name, never as "mom" or "dad." The underlying assumption was that every adult member could and should be a parental figure to every child, and that the supreme parent, the highest educational authority, was the kibbutz itself. The community explicitly claimed the symbolic functions traditionally attached to family, while relegating biology to mere fact.

This radical reconfiguration of kinship expressed a generational ethos. All socialist pioneers embraced some version of "out with the old, in with the new," but Hashomer Hatzair pursued the impulse to an extreme. Members imagined themselves as "newly made human beings," actively inventing a new mode of being human, committed to discarding everything associated with their parents' world. The conviction that youth, rather than inherited family tradition, would redeem humanity was also inscribed in space: from the 1950s onward, kibbutzim undertook what Muki calls "a huge project of building comprehensive houses," architectural ensembles in which children were meant to experience the collective, rather than the private home, as their primary world.

Saying Goodbye to Parents

The rejection of the biological family was not only ideological; it was also biographical. Muki notes a recurrent element in early kibbutz life histories up to the 1930s: "Most people who tell their story always tell part of it: how we said goodbye to parents. This is an integral part of a kibbutz biography. Some parted in peace, and some parted in shiva."

Parting in *shiva* meant that the parent mourned the children as if they had died: "We're sitting shiva. We don't have them. These children are not ours." One story Muki recounts is stark: a father lies across the doorway to prevent his son from leaving for Palestine; the son lifts him, lays him on the bed, and walks out. Emigration meant not only geographic departure but a dramatized severing of ties. Reconciliation, when it occurred, usually came through grandchildren: "Grandchildren always bridge between parents and their sons."

These founding biographies are essential context for everything that follows. The kibbutz that built communal childrearing was a kibbutz whose members had themselves enacted the most radical break possible with their own parents. The children's house was, in part, the institutional form of that break. Later, when the generation that had cut itself off finally began to speak, its message to its own children would unsettle the whole arrangement.

Dilemma 1: Can Revolutionary Values Be Transmitted to Generations That Never Lived the Revolution?

Heretics, Ignoramuses, and the Deep Error

From its earliest years, the kibbutz treated education not as one function among many, but as the central mechanism through which the revolutionary experiment would reproduce itself. Tsuk notes that intentional communities with distinctive life and organizational patterns "tend to develop comprehensive, vigorous and isolationist education systems which aim to transfer the ideological identity of the parents' or founders' generation to their offspring" (Tsuk, 2005, p. 62). In this sense, kibbutz education was "a classic case of communal education": children were understood as belonging to the kibbutz as a whole, which assumed the role of collective parent and took direct responsibility for all their needs, minimizing the mediating role of the nuclear family (Tsuk, 2005, p. 65).

The entire ecology, economy, institutional life, history, and philosophy of the kibbutz were mobilized as educational resources. Rites of passage, school entry, year's end, and graduation, became community festivals; work was integrated into the curriculum from childhood; and moral behavior and contribution to society were ranked above academic achievement. The theory of "joint education" sought to form future kibbutz members and loyal Zionist socialists through a synthetic education addressing all dimensions of the child's personality. This rested on a crucial institutional fact: kibbutz schools enjoyed a quasi-autonomous status vis-à-vis the national system, with their own curricula, rites, and standards.

Communal education in the 1930s thus turned from improvisation into a movement-wide doctrine that treated children as the kibbutz's paramount collective project. Balberg notes that kibbutz children, though cherished, were also "in many ways lab animals," exposed to successive experiments in how to produce courageous, hardworking socialists. Muki's recollections let us see this architecture from the inside: the comprehensive house, where children slept, ate, and studied under one roof, embodied an organic conception of educational work. Parents organized, designed, and argued over the children's yard, producing "beautiful programs" about how to build the space pedagogically, and insisting that children feel they "create in the world," not merely enter it.

Yet this extraordinary investment in education harbored a paradox that became visible only across generations. Kibbutz education drew on Jewish tradition, socialist pedagogy, and progressive education, and tried to fuse them into a single synthetic project; but the synthesis contained a deep tension. Leaders idealized a physically robust, psychologically uncomplicated worker whose attachment to the land would be natural rather than reflective, even as they charged education with cultivating ideological consciousness and continuity. The outcome was, in Balberg's phrase, "a model of self-defeating education": enormous resources were devoted to educating people who were meant, in principle, to have no need for such education and might even come to despise it.

The bitter joke, "We wanted to raise heretics, but we raised ignoramuses," captures this dynamic. The founders sought children who would reject the old world their parents had rejected, but produced a generation that no longer even knew what had been rejected. Muki names the same problem from within as "the deep error of the founding generation." The founders acutely felt the painful gap between their ideals and their lived capacities, but assumed this tension was temporary, and that children raised entirely inside the kibbutz would grow up without it. In reality, "the second generation born in the place was not less tormented than the first generation, though not with the same torments": agricultural work posed no difficulty, but "dealing with the idea was harder for them."

Balberg describes how the parents looked at this tanned, strong, confident, Hebrew-speaking generation with mingled admiration and disappointment. They had become the bodies the founders dreamed of, but lacked the revolutionary consciousness that had animated the dream, producing twice as much as their parents while quoting neither Gordon nor Marx.

The Weight of Holocaust Silences

If the second generation's torment was the weight of ideas they had inherited but could not inhabit, the third generation's was different still. Muki describes how "this community becomes problematic when the third generation arrives. There, it's already complicated, because you don't start from the beginning." The demand of later generations was, in essence, a demand for normalcy: "Now we do everything sane. Everything needs to be normal."

The wounds were deepened by a specific historical trauma. A significant part of the grandparent generation, survivors of or mourners for the Holocaust, were, as Muki puts it, "in the stage of mourning for their parents," and their message to their children was shattering: "Don't be crazy like us. We left the parents, you won't leave the parents." This, Muki says, "is an earthquake." The very generation that had enacted the most radical break with the parental home now insisted that its children must not repeat that break. The educational project of the kibbutz, built on the premise of separation from the family, was thus undermined from within, not by ideological opponents but by the accumulated grief of its own founders.

Two further dimensions of this trauma deserve attention, because they shape what later became thinkable about the kibbutz as a place to raise children. The first is the silence of the 1930s arrivals.

> "Everyone who came in the 30s doesn't have a story of leaving the parents," Muki explains, "because either he managed to bring the parents here, or he looks at the other parents who didn't manage to bring the parents and says: I won't tell this story, because this is a story of victory versus their mourning. At one kibbutz, of roughly 160 members who had applied to bring their parents from Europe, only sixteen parents arrived. Silence became a form of solidarity with those who had lost everything. People told their children how they had departed from their own parents only at the age of eighty. The children knew something had happened, but the silence did not make it go away. It often increased its impact."

The same pattern governed other traumas inside the kibbutz itself. In one children's house in the 1930s, several children fell ill; three died in close succession despite the best doctors. They were not buried in the kibbutz cemetery; a memorial booklet was printed, but within their families the surviving siblings were never told. When a child later saw a photograph and asked "Who is this?", the parents answered: "That's you when you were little." Only thirty years later, when one sibling went to the cemetery and saw the graves, did the truth erupt, "like an earthquake." The tragic deaths of these children threatened the kibbutz's self-understanding as a place where children would flourish. The response, erasure and silence, protected that identity at the cost of unprocessed grief.

These unspoken traumas, bound up with broken genealogies and missing grandparents, would matter profoundly when the question of family sleeping returned. The shift from communal to family sleeping, traced in Chapter 4 from the standpoint of women's labor, cannot be read only as a response to feminist critique, sociological research, or economic change. It also enacts the insistence of a traumatized generation that its children not repeat its own radical break with the parental home. The return of children to their parents' bedrooms at night embodies both a critique of earlier communal practices and an attempt to heal an intergenerational wound.

The Kibbutz as Substitute Family

Paradoxically, while the biological family reasserted itself for members, the kibbutz simultaneously fulfilled its original promise as a substitute family for those who had none. Between 1946 and 1948, some 15,000 thousand children arrived in Palestine through Youth Aliyah; about two-thirds were placed in kibbutzim. For them, the kibbutz "functioned in the deepest sense as what it was always supposed to be: a substitute for a family." Where biological kin were absent, the collective could successfully serve as family. Where biological families existed, the kibbutz could not permanently displace them. The reinvention of kinship therefore worked best precisely where there was no longer any kinship to compete with it.

The Structural Frame

Tsuk's structural analysis situates this emotional and generational crisis in a broader institutional framework. The kibbutz education system, he notes, was supported by "the isolation of kibbutz education from the general Jewish and Israeli education system, with a kind of privileged charter given to the kibbutz movement to develop, organize, run and evaluate its educational institutions in relative freedom" (Tsuk, 2005, p. 66). This isolation was both the system's strength and its vulnerability. As long as the kibbutz remained a world unto itself, its educational project could maintain its coherence. But as Israel's state institutions grew stronger, as the kibbutz's national prestige declined after the political upheaval of 1977, and as members increasingly pursued lives beyond the kibbutz's borders, the enclosed educational ecosystem began to leak. Tsuk identifies two other continua that shaped educational decisions in each kibbutz: from ideological openness to rigidity, and from the cultivation of the individual to the primacy of the group. Under external pressure and internal doubt, most kibbutzim shifted toward the individual end of this spectrum, and the communal system that was to reproduce revolutionary values gradually loosened its grip.

The German Comparison: What Transmission Actually Requires

The question of whether revolutionary values can survive their own success is not unique to the kibbutz. Scholars of political culture have long observed that values instilled through struggle tend to erode once the conditions that produced them disappear (Tocqueville, 1835/2000). My comparison with post-war Germany brings this into focus. In West Germany, democratic socialization began as an instruction from above, and was sustained through a deliberate, decades-long investment in the education system. I remember in school, the teachers pushed into us the feeling of responsibility, not guilt, because we were young, but the agenda was clear: as Germans we had to take over responsibility for the deeds of our parents' generation. In East Germany, due to political circumstances, it did not work like that. My account resonates with scholarship on German *Erinnerungskultur* (culture of memory). Adorno's "Education After Auschwitz" argued that the primary task of post-war education was not the transmission of knowledge but the cultivation of a reflective moral conscience capable of resisting conformity and authoritarian seduction (Adorno, 1966/1998). West Germany's sustained commitment to this project, through school curricula, memorials, and civic pedagogy, helped to produce what Jan-Werner Müller calls "constitutional patriotism": attachment to democratic norms grounded not in national pride but in critical self-reckoning (Müller, 2008). East Germany, by contrast, channeled its anti-fascist narrative through a state ideology that left little room for individual moral reflection, with consequences visible after reunification in patterns of political distrust and democratic disengagement (Fulbrook, 1999; Welzer, Moller, & Tschuggnall, 2014).

The divided German experience suggests that values can be transmitted across generations, but only through sustained, deliberate, and often uncomfortable institutional effort, and not through the mere fact of being born into a particular environment. Research on civic socialization indicates that exposure to moral complexity, including historical guilt and institutional failure, is a stronger predictor of democratic commitment than passive inheritance of a favorable milieu (Torney-Purta et al., 2001; Gibson & Gouws, 2003). This is a lesson Israelis would do well to consider today. The kibbutz founders hoped to avoid such discomfort by environmental design alone, trusting that children raised in conditions of equality and cooperation would absorb those values naturally. The German case suggests they underestimated what transmission actually requires.

Muki's response to my reading is revealing. He does not dispute the diagnosis of Israel's own socialization failures, but insists that the response must be sought not in politics but in civic and educational institutions. "Underneath all this there are tons of forces: educational forces, public forces, community forces. Let's do this not through politics. Let's do this through the public sector, through education, through universities, through academic education." This is the kibbutz educator's credo: the conviction that values are made and remade through pedagogical and communal practice, not through political power alone. It is also a tacit acknowledgement that the kibbutz's own educational experiment, for all its failures, pointed toward an important insight. A society's deepest commitments cannot simply be declared or legislated. They must be cultivated, generation after generation, through the patient, imperfect work of education.

Our first dilemma, then, remains unresolved. The founders' deep error was to believe that the right environment would be sufficient, that children raised in freedom and equality would naturally absorb the values that had motivated the revolution. The second generation's rebellion was to reject the very intellectualism through which those values had been articulated, producing what Balberg calls "the paradox of conservative revolutionism." The third generation demanded normalcy, and normalcy, by definition, is the opposite of revolutionary commitment. Yet the German comparison suggests that transmission is not impossible, only that it requires something more deliberate, more uncomfortable, and more ongoing than the kibbutz's early ideologues imagined.

Muki's concept of parental transmission acknowledges this reality. After the great crisis, kibbutz pedagogues had to accept that there is a parental culture that directs the thing, and that the community cannot simply override it. But he also points to something beyond parental transmission: the parents who come to the kibbutz today "because of education," who choose it not out of inherited loyalty but out of a conviction that it still offers something their children cannot find elsewhere. These newcomers must "choose anew in kibbutz education." Their choice is not a continuation of the revolution; it is, perhaps, a different kind of beginning. Whether that beginning can sustain the values that the revolution carried, or whether each generation must simply start again because, as Muki suggests, "you never start from the beginning, but the parent always starts from the beginning," is the question this dilemma leaves open.

Dilemma 2: Can Education Remain a Communal Mission When the Community Itself Transforms?

In its ideal form, kibbutz education was not merely a service the community provided, but the primary mechanism through which the community attempted to reproduce itself. Children were not just "the sons and daughters of the kibbutz" in a metaphorical sense; they were the site on which the kibbutz tried to refashion kinship, gender roles, and belonging. As Tsuk puts it, the community assumed "comprehensive responsibility" for children's needs, positioning itself as a collective parent and relegating the nuclear family to the margins. Education was thus entangled with the kibbutz's ecology, economy, institutions, and moral imagination: children's work was integrated into the general work scheme, and the boundaries between educator and community member, curriculum and daily life, were deliberately dissolved.

In this world, the educator was not a hired professional but a selected bearer of the collective ethos. I recall that kibbutzim sent "the most successful people, the best and most gifted women" to Oranim and the Kibbutz Seminar, with the clear expectation that they would return as kindergarten teachers and schoolteachers. Their social status was high not because they represented a separate profession, but because they stood at the point where the community's future was made present. The same closed women's sector traced in Chapter 4, including kitchens, laundries, and children's houses, was here reimagined as the vanguard of the new society, even as it remained structured by gendered divisions of labor.

The paradox Chapter 4 traces around gender liberation, that emancipation was built on "dirty work" and that equality reinscribed hierarchy, thus runs straight through the educational field. Women's concentration in childcare both sustained the communal project and constrained their own horizons. This circuit was fragile. From the 1990s onward, privatization and outsourcing broke it at every link. Where once the triangle of state, market, and community buttressed communal education, it now rearranged it: non-member workers entered the kindergartens while members increasingly moved into managerial, professional, or external employment. What had been a closed women's sector began to open, but in a way that also hollowed out the communal character of education. As Muki notes, "there's a problem how to instill in workers from outside the educational ethos of the kibbutz educational system." Routine can be transmitted through orientation sessions; but what he calls "content," the tacit understanding of what the community is trying to do, requires a thick, lived immersion in a shared way of life.

Re-familization: Talmon-Garber and the Return of Kinship

By the 1960s, the sociologist Yonina Talmon-Garber (Talmon-Garber, 2020) had already identified a clear trend: individualism and kinship relations were becoming increasingly prominent inside the kibbutz. The growing centrality of the family led to the emergence of new foci of power, including extended kinship networks and inter-family cliques, and to an expanded family influence in education, housing, and consumption budgets. What emerged was not a simple restoration of the pre-kibbutz nuclear family, but a new formation: multi-generational extended families that operated as power blocs within the communal framework, coordinating children's educational tracks, employment trajectories, and housing opportunities. From the 1970s onward, economic pressures, cultural shifts, and internal critique accelerated what researchers came to call *re-familization*.

Sociologically, this trajectory exemplifies, to a certain extent, what Ferdinand Tönnies described as the shift from *Gemeinschaft* (community) to *Gesellschaft* (society) (Tönnies, 1887). In early kibbutzim, children's houses meant that parents of the same age group met every evening, creating dense webs of interaction. With family sleeping, parents of children in the same peer group no longer met at the children's house every evening. Together with the decline of communal dining and the rise of outside employment, the result was less social contact, reduced intimacy of social relations, and the loss of a major form of social participation.

Generational Change and the Newcomers

Generational change sharpened this crisis. As Muki remarks, "things became even more problematic when the third generation arrives. You don't start from the beginning." The first generation of founders had broken with their families of origin and consciously chosen communal childrearing; the second still experienced the children's house as part of an ongoing revolution. By the time the third and fourth generations grew up, communal sleeping and collective education had become normality rather than rupture. The departure of many from the kibbutzim, a decline from roughly 3.5 percent to 1.5 percent of the Jewish population, mirrored the re-familization processes traced above: the strengthening of extended kin networks, the rise of family power blocs, and the increasing weight of biological ties in decisions about education, housing, and work. The educational system, designed for a homogeneous, self-confident collective, now confronted a social body in which many members were temporary, ambivalent, or oriented primarily toward their own families.

At this point, the dilemma acquires the generational inflection captured in Muki's aphorism: "You never start from the beginning, but the parent always starts from the beginning." The community accumulates institutions, habits, and scars; the parent arrives with a newborn child and asks, for the first time, what stories to tell, what schedule to follow, what kind of life to imagine. When parents themselves had grown up in children's houses, this asymmetry could be managed; they knew the system from the inside and understood its compromises. But as more newcomers joined the kibbutzim, often marrying in from outside and choosing the kibbutz precisely "because of education" rather than because of ideology or economics, the gap widened. These parents came seeking what they imagined as a better, freer, more nature-oriented childhood, "less in the race of urban culture." They brought energy and commitment, yet they did not carry the tacit knowledge on which the communal system had been built. Their beginning did not coincide with the community's accumulated history.

The Mezuzah on the Children's House Door

This mismatch is intensified by the transformations in kinship and gender analyzed in Chapter 4. When a woman from a Haredi Mizrahi family demands a *mezuzah* on the children's house door, she is not simply asking for a religious symbol. She is importing another kinship universe into a space that once derived its authority from secular, socialist, and often explicitly anti-familial premises. The victory of the mezuzah, Muki suggests, reflects not only the kibbutz's liberalism, in other words its requirement of tolerance and accommodation, but also its weakened capacity to define a shared educational horizon. In earlier decades, the same space had been used to abolish the father, to downplay biological parents in favor of the collective, or to reassign mothers' guilt from the home to the children's house. Now it becomes the arena where conflicting family narratives, secular, religious, traditional, liberal, are negotiated without an agreed-upon meta-story.

The gender dynamics of this new situation echo Chapter 4's first dilemma. The move to family sleeping liberated some women by opening the women's sector and enabling professional careers, but often at the cost of increased domestic responsibility and reliance on hired caregivers. Similarly, the erosion of the communal education circuit allows some women to leave the children's houses for external work, while others remain in what they themselves call the "dirty work" of childcare, this time under conditions of weaker collective ethos and stronger parental demands. The women's strike Muki recalls in Chapter 4, between those who felt "left with the floor rag" and those who "go to teach," therefore prefigures the differentiated positions of women within the reconfigured educational field. Liberation in this context is never simply an individual achievement; it is redistributed burden.

Seen from this angle, the contemporary kibbutz faces not one but two overlapping questions. The first is the explicit one: can it keep its schools communal when privatization, external employment, and demographic change reshape the triangle of state, market, and community? The second is more hidden: can it sustain an educational mission that once depended on a relatively homogeneous, self-sacrificing collective when parents now arrive with strong, diverse, and sometimes contradictory expectations grounded in their own family histories? The dilemma is not only whether a kibbutz can preserve communal schools in an era of privatization, but whether a communal educational mission is still possible when the community itself is no longer given but continuously remade.

Can a pedagogy born in a movement that wanted to reinvent kinship withstand a situation in which kinship has already been reinvented in the direction of multi-generational families, differentiated membership categories, and hybrid local societies of members and non-members? And if, as Chapter 4 suggests, each generation inherits a set of arrangements it did not choose, and must decide anew what to preserve, what to discard, and what to reimagine, what does it mean for education that every new generation of parents starts from the beginning? Is this perpetual beginning a sign of failure, the inability to transmit a stable communal ethos? Or could it be reinterpreted as the basis for a more modest, more fragile, but perhaps more honest form of communal education, one that accepts parents' and children's singularity without relinquishing the aspiration to shared responsibility?

Kibbutz education's turn from a thick socialist-Zionist worldview to a neutral arena of tolerance can be framed, explicitly, as a paradigm case of the liberal-left's self-disarmament: the abandonment of its own formative institutions and meta-story in the name of openness, unity, and state conformity. It is to this argument that I now turn.

Dilemma 3: Did Kibbutz Education Defend Liberal Democracy or Disarm It?

From Aristocratic Proletarians to Neutral Consumers of Narratives

For several decades, the kibbutz school did not merely "offer an educational alternative" but operated as the institutional heart of a thick, unapologetic political culture. Drawing on New Education pedagogies and on Marxian and psychoanalytic thought, kibbutz pedagogy sought to form a particular kind of human being: intellectually curious, artistically cultivated, committed to productive labor, and embedded in a collective life where moral behavior and contribution to society mattered more than grades. Balberg's phrase "aristocratic proletariat education" condenses the paradox of these schools, combining an elite humanistic curriculum with the explicit goal of producing hard-working socialist-Zionist laborers. Tsuk shows how this vision translated into practice: flexible assessment, rejection of selection, twelve years of schooling for all, and a tight fusion of school and community within the "educating settlement," backed by a quasi-autonomous "charter" from the state.

Muki maintains that the most radical expression of this project, *Shomria* at Mishmar HaEmek, was imagined as a "republic of youth," a training ground for self-governing socialist citizens rather than future consumers in a national marketplace of credentials. Adults intervened minimally; adolescents ran committees, debates, and work assignments, rehearsing the democratic-collectivist order they were expected to build in the kibbutz and the state. Within this worldview, the refusal of matriculation exams was not a quaint quirk but a political statement. External certification was condemned as bourgeois individualism, and the very notion that knowledge could be hierarchically measured and ranked was treated as an attack on equality. Muki's instinctive "God forbid matriculation certificates" captured a conviction that authentic learning should be intrinsically motivated and that the community's moral economy outweighed the state's systems of evaluation.

The Political Price of Tolerance: Surrendering the Meta-Story

Over time, however, this counter-hegemonic educational republic not only moderated its practices but, unfortunately, surrendered the very idea that it possessed a legitimate, particularistic worldview to transmit. The first breach came not from universities but from the army. Kibbutzim began aligning their curricula with state matriculation standards in the 1960s and 1970s, especially when it turned out that the lack of a high school diploma could negatively impact one's prospects of advancement in the military. What began as a tactical concession became, gradually, a strategic abandonment. By the 1990s, kibbutz schooling had largely dissolved into general state education, and its socialist-Zionist horizon was recoded as "heritage" rather than a living project of formation. The school that had once functioned as a state within a state accepted the status of local franchise of a supposedly neutral national system.

This transition can be read as a local instance of a wider asymmetry that reshaped Israeli politics. In 1953, the State Education Law abolished the ideological "streams" for the secular sector, merging the Labor-stream and General-stream into a single, ostensibly universal state education, while preserving and even reinforcing the autonomy of the religious-Zionist and ultra-Orthodox systems. The religious right maintained an entire ecosystem of formation, schools, *yeshivot*, *mechinot*, universities, youth movements, invested with a clear, thick narrative of people, land, Torah, and state. The secular-liberal camp, by contrast, folded its once-dense network of kibbutz schools, Labor-stream institutions, and youth movements into a framework that defined itself by neutrality, pluralism, and the refusal to impose one comprehensive worldview. The kibbutz movement, once the most radical defender of its pedagogical sovereignty, offered an exemplary case of this self-neutralization. In the name of tolerance and national integration, it relinquished its privileged educational charter and the right to treat its own narrative as binding rather than optional.

The quote that "now the school becomes the arena where conflicting family narratives, the secular, religious, traditional, liberal, are negotiated without an agreed-upon meta-story" crystallizes this shift. What is presented as an advance in pluralism can also be read, politically, as the liberal-left's greatest mistake. It was indeed a mistake with a devastating outcome: confusing the renunciation of its own meta-story for fairness, and failing to see that other camps were not reciprocating. As Asaf Sharon (Sharon, 2025) argues, the discourse of "unity" and the fear of internal conflict functioned as one-sided disarmament. The right waged a long war of position, building institutions that reproduced its worldview, while the liberal majority retreated from ideological struggle under the banner of national cohesion and procedural democracy. The kibbutz school's journey, from a republic of youth with a clear collective telos to a tolerant clearing house of private narratives, is thus not only a pedagogical story but a political cautionary tale.

The Asymmetry of Formation: Who Kept Their Schools?

Seen through the lens of the asymmetry of formation, the kibbutz's educational choices help explain why the camp that built the state now struggles to articulate, even to its own children, what it stands for. Religious Zionism preserved and expanded a coherent pipeline: national-religious elementary and secondary schools; *Hesder yeshivot* that combine intensive Torah study with high-commitment military service; ideologically dense *mechinot*; universities like Bar-Ilan and Ariel that embed religious-nationalist commitments within academic frameworks; and youth movements like *Bnei-Akiva* that turn values into lived community and mission. Graduates of this system enter the army, the legal establishment, and politics with a highly formed sense of what Israel is and ought to be.

The secular-liberal world, including the kibbutzim, systematically dismantled its own equivalents. It de-ideologized its schools, shrank or depoliticized its youth movements, privatized its communal institutions, and defined its universities as spaces of value-neutral expertise rather than sites of civic and political formation. In this light, the kibbutz movement's failure or refusal to found a Bar-Ilan of the left, the long-dreamt-of "kibbutz university," acquires sharp political meaning. Muki recalls that educators imagined an institution that would mirror Bar-Ilan: nationally recognized, academically rigorous, but explicitly anchored in the kibbutz's egalitarian, socialist-Zionist vision. That project never materialized, and Muki confesses that he is "personally glad" it did not, a gladness that itself reflects the liberal discomfort with institutionalizing a particular worldview, with becoming "like" one's ideological rival.

Yet the absence of such institutions is precisely what underlies the current asymmetry: the right was willing to build structures that bind, while the left preferred dispersion, individual conscience, and the imagined neutrality of the state. The result, as Eva Illouz (Illouz & Sicron, 2023) and Uri Ram (Ram, 2024) suggest, is that the religious right now enjoys an entrenched educational hegemony, while the secular-liberal camp finds itself in what Sharon describes as a 'cold civil war' for which it has neither the institutional infrastructure nor the habituated confidence to fight. Thus, Muki's position is probably a mistake.

The Urban Kibbutz in Harish

Within this broader story, experiments like the urban kibbutz in Harish appear as late attempts to square a circle. When its radical Hashomer Hatzair founders decided to offer full matriculation, they justified it as a tool of empowerment: "We'll do matriculation certificates, but for everyone." Politically, this is both an act of adaptation and a symptom of earlier abdications. On the one hand, insisting that all students, especially those from disadvantaged backgrounds, obtain the credential subverts the stratifying logic of exams and uses the national standard against its own sorting mechanisms. On the other hand, it accepts the disappearance of the kibbutz school as a protected space of alternative formation and confirms that the real ideological work will now be done elsewhere, primarily in institutions owned and run by the religious right. The kibbutz movement's ethos of equality is thus preserved at the micro level of classroom practice, even as it cedes the macro arena of narrative and identity formation to a rival camp that never abandoned the idea of partisan schools. (The wider fate of the urban kibbutzim is taken up in Chapter 11.)

The Dilemma Reframed

If we take seriously the arguments of Asaf Sharon and the analysis of educational asymmetry, the question is no longer "Should kibbutz education preserve its pedagogical distinctiveness or conform to national standards?" but rather: Can a liberal-left movement survive if it refuses to treat education as an arena of open political struggle? The kibbutz school's evolution suggests that what looked like tolerance, neutrality, and responsible nation-building, opening the gates to state curricula, neutralizing ideological content into "heritage," presenting the school as a forum where competing narratives coexist without a shared meta-story, was, in fact, a quiet surrender of the very institutions that once reproduced the liberal-socialist project. Meanwhile, the religious right understood, perhaps instinctively, a Gramscian lesson: whoever keeps their schools, wins the future.

The dilemma, then, is stark. To remain faithful to its liberal instincts, the kibbutz, and the broader Israeli left, recoils from building its own "ideological machine," fearing indoctrination and civil strife. But to abstain is to leave the field to those for whom "unity" is merely a tactic and for whom education is already a theatre of civil war by other means. The kibbutz story exposes this contradiction at its most intimate level. A movement that once claimed the right to raise its children in a consciously partisan, egalitarian project now finds itself defending an educational neutrality that, in practice, entrenches the hegemony of its opponents.

Whether kibbutz education can reinvent a thick, explicitly liberal-democratic story, one that is neither dogmatic nor ashamed of its commitments, may be a microcosmic test of whether the Israeli liberal camp can recover the will not only to argue for its values, but to institutionalize them again. In a society where the religious right has invested for decades in unapologetically partisan schools, mechinot, yeshivot, and universities, can a liberal-democratic camp that refuses to build its own explicitly formative educational institutions still hope to shape Israel's future, or is the insistence on "neutral" education itself a political luxury that the kibbutz, and the Israeli left more broadly, can no longer afford?

What the Kibbutz Teaches Beyond Itself

The concrete scenes that thread this chapter, the ornamental garden and the junk garden, communal sleeping and its undoing, the women's strike over the "floor rag," the mezuzah on the children's house door, parents who come "because of education," the radical kibbutz in Harish that chooses matriculation "but for everyone," are all local stories, but they point beyond themselves. They show what happens when a community tries to make education carry the weight of a revolution, and what happens when it slowly stops trying.

One lesson is that environment is never enough. The founders believed that a new ecology, shared childhood, joint work, the erasure of bourgeois domesticity, would allow values to pass almost by osmosis. The second and third generations showed otherwise: what had been a rupture for their parents became their normality, and the call that "everything needs to be normal" signaled not the disappearance of ideology but its replacement. The kibbutz experience suggests that there is no substitute for the explicit, sometimes uncomfortable work of narration, conflict, and institutional design when it comes to transmission.

A second lesson concerns liberation. Many of the changes traced here, family sleeping, private appliances, external employment, the opening of the women's sector, greater parental say, were rightly experienced as releases from earlier constraints. Yet they were bought at the price of new dependencies and inequalities: "dirty work" outsourced to non-members, a thinning communal ethos, a heavier load on individual mothers even as some women moved into professional roles. The kibbutz shows how projects born from a promise of equality often falter not because the promise is rejected, but because the practices that sustained it become asymmetrically distributed and increasingly hard to defend.

A third lesson is that refusing a shared meta-story does not produce neutrality. When the children's house becomes "the arena where conflicting family narratives are negotiated without an agreed-upon meta-story," this can be named tolerance, but it also marks a retreat from the earlier conviction that the kibbutz had something definite to say about a good life and a good childhood. A horizon that is no longer articulated does not vanish; it is displaced by others that are backed by stronger institutions. In that sense, the kibbutz story captures a broader liberal predicament: the fear of imposing values can easily become the mechanism through which other, less hesitant projects prevail.

The Asymmetry of Formation in Israel Today

Placed against the wider Israeli canvas, these lessons converge in what this chapter has called the asymmetry of formation. Religious Zionism has, over decades, built and guarded a dense ecosystem of formative institutions. Schools, yeshivot, mechinot, universities, and youth movements transmit a thick narrative of people, land, Torah, and state. The secular-liberal camp, including the kibbutzim, progressively folded its parallel institutions into a thin state framework that presents itself as neutral, and trusted that a once-hegemonic culture and universal values would reproduce themselves without partisan schools.

The kibbutz offers a distilled version of this process. Its education system once enjoyed a privileged charter vis-à-vis the national system: its own curricula, rites, evaluation, and a principled refusal of matriculation certificates as instruments of bourgeois hierarchy. Step by step, in the name of fairness, mobility, and national integration, this autonomy was relinquished. Curricula were aligned, matriculation introduced, communal arrangements loosened, the children's house recast as one option among others. What appeared as normalization was also a steady renunciation of the right to form heirs according to a particular vision.

Seen from here, Israel's present 'cold civil war' is not only a matter of elections or constitutional struggles. It is the long-term result of this asymmetry. One camp invested in slowly building institutions of formation that could survive electoral cycles. The other allowed its central formative structures to be absorbed, privatized, or emptied of thick content, while continuing to imagine that the state education system and the market were neutral spaces. The kibbutz, which once concentrated the secular-socialist project, thus becomes a small but exact lens on a national transformation.

Education as a Non-Neutral Arena

The thread binding these stories is the refusal, or inability, or both, to treat education as anything other than an apparently technical field. For the founding generation, this was inconceivable: they designed gardens, children's houses, work schedules, and rites of passage as the core infrastructure of the new society. For later generations, the same spaces increasingly appeared as a bundle of services and choices, between communal and family arrangements, religious and secular symbols, different paths through the school system, within a framework that no longer offered a binding horizon but tried to accommodate many.

Muki's late insistence that hope lies "not through politics" but "through the public sector, through education, through universities, through academic education" both continues and revises the kibbutz educator's faith in formation. It continues it by locating the possibility of renewal in schools, communities, and civic institutions rather than in state power alone. It revises it by acknowledging that the kibbutz's own educational experiment did not solve the problem of how to build institutions that are at once formative and self-critical. The question is no longer whether education is political, but how to inhabit that fact under democratic and egalitarian commitments.

From this perspective, the kibbutz story does not offer a ready-made model for the present; it offers a record of experiments, blind spots, and renunciations from which to think again. It suggests that a liberal-democratic camp which continues to speak the language of equality, responsibility, and shared fate cannot indefinitely avoid the question of formation by appealing to neutrality or to the market. It must decide whether and how to build institutions thick enough to transmit a horizon, and modest enough to remain revisable. In a country where the religious right has spent decades building unapologetically partisan schools, mechinot, yeshivot, and universities, what would it mean for those who still speak in the name of liberal, egalitarian democracy to take formation as seriously, and to create educational institutions that are neither neutral nor indoctrinating, but thick enough to fight for their values without repeating the kibbutz's beautiful errors?

6. Will the Lazy and the Diligent Balance Out?

Work, Motivation, and Evolving Contributions

Women working in the factory of Ein Gev, 1950s

Source: Archives Ein Gev, photographer unknown

The Morning Note: A Personal Entry Point

When I first arrived at Kibbutz Barkai in 1977, there was a ritual that defined my relationship to labor in ways I had not anticipated. Each evening, I would find a small slip of paper in my postbox, a note telling me where and when to go to work the following day. The responsibility for working, for finding a place to contribute my hours, belonged not to me but to the kibbutz itself, mediated through the work organizer, then one of the most important offices in every kibbutz. As long as I lacked a stable work assignment, this daily choreography of collective coordination would determine my morning destination. For a newcomer like me, the ritual was a daily reminder that my time belonged not to me, but to the kibbutz community.

This seemingly simple arrangement contained within it a profound philosophical statement about the nature of work, responsibility, and belonging. The individual worker was not atomized, left to navigate the labor market alone, but embedded within a system of mutual care and collective planning. Yet the same system raised questions that would echo throughout the evolution of the kibbutz movement. What happens when individual aspirations clash with collective needs? How does a community balance personal fulfillment with productive necessity? And what occurs when the very meaning of "contribution" begins to shift?

The tensions I explore in this chapter concern the evolving boundaries between individual responsibility and collective obligation, the ongoing negotiation between ideals of collectivism and the reality of human difference, the shifting meanings of what constitutes valuable contribution, and the emergence of what is termed in the kibbutz jargon "livelihood discourse": a fundamental reframing of work.

These dilemmas are not merely historical curiosities but living questions that continue to shape both the kibbutz and broader conversations about work, meaning, and community in an era of economic uncertainty. As we witness the rise of the gig economy, debates over universal basic income, and growing concerns about the impact of automation and artificial intelligence on employment, the kibbutz's wrestling with these fundamental questions offers crucial insights into alternative ways of organizing human productivity and purpose.

The Philosophical Foundation: A. D. Gordon's Vision

To understand the depth of these dilemmas in the kibbutz context, I return to their philosophical origins in the thought of Aaron David Gordon (1856–1922), one of the most influential thinkers in the development of Labor Zionism and the kibbutz movement. Unlike many Zionist pioneers who arrived in Palestine as young revolutionaries, Gordon immigrated in 1904 at the age of forty-eight, having spent decades as an estate manager in Russia. Despite having no previous experience with manual labor, Gordon insisted on working the land, declaring that the Land of Israel is acquired through labor, not through fire and not through blood. Gordon's philosophy (as documented in his Selected Essays published in 1973) centered on what he called the "religion of labor," a vision that elevated physical agricultural work from economic necessity to spiritual imperative. This ethos quickly took root in kibbutz routines, transforming work from a mere economic function into a spiritual calling, a way to rejoin history itself. For Gordon, Diaspora existence had severed Jews from their essential source of sustenance: direct connection with the land. The disconnection had forced them to survive through what he saw as the dried-up resources of history and religion. In his view, the revival of the Jewish people required not only political independence but a fundamental reconnection with the soil of the ancestral homeland through the transformative power of physical labor.

This was no mere romanticism about rural life. Gordon's philosophy was deeply influential among the idealistic young pioneers of the Second Aliyah (1904–1914), who embraced his vision of spiritual regeneration through labor as essential to their project of creating a new kind of person. Though Gordon himself refused to label his philosophy with terms like socialism or anarchism, his ideas about humanity's organic connection to nature and non-hierarchical social organization resonated powerfully with anarchist thought and would profoundly shape the kibbutz's approach to work organization. (Gordon's broader place in the kibbutz's intellectual genealogy is discussed in Chapter 2.)

Historical Context: Rethinking Work Itself

To grasp the revolutionary nature of the kibbutz's approach to work, it helps to situate it within a broader historical understanding of labor. Andrea Komlosy's global and comparative analysis in Work: The Last 1000 Years invites us to reconsider work not as a static, narrow category of gainful employment, but as an evolving form of human activity shaped by changing social, cultural, and economic contexts (Komlosy, 2018). Her framework challenges the conventional, modern, and fundamentally Eurocentric definitions that dominate contemporary discourse, and reminds us that the meaning and value of work are historically contingent.

Two of her insights are crucial for understanding the kibbutz experience. First, for most of human history, work has encompassed unpaid, forced, and informal labor, often existing outside the boundaries of today's regulated employment. Work is not a monolith but a dynamic negotiation between individual circumstances and community needs. The kibbutz's attempt to transcend traditional distinctions between mental and manual labor, between productive and reproductive work, and between individual achievement and collective benefit, represented a radical reimagining of these established hierarchies. Second, as societies industrialize, the meanings attached to work undergo fundamental shifts: from necessity and communal duty, to creativity and professionalization, and more recently to what the kibbutz idiom calls livelihood discourse. The emergence of the livelihood framework reflects a broader transition from collective survival and shared enterprise to an individualized pursuit of economic and personal security.

Situating the kibbutz within this longer history opens space for critical reflection on enduring questions. What counts as meaningful labor? Who has the authority to assign value to different forms of contribution? How might communities renegotiate the balance between solidarity and differentiation? As Muki and I take up these questions, we remain mindful that the story we tell is not one of simple success or failure, but of ongoing dialogue between ideals and reality, between individual aspirations and collective needs, between the transformative vision of the founding generation and the evolving challenges of subsequent eras.

Motivation to Work: From Collectivism to Individualism

The transformation of work motivation within the kibbutz movement represents one of the most profound shifts in the community's philosophical foundations. This evolution from deeply held collectivist ideals to increasingly individualistic orientations illuminates broader questions about human motivation, social belonging, and the sustainability of utopian projects in the face of changing historical circumstances. (Some of these themes were introduced in Chapter 2.)

> In the founding decades of the kibbutz movement, work motivation drew its power from sources that transcended individual material concerns. Members were driven by what can only be described as a transcendent sense of purpose, one that transformed even the most demanding physical labor into an act of historical significance. When I asked Muki about this transformation, he painted a vivid picture of how things had changed: "In the first stage of the kibbutzim, say until the establishment of the state but also after, people worked in terrible jobs. The ideology actually filled the motivation to work. And later, with time, when there was no existential question for the kibbutzim, you can really divide the population into two: those who enjoyed their work, and those who went to work because you have to go to work. And then, if you go to work because you have to and you don't get what you expect, of course it is much more problematic."

Muki's Two Motivators: Creativity and Belonging

Muki captured a fundamental truth about the early kibbutz experience: ideology served as a powerful motivational force capable of sustaining commitment even under difficult material conditions. The existential urgency of building a new society, of literally creating the infrastructure for Jewish renewal in the ancestral homeland, provided a framework within which individual sacrifice made collective sense. "What motivates a person to work are two things," he explained, with the conviction of someone who had lived through these changes. "First, his creativity. People want to express themselves creatively. The second is his desire to express his belonging to society, the social side. These are the two motivators that drive people to work. By the way, I have to say that I personally believe that this is still relevant today."

Muki's formulation reveals the understanding that early kibbutz members developed about the relationship between individual fulfillment and social contribution. Work was conceived not as mere economic exchange but as a dual expression of personal creativity and communal belonging. This vision aligned with Gordon's philosophy of labor as spiritual practice, transforming daily tasks into opportunities for both self-realization and social connection.

The depth of the kibbutz's commitment to collective work motivation can be measured in part through the language used to describe economic activity. For decades, the very vocabulary employed by kibbutz members reflected a fundamental orientation toward shared enterprise rather than individual accumulation.

> "The word livelihood did not exist," Muki told me, emphasizing how complete this linguistic transformation had been. "There was only one word: the economy. The idea behind it is very clear. But the word livelihood is a Diaspora word. In the mid-1980s suddenly the word livelihood started to appear as a statement: you are not supporting the collective. The current system that does not encourage livelihood is a system that paralyzes the kibbutz economically."

In other words, the kibbutz had economically failed as a collective enterprise. The transfer from "economy" (a collective enterprise) to "livelihood" (individual sustenance) represented more than semantic change; it reflected a fundamental reorientation of consciousness from communal to personal concerns. The emergence of livelihood discourse marked the beginning of a new era in kibbutz thinking about work and motivation.

Scholarly analysis of kibbutz development documents a systematic transformation that extended far beyond questions of work motivation to encompass the entire social fabric of these communities (Ben-Rafael & Shemer, 2020; Palgi & Reinharz, 2011; Russell, Hanneman & Getz, 2013). Researchers have identified a comprehensive shift in fundamental values and orientations that reshaped every aspect of kibbutz life. The transformation moved kibbutz society away from its foundational principles of egalitarian cooperation toward models that prioritized individual achievement and family-centered concerns. The change manifested most clearly in evolving attitudes toward work itself. Where once the contribution to the common enterprise had served as the primary measure of valuable labor, increasingly the contribution to income became the dominant criterion for assessing worth. This shift reflected a broader adoption of market-based thinking that fundamentally altered how kibbutz members understood the purpose and value of their daily activities.

The kibbutz movement's very success in achieving its original goals (establishing viable agricultural communities, contributing to the creation of the State of Israel, demonstrating the feasibility of cooperative economic organization) paradoxically undermined the existential urgency that had powered the original commitment to collective work. As Muki observed, once there was no existential question for the kibbutzim, the community could be divided between those who enjoyed their work and those who went to work because they had to. This division revealed a fundamental tension that had perhaps always existed but had been obscured by the pressing demands of community survival and nation-building. When ideology no longer provided sufficient motivation for difficult or unrewarding work, the question of individual satisfaction became paramount. Members who found their work fulfilling remained committed regardless of material rewards, while those who worked primarily from duty or obligation became increasingly dissatisfied when their expectations for recognition or compensation went unmet.

The dream that individual differences in motivation and capability would somehow balance out to create a harmonious whole persisted alongside the growing recognition that such balance could not be assumed or mandated. As Muki put it, with a mixture of idealism and realism, the utopia was that there would be lazy people in some areas and diligent ones in others, and that it would work out. The chapter takes its title from precisely this proposition, and from the question that the rest of the kibbutz movement's history would press against it.

The diverse contemporary kibbutz landscape reveals the complexity of this ongoing negotiation. Individual cases illustrate the contradictions and tensions that persist. Muki offered a telling example: "It is interesting that a kibbutz can raise a smart woman, very involved in the kibbutz, who volunteers for holidays and communal initiatives, but who does not like to work. She would be super happy if she could retire now at sixty-three. That is all she is waiting for." The example demonstrates how individual kibbutz members can simultaneously embody both collectivist values (through voluntary community involvement) and individualist motivations (through a desire to minimize work obligations). Such hybrid orientations suggest that the transformation from collectivism to individualism has not simply replaced one coherent system with another but has produced a complex landscape where multiple motivational frameworks coexist.

The Crisis of Contribution: From Collective Value to Market Logic

The transformation in how kibbutz communities understood and valued different forms of contribution represents perhaps one of the most profound challenges to their founding principles. The shift reflects fundamental questions about the nature of human worth, the relationship between productivity and value, and the possibility of maintaining alternative economic logic in the face of market pressures. (A related set of questions, about how kibbutz industries handled these same pressures, is taken up in Chapter 8.)

The Complementarity Principle and Its Limits

In the early period of the kibbutz, the vision about how people would contribute to the community leaned upon what we can call a complementarity principle. The principle echoed the belief that different people would naturally excel in different areas, and that these variations would ultimately serve the common good.

> "The utopia is that there will be lazy people in some areas and diligent in others and that it will work out," Muki explained, though his tone suggested he knew this ideal was easier to articulate than to achieve. "The utopia does not happen. There is a lot of tension around this. It does not happen with hugs. But there is a utopia behind it, a belief that a diverse human community can find a way where each person is diligent in one area and lazy in another."

This understanding represented more than wishful thinking; it embodied a fundamental philosophical commitment to human dignity that transcended narrow definitions of productivity. The kibbutz aspired to create a community where individual worth was not reduced to economic output, and where the full spectrum of human capabilities (emotional, intellectual, artistic, social) could find recognition and value. But how does one measure and compare radically different types of contribution? When I pressed Muki on this practical challenge, he acknowledged the complexity: "Overall, you have to take into account that what we call being active in the kibbutz is not measured. So there is a problem, because it could be that the same woman, in terms of her paid work, the work that brings in money, is lazy. In terms of her social activity, if it were funded, then she would be considered diligent."

This observation reveals the profound difficulty of creating systems that could adequately capture the full range of valuable activities within a community. The woman Muki described embodies the contradiction: simultaneously "lazy" according to market criteria and "diligent" according to social contribution measures. The paradox highlights the impossibility of reducing human worth to any single metric, while also exposing the practical challenges facing communities that attempt to operate according to non-market principles.

Prevalent scholarly literature on kibbutzim documents how the businesslike instrumental approach replaced an intrinsic attitude emphasizing the contribution of work to the common good, which in turn replaced the early expressive and idealistic outlook (Palgi & Reinharz, 2011). The contribution to income became important rather than the contribution to the common enterprise. This progression from expressive idealism, to common-good orientation, to instrumental income focus traces the gradual erosion of the kibbutz's capacity to maintain alternative systems of value.

Over the years, the relationship between personal fulfillment and community benefit became increasingly problematic. Members found themselves pursuing interests and developing expertise that, while personally meaningful, bore little relationship to collective needs or priorities. Muki offered his own experience as an example: "Each of us has these areas, and how focused we are on things inside the kibbutz circle, and how much outside the kibbutz circle. I am very diligent in my area of collecting books, but what does that have to do with the kibbutz? It really does not." His confession illustrates a fundamental challenge facing any community that seeks to balance individual self-realization with collective welfare. Muki's passion for book collecting represents a form of diligence and commitment that is undeniably real and valuable to him as an individual, yet its contribution to the community remains questionable. The scenario repeats across countless variations: the member who develops expertise in obscure academic subjects, the artist whose work finds no audience within the community, the entrepreneur whose innovations serve external markets rather than internal needs.

Interestingly, the challenge of balancing individual economic activity with collective welfare was not entirely unprecedented in kibbutz history. "At the beginning of the kibbutz there was no work in the kibbutz," Muki reminded me. "And there were periods before 1948, when a kibbutz of thirty people would produce three days of work to support all thirty. So half the kibbutz members would go to work outside. And now that is what is happening in the kibbutz again." This historical perspective reveals that the tension between internal and external economic orientation has been a recurring theme throughout kibbutz development. The difference, however, lies in the context and meaning of this external work. In the early period, members working outside the kibbutz were understood to be making temporary sacrifices for collective survival. In the contemporary period, external work increasingly represents individual career development and personal economic advancement, with the connection to collective welfare becoming ever more attenuated.

Bureaucracy and the Loss of Voluntary Initiative

Faced with these mounting tensions around contribution and value, many kibbutz communities turned to increasingly complex bureaucratic systems designed to regulate every aspect of member activity and compensation. Research indicates that, in seeking to control what each member could receive from the kibbutz and what each was expected to contribute, kibbutzim produced an endless array of bylaws, rules, sub-rules, and protocols covering virtually every aspect of life (Russell, Hanneman & Getz, 2013). This attempt to regulate members' lives in such detail both reflected their growing dissatisfaction and further fueled feelings of resentment and unhappiness.

The bureaucratic explosion represented both a symptom of deeper problems and a cause of further deterioration. The multiplication of rules reflected the community's loss of shared understanding about value and contribution, while simultaneously stifling the voluntary initiative and spontaneous generosity that had characterized earlier periods. Members began to operate according to rules rather than outdo them (Avrahami, 1996; Russell, Hanneman & Getz, 2013). This mentality directly contradicted the spirit of voluntary contribution that had originally animated kibbutz life.

Despite these mounting challenges, many kibbutz communities maintained mechanisms for evaluating individual activities according to collective criteria, though applying those standards became increasingly contested and difficult to implement consistently. Muki shared his own experience with the evaluation process: "There was always a criterion: what is good for the kibbutz. When I went to study philosophy and Kabbalah, they asked me: how much Kabbalah do you distribute to kibbutz members? What will you do with this thing? But I went to be a teacher, so they let me study as a teacher."

The anecdote illustrates both the persistence of collective thinking and its practical limitations. The question about distributing Kabbalah knowledge to other members reflects a genuine attempt to maintain a connection between individual development and community benefit. Yet the seemingly arbitrary distinction (accepting teacher training while questioning philosophical study) reveals the difficulty of applying such criteria consistently and fairly. Despite the pressures toward market-based evaluation, some kibbutz members and communities maintained alternative definitions of success and contribution that preserved elements of the original vision. Muki reflects: "It is a social experiment that created a wonderful reality where success is not measured only by climbing the economic hierarchy, but by influence through involvement, responsibility and caring. We created a special partnership."

This is an attempt to articulate a counter-narrative to the dominance of economic criteria. The emphasis on "influence through involvement, responsibility and caring" offers an alternative framework for understanding achievement and contribution that remains rooted in social rather than individual terms. The transformation in the meaning of contribution has not resulted in a stable new equilibrium but rather in ongoing tension and negotiation. Individual kibbutz members continue to embody contradictory orientations. The sixty-threeyearold woman waiting for retirement captures, in my view, the complexity of contemporary kibbutz experience: individuals simultaneously maintain commitment to collective values (through voluntary involvement in community activities) while harboring thoroughly individualistic attitudes toward paid work (counting the days until retirement). Such hybrid orientations suggest that the crisis of contribution has not been resolved through the adoption of market logic but has instead created a fragmented landscape where multiple, often contradictory, systems of value coexist uneasily.

The Emergence of Livelihood Discourse: A Linguistic Revolution with Profound Consequences

The most dramatic and revealing transformation in kibbutz consciousness occurred not through policy changes or institutional reforms, but through a fundamental shift in language itself. The emergence of what members came to call livelihood discourse in the mid-1980s marked nothing less than a conceptual revolution that would reshape every aspect of kibbutz life. This linguistic transformation opens a uniquely clear window into the deeper philosophical and cultural changes that were reshaping these communities, revealing how changes in vocabulary both reflected and accelerated the movement away from collective principles toward individualistic orientations.

The power of this transformation can be measured by its suddenness and the consciousness with which kibbutz members experienced it. When I asked Muki about the shift, his explanation was both precise and dramatic:

> "In the kibbutz until the 1980s, mid-1980s, the word livelihood did not exist. There was only one word: the economy. The idea behind it is very clear. But the word livelihood is a Diaspora word. In the mid-1980s suddenly the word livelihood started to appear as a statement: you are not supporting the collective. The current system that does not encourage livelihood is a system that paralyzes the kibbutz economically."

The movement from "economy" to "livelihood" was not gradual but sudden, not unconscious but deliberate, not merely descriptive but actively prescriptive. The new language did not simply describe changing reality; it actively worked to reshape that reality by introducing new frameworks for understanding the relationship between individual and collective welfare. The historical significance of this linguistic transformation becomes clearer when we understand what Muki means by calling livelihood a Diaspora word. The designation carries profound ideological weight within the context of Zionist thought and kibbutz philosophy. "What is a Diaspora word?" Muki explained. "It is the word that says: for a spiritual life, you have to make a living. Which we know to this day in the ultra-Orthodox community. That is the term: if you want to influence an ultra-Orthodox person to go to work, you tell him, support your family's ability to live with low economic life and great spiritual life." By identifying livelihood as a Diaspora word, Muki indicates that its introduction represented a fundamental betrayal of the kibbutz's founding vision. The Diaspora model separated spiritual and material life, requiring individuals to engage in economic activity primarily to sustain themselves and their families while seeking meaning and fulfillment elsewhere. The kibbutz had originally sought to transcend this division through the integration of spiritual purpose and productive labor within a collective framework. The emergence of livelihood discourse thus marked not merely a practical adaptation but a philosophical capitulation to the very model of existence that the kibbutz had been created to overcome.

The introduction of livelihood language was triggered by a fundamental crisis in the kibbutz's capacity to fulfill its basic promise to members. The community's growing inability to provide economic security for all its members created the conditions in which livelihood discourse could take root. "The turnaround began the moment they said the kibbutz cannot support its people," Muki explained. "The kibbutz cannot support all its members. In 1985 they said: the kibbutz does not support its members, and the responsibility for livelihood should be transferred to the members. That is a very bold statement." The 1985 turn is the same moment around which Chapter 5 organizes its discussion of the broader kibbutz crisis (Balberg, 2024; Tsuk, 2005). What that chapter analyzed in terms of the kibbutz's relationship to the state, the market, and the surrounding community appears here at the level of the daily vocabulary of work. The transformation represented a complete reversal of the original kibbutz social contract. Instead of the collective taking responsibility for individual welfare, individuals were now expected to take responsibility for their own economic survival. The "bold statement" Muki described effectively dissolved the fundamental premise upon which kibbutz life had been organized: that the community would provide for its members' material needs in exchange for their contribution to the common enterprise.

The broader context of this crisis extended beyond individual kibbutz communities to encompass the entire institutional framework of Israeli cooperative agriculture. Muki noted that in the cooperative agricultural villages, the moshavim, people were also saying, "We cannot take this anymore." Back then, the moshav operated with a joint fund: everyone contributed all their agricultural products to a communal pool. (The moshav as a contrasting settlement form was introduced in Chapter 3.) But in the 1980s and 1990s the joint system fell apart, for reasons similar to those in the kibbutzim: financial pressures took over, replacing the spirit of cooperation and the focus on productive work. The kibbutz transformation was taking place within a broader pattern of change affecting all forms of cooperative economic organization in Israel during this period. The shift from "economy" to "finances," from production-focused thinking to money-focused thinking, represented a fundamental reorientation that extended far beyond the kibbutz movement itself.

Why Livelihood Discourse Did Not Solve the Problem

Despite its adoption as the new organizing principle for kibbutz economic life, livelihood discourse failed to resolve the motivational and organizational problems it was intended to address. The persistence of these problems revealed the limitations of purely individualistic approaches to work motivation. "But I look to this day," Muki observed with something approaching wry amusement, "I look at the literature dealing with the question of work motivation and I see that the literature discussing livelihood still has not stopped publishing new books, because they have not succeeded in motivating everyone." I believe that the shift to individual economic responsibility, while solving certain practical problems, created or intensified others. The continued proliferation of literature on work motivation indicates that replacing collective purpose with individual economic incentives did not eliminate the fundamental challenges of motivating human labor but merely displaced them to a different level.

In the kibbutz communities, despite the apparent triumph of livelihood discourse, alternative voices and visions persist to this day. Many kibbutz members maintain their commitment to collective values while acknowledging the reality of changed circumstances. As Muki has put it, the kibbutz is a social experiment that created a wonderful reality where success is not measured only by climbing the economic hierarchy, but by influence through involvement, responsibility and caring: a special form of partnership. The emphasis on "influence through involvement, responsibility and caring" offers a counter-narrative to purely economic definitions of success, suggesting possibilities for maintaining collective values within transformed institutional frameworks. Accordingly, the emergence of livelihood discourse has not resulted in the complete abandonment of collective thinking but in complex hybrid forms that combine individual and collective orientations in ongoing tension. Contemporary kibbutz members often embody contradictory relationships to work and community that reflect the unresolved nature of these transformations.

Concluding Thoughts

The journey traced through this chapter, from the morning note that assigned my daily labor to the contemporary landscape of individual economic responsibility, reveals the profound challenges facing any community that seeks to create alternatives to conventional economic arrangements. The transformation of motivation from collective purpose to individual satisfaction, the shift in understanding contribution from social value to market worth, and the emergence of livelihood discourse as the dominant framework for thinking about work and economic life, all illuminate broader questions about human nature, social organization, and the possibility of sustainable alternatives to capitalism.

The kibbutz experience offers no simple lessons or easy answers to these enduring questions. Instead, it provides a complex and often contradictory record of human attempts to balance individual fulfillment with collective responsibility, personal autonomy with social solidarity, economic efficiency with social justice. The tensions and contradictions revealed through this analysis are not merely historical artifacts but living dilemmas that continue to shape contemporary attempts to create more just and meaningful forms of economic organization.

The disappearance of the morning note that once directed my daily labor may symbolize the end of one particular part of an experiment in collective organization. But the questions that note embodied, about responsibility, belonging, contribution, and the relationship between individual fulfillment and collective welfare, remain as urgent today as they were when the first kibbutz pioneers began their remarkable experiment in social transformation over a century ago. How we answer these questions will determine not only the future of intentional communities like the kibbutz but the broader possibilities for creating more just and meaningful forms of human association in a rapidly changing world.

7. Can the Artist Be a Worker?[1]

Art, Culture, and the Question of Productivity

Inflatable-submarine installations at a demonstration in 2023 against the judicial overhaul, invoking the "Case 3000" affair

Source: Erez Harodi, photographer

1 My special thanks go to my son Ran Heilbrunn, who played a key role in the creation of this chapter through his thoughtful contributions and active collaboration. Responsibility for the text remains ours.

Introduction

The history of the kibbutz is conventionally narrated through land, labor, and political organization, yet it is equally a history of choirs and amateur orchestras, of seasonal festivals and reinvented Seders, of murals, sculptures, and shows. It is also, crucially, a history of demonstrations and protests. Cultural practices did not simply ornament a pre-given social order; they were among the primary arenas in which the meaning of work, community, and socialism was produced, contested, and continuously re-imagined. Raymond Williams's insistence that culture is "ordinary," not a rarefied supplement to "real" economic life but something woven into its very fabric, finds a particularly vivid illustration in the kibbutz (Williams, 1958). Here, the same people who milked cows wrote festival pageants, painted dining halls, and rehearsed evening choirs. The kibbutz created, in this sense, something not too far off from Marx and Engels's famous description in *The German Ideology* of life "in a communist society, where nobody has one exclusive sphere of activity but each can become accomplished in any branch he wishes." Communal organization of production, as Marx and Engels explained, relaxes the relation between one's livelihood and one's labor. It thus becomes "possible for me to do one thing today and another tomorrow, to hunt in the morning, fish in the afternoon, rear cattle in the evening, criticize after dinner, just as I have a mind, without ever becoming hunter, fisherman, herdsman or critic."

And yet, the abolition of vocational exclusivity, the ability to be both a milkman and a poet, a herdsman in the morning and an art critic in the evening, does not mean that one's work becomes voluntary, or free from social pressures. Indeed, precisely because art and culture were embedded in the kibbutz's sphere of social reproduction and economic productivity, there emerged the expectation that every artist must also be a worker. This situation is indicative of a broader tension inherent in the kibbutz's understanding of art and culture. On the one hand, as Muki puts it, the kibbutz "terribly believes in art." In this deeply secular society, art and culture were seen as "the highest spiritual activity": not a personal recreational activity, but a collective endeavor and an integral element of the community's identity. On the other hand, this insistence on embedding aesthetic production into the social fabric, and on treating its members' creative capabilities almost as a kind of common good, had the effect of undermining art's uniqueness, making it mundane. Paradoxically, art was both sacred and amateurish, both a lionized social purpose and a prosaic collective hobby. In a society in which everyone is an artist, no one is. A community that "terribly believes in art" is also one that becomes impatient with the ethos of artistic genius, of a life dedicated to artistic excellence. Productivity is the axis on which these tensions turn. The kibbutz never doubted that art mattered; what it would not stop renegotiating was whether making art counted as productive labor.[2]

One is reminded, in this context, of an anecdote recounted by the late Amos Oz in a 2018 interview.[3] Oz, a former member of Kibbutz Hulda and probably the single most influential figure in Israeli literature, recalled how, as an aspiring young writer in the 1960s, he "went to the kibbutz secretariat and asked for one day a week to write." As a result, "a heated argument broke out." Some members objected that "anyone can say he's an artist. One will want to be a photographer, one a dancer, one a sculptor and one a movie maker. So who will milk the cows?" Furthermore, they claimed, allowing Oz to withdraw into his study would be inegalitarian: "If we give Amos time to write, we'll have to give time to everyone else who asks for it. After all, we have no way of ranking self-proclaimed artists." Far from being resentful, Oz himself, as the true kibbutz member that he was, found that this "was a solid argument. I had no answer for it. I couldn't stand there like a gorilla pounding its chest and say, 'No, but I'm special. I'm not like anyone else.'" An old kibbutz member sitting there, Oz further recalled, said that "young Amos might be a new Tolstoy. But at the age of twenty-two, what does he know about life? Let him work in the fields with us for another twenty, twenty-five years, and then he can write *War and Peace* for us." Commenting on the old man's objection, Oz again found it difficult to dismiss the kibbutz's collective claim upon his personal and artistic self-fullfilment: "That was a weighty reason. To this day I'm not entirely convinced there wasn't something in what he said." In the end, Oz's request was

2 The named artists and theorists discussed in this chapter (Atar, Bickels, Geva, Grossman, Ofrat, Ullman, Or Ner, Gershuni, Tabenkin, Gordon) are uniformly male. Female figures appear here primarily as critics or curators: Chinski as theorist, Tamir and Lidror as curators of the Metzer–Meiser: Take 2 exhibition. This pattern is partly an artifact of the period under discussion and partly continuous with the gendered division of labor analyzed in Chapter 4. The women's labor of singing, festival preparation, ritual reinvention, and seasonal cultural production was no less constitutive of kibbutz culture; its under-representation among "named artists" is itself a feature of the structure this chapter describes.

3 The paragraph that follows is based on "A Room of One's Own: A Conversation between Amos Oz and Shira Hadad," translated by Sondra Silverston and published in Granta (https://granta.com/a-room-of-ones-own/) in 2018.

approved, but not simply out of respect for the intrinsic worth of artistic vocation. Rather, the kibbutz recognized the profitability of Oz's talent: "I published another book and another one, increasing the kibbutz income, and in the end I was given three days to write, which was the maximum." The artist's partial exception from ordinary labor was thus permitted, but only once that exception could itself be justified as an economic contribution.

What this set of themes and problems shows is that the kibbutz gave a concrete, real-life expression to one of the oldest questions in modern debates about art: the question of art's autonomy. Like several traditions of Marxist art theory and 1960s–70s New Left radicalism, the kibbutz tended to regard the separation between everyday life and aesthetic experience with suspicion. According to this line of thinking, the isolation of art from the rhythms of ordinary experience, its confinement to the separate space of the museum, is an expression of capitalist culture. Capitalism, in other words, commercializes art not only by turning it into a commodity, but also by turning it into a revered object: something separated from the ordinary masses and presented on the walls of museums and galleries to be viewed, or consumed, by the bourgeoisie. The kibbutz's artistic tradition, in a way that echoes twentieth-century traditions of revolutionary art-making, consequently sought to democratize art, abolish the boundary between aesthetic experience and everyday life, and embed art in the fabric of the community.

This chapter explores three instances in which kibbutz art gave expression to this effort. First, we discuss the unique phenomenon of the kibbutz art museum, and ask how it differs from the art museum of the city. We then turn to two well-known collective artistic projects created by kibbutz artists that left a significant mark both nationally and internationally: Avital Geva's *Hamama* (The Greenhouse), which represented Israel at the 1993 Venice Biennale, and the 1972 Metzer–Meiser Project, a groundbreaking conceptual art project and a landmark attempt to place art in the service of progressive left-wing politics. Each of these examples corresponds to a specific social and thematic dilemma that emerges from the place of art and culture in the kibbutz. The kibbutz art museum allows us to examine the tension between the figure of the artist and the figure of the worker; the *Hamama* raises the question of when communal cultural practice becomes communal coercion; and Metzer–Meiser brings into focus the problem of art as a form of political protest. Taken together, these examples show that culture in the kibbutz was a dense site where productivity, belonging, authority, and dissent were continuously renegotiated.

First Dilemma: The Artist in a Working Community and the Museum at the Center

The first dilemma is not whether art existed in the kibbutz, but how it could be legitimized inside a society that defined itself through labor, equality, and collective discipline. Muki's account begins not with an individual genius but with this structural problem. "In the kibbutz there's a very strong work obligation," he says. "So what will the artist do? Will the artist be a worker or will he be an artist?" In the wider twentieth-century art world, the modern artist could always fall back on what Muki calls a negative privilege: "the artists, they have one right: not to eat, to starve, to be poor and make art." This right, he insists, "doesn't exist in the kibbutz, because in the kibbutz you eat even if you don't do anything." Collective security thus removes the material conditions that have conventionally underpinned artistic autonomy, while the collective's demand for work subjects the artist to an ethos of productivity that is indifferent to the special pleading of art. And yet, as we have seen, the kibbutz did not treat art as a bourgeois luxury to be discarded once the "real" work of agriculture and industry had begun, but as a privileged form of spiritual labor that could elevate the collective. The figure of the artist in a working community is therefore structurally unstable: neither free nor hungry, simultaneously idealized and suspected. Nowhere is this tension more visible than in the institution that came to occupy the symbolic summit of kibbutz life: the museum.

Bar Or's analysis of kibbutz museums is crucial here, because it shifts attention away from the romantic story of the solitary founder and toward the broader institutional and ideological conditions that made a museum possible in the first place (Bar Or, 2016). The familiar narrative credits Haim Atar with the founding of the Mishkan Museum of Art at Ein Harod, and Atar was indeed indispensable. However, as Bar Or stresses, in a kibbutz where the individual owns neither land, nor capital, nor full control over working time, even a charismatic artist "obsessed with the idea" cannot establish a museum without a supportive local public context. The Mishkan therefore tells a double story: of Atar's initiative and of a movement that was unusually willing to grant cultural work a constitutive place within communal life. This willingness was rooted in the *Kibbutz Meuhad* vision of the "large group" or "city-village," articulated early at Ein Harod, in which the artist is not a tolerated deviation from a pure agrarian norm but one possible figure of "mental work" within a socialist settlement that aims to abolish the division between brain and hand (Bar Or, 2016). Atar himself warned that without such cultivation the kibbutz would sink into "that which is insignificant in life," a worry Muki echoes when he insists that socialism without art would collapse into routine. In this light, the artist in the working community appears not as an ornamental figure but as a guardian against the reduction of the collective project to technical organization.

Muki's testimony allows these abstract formulations to be anchored in concrete curatorial decisions. He recalls that already in 1947, before the permanent museum building existed, Atar staged an exhibition of reproductions of Van Gogh in the wooden shack that served as the kibbutz art center. When I asked Muki why Van Gogh, he answered: "Atar did not want pedagogical art. He wanted art. Not Jewish art, not kibbutz art but art. That's why he staged a Van Gogh exhibition, believing that it will shape the future of art in the kibbutz." Within a kibbutz culture capable of reading art as "the highest spiritual activity," Atar refused both nationalist illustration and socialist realism, even at the cost, as Muki puts it, of "importing the icon of the starving modern artist into a society that has, at least in principle, abolished the right to starve." The same refusal is visible in his own painting practice: he lived in the kibbutz but, Muki notes, "the only paintings he paints are never of the kibbutz, but always of people's faces. Only people's faces. Not focusing on the collective enterprise." Atar's portraits mark a subtle but decisive resistance to the instrumentalization of art: he does not turn the kibbutz into an icon of itself, but insists on the irreducibility of individual faces within the collective. If the hilltop museum signals the community's commitment to art, everyday practices reveal how incomplete that commitment remained. Muki compresses the tension into a small, almost comic scene: "So we have, for example, an artist who, when he goes to his studio, he goes with a pile of bricks, to show as if he's going to work." The bricks serve as a prop in a tiny performance of manual labor that legitimizes his withdrawal into the studio. The gesture reveals an underlying regime in which art does not obviously count as work unless it can be made to look like work in the narrow, bodily, productive sense. The very need for this performance indicates that art is not fully expelled from the realm of legitimate activity; instead it must be continuously translated into the language of effort, contribution, and fatigue. Here Muki's formulation is again helpful: "the kibbutz can do something very, very big for arts; it can provide material security, collective infrastructure, and an audience." Thus, artists inhabit a position of both privilege and suspicion, supported yet constantly required to justify their difference. The bricks carried to the studio, the refusal to paint someone with a kippah, and the wager on Van Gogh as model are all small techniques for navigating this position.

From this angle, the Mishkan's central location takes on its full meaning. In the classic kibbutz diagram, the dining room at the center embodies equality through shared meals and the everyday reproduction of the collective. In Ein Harod, however, the museum displaces the dining room from the highest point and claims centrality for a different kind of practice: concentrated looking, historical memory, and aesthetic reflection. The topography stages the argument that a working society requires more than the administration of labor and consumption; it also requires a permanent institution where "spiritual matters" are given collective form (Bar Or, 2016). The building itself, designed by Samuel (Milek) Bickels and opened in 1948, was the first purpose-built art museum in pre-state Israel, preceding the permanent buildings of the Israel Museum in Jerusalem and the Tel Aviv Museum by many years, and its inward-oriented galleries and carefully modulated natural light create a space of concentration rather than spectacle (Bar Or, 2016). Because this space sits physically at the heart of the settlement, its slower, attentive rhythm is not exiled from communal existence but punctuates the paths between workshops, fields, and homes. The working community does not merely tolerate an enclave of "culture" at the margins; it organizes a central place in which the non-instrumental and reflective dimensions of life can be practiced collectively.

This section can therefore make a broader claim. In the Ein Harod case, the artist was legitimated not because the kibbutz ceased to be a working community, but because part of that community came to believe that work alone could not sustain human depth, historical continuity, or social imagination. The museum at the center made that belief visible in built form. It converted the artist's ambiguous place in the collective into an institution that educated children, hosted members and guests, gathered the traces of a threatened Jewish world, and offered a secular site of inwardness within everyday socialist life. Muki's formula remains the best shorthand for the unresolved tension: "the artist as worker, with all the censorship, and on the other hand the kibbutz that believes in arts." The Mishkan's centrality shows that this tension was not pushed to the margins but institutionalized at the very heart of the working community.

Second Dilemma: When Communal Practice Becomes Coercion

If the first dilemma turned on the figure of the artist alone, the painter with his pile of bricks, the writer asking permission to leave the milking shift, the second turns on the figure of the collective itself. What happens when art is not produced by one person inside a working community, but produced by the community as a single body? When the artwork is no longer a painting in a frame but a working enterprise, a choir of voices, a building full of people? At what point does the *togetherness* that makes the kibbutz the kibbutz become something else: a discipline, a mass ritual, an apparatus of coercion? Two cases let us examine the question at very different registers. The first, Avital Geva's *Hamama* (The Greenhouse) at Kibbutz Ein Shemer, takes us into the spatial and institutional dimension: a working educational greenhouse that represented Israel at the 1993 Venice Biennale and became the object of one of the most theoretically charged debates in Israeli art history. The second, the tradition of kibbutz choral singing, takes us into the affective and embodied dimension: the voice produced by many bodies in unison, which Muki hears as secular prayer and I hear as something closer to a different kind of ritual altogether. Both raise the same question: when does communal cultural practice become communal coercion?

Part 1: The Greenhouse, Utopia or Panopticon?

Avital Geva, born in 1941, was a member of Kibbutz Ein Shemer and one of the major figures of Israeli conceptual art of the 1970s and beyond. From 1977 he developed at Ein Shemer an unusual project: a working educational greenhouse, 1,700 square meters of plastic sheeting, operated as part of the *Mevo'ot Iron* regional school. Inside it, advanced technology (computers, sensors, electronic instrumentation) was integrated with experimental ecological practice: closed-circuit fish ponds whose water irrigated cucumbers, solar irrigation, hydroponic tomatoes, alternative growing substrates. The greenhouse was run by a shifting team of youth, scientists from the Volcani Institute, and agricultural researchers. Around 1980 Geva withdrew from individual authorship and from the gallery economy of conventional contemporary art. He refused interviews, refused to be named publicly as a singular author, refused all theoretical discourse about his own work; the greenhouse, not the artist, was to be exhibited. In 1993, working and intact, the *Hamama* was transplanted to the Israeli pavilion at the Venice Biennale, where it served as the proving case of that withdrawal: Geva did not present a painting *about* the kibbutz but the kibbutz he had built. For Muki, the *Hamama* is the paradigmatic case of what kibbutz art *should* be. "Avital Geva," he says, "is a very, very prominent example of the piece that says work and art are connected: the work needs to be artistic creation, and the artistic creation needs to be work." Geva's tea-pouring at the greenhouse, the smallest social gesture, is for Muki diagnostic of the larger move: it is *workers'* tea, "not bank tea," and, as I added in our conversation, not intellectuals' tea either. Muki agreed: "It's such a double rebellion," against an art that has withdrawn from labor and against a labor that has withdrawn from reflection. Geva's animating idea, Muki explained, began as a diagnosis of a problem inside the kibbutz: "you're distancing yourselves from the land, and I'll establish here a place where you can return to the land, and that's my art." For my part, I remembered Avital from the many gatherings I had attended in the greenhouse over the years, events that were, as I put it to Muki, "very geriatric," and where Avital functioned, I thought, as a kind of intellectual father of the place. Something intellectual happened there.

Muki then insisted on something that complicates the heroic-artist version of the story. "Avital wouldn't have done what he did without Avishai," Avishai Grossman, the kibbutz educator and thinker. Avital was "an adventurer, artistic, visionary," but Avishai was the one who anchored the project in the kibbutz, conceiving the greenhouse not as an exit from the kibbutz idea but as its deepening. Avital was an optimist to the point of obsession, Avishai a pessimist; the two of them, in Muki's phrase, "played tango for two." The greenhouse's eventual integration into the regional educational institution was what enabled the whole enterprise. The collective of the greenhouse, in other words, was not anonymous teamwork but a specific, named partnership, a qualifier that matters for the academic debate we are about to enter.

That debate unfolded across 1993–94 in the pages of *Theory and Criticism* and remains the most theoretically charged exchange in the historiography of kibbutz art. Gideon Ofrat's catalog essay for the Venice pavilion framed Geva's gesture as an inversion of Duchamp: where Duchamp had annexed a slice of life into the museum, Geva annexes the museum into a slice of life (Ofrat, 1993). Ofrat placed Geva inside a specific intellectual genealogy, running from A. D. Gordon, who had taught the unity of person and nature through agricultural labor, through Yitzhak Tabenkin's vision of the kibbutz as the humanization of nature, what Ofrat called a "kibbutz dimension" in which nature is neither subject nor object but is mediated by human labor in symbiosis. The greenhouse, in this reading, is a constructive utopia in which signifier and signified have not been pulled apart, because the cucumbers are actual cucumbers and the youth are actual youth; it is at once an ecological experiment, an educational program informed by A. S. Neill's Summerhill, and a collective creative process. Geva's refusal of personal authorship is not eccentricity but the expression of a kibbutz-derived rejection of the Western myth of the artist-genius.

A year later, in the same journal, the art historian Sara Chinski published a response that turned every one of Ofrat's terms inside out (Chinski, 1994). Her argument unfolds on three fronts that bear directly on the question of communal cultural practice and communal coercion. The first concerns "nature." Where Ofrat treats nature as a philosophical given through which the greenhouse mediates labor, Chinski reads it as a culturally constructed concept, "the DNA strand" of dominant Zionist discourse, whose invocation works as a symbolic act confirming "the validity of the bond between Zionist man and his territory." The greenhouse's luminous interior, in this reading, is constituted by what is *outside* its plastic sheeting: practices of removal, displacement, and colonization that its frame does not allow us to see. Muki's account of Avital's animating idea, that the kibbutz members were drifting from the land, and Geva would build a place to bring them back, appears, read this way, not innocent but symptomatic. The second front is the disciplinary reading. Drawing on Foucault, Chinski reads the greenhouse as an embodiment of the panoptic principle: a built space of cells in which surveillance, schedule, monitoring, and behavior-management produce what Foucault called *docile bodies*. The greenhouse is "educational" rather than "instructional," and education, in Foucault's sense, is the most refined of disciplinary technologies. The discipline operates on two fronts at once: on the youth being educated, and on nature itself, the cucumbers and fish "supervised, managed, exploited," serialized and severed from their life-function. Ofrat would push back forcefully on this reading in a 1994 reply (Ofrat, 1994). Empirically, he insisted, Chinski had never visited the greenhouse, and had she gone, she would have seen that the supposed panoptic supervisors are *the youth themselves*: there is no Big Brother, no surveillance from above, only collective self-management. The third front, and the one that strikes hardest, is Chinski's attack on the imagery of "community" and the "bee colony" that Ofrat had used to celebrate the greenhouse's collective dimension. Where Ofrat sees harmonious organic collectivity, Chinski sees "complete subjugation of the individual to the systemic super-organism." That single formulation names a possibility the kibbutz tradition has rarely wanted to think about its own collective forms: that what looks like solidarity from inside may look like the dissolution of the individual into a single body of organized labor from outside, and that the difference between these two descriptions may not be decidable from any neutral standpoint. The line landed with me in our conversation in an unexpected way. Earlier I had remarked to Muki that Avital "knew how to create excellent public relations for himself and almost complete support from the not simple kibbutz, while at the same time didn't give to others," an everyday kibbutz observation about distribution and access. In light of Chinski's argument it carries a sharper edge: the greenhouse's collective form, even from inside the kibbutz, was perhaps less collective in its allocation of resources and recognition than its rhetoric proposed. Ofrat's 1994 reply offered one final move worth attending to. He distinguished between *idealization*, which anesthetizes, and *ideal*, which energizes critique. Utopian universals, he argued, are genuinely useful precisely under conditions of empirical oppression. The kibbutz greenhouse, in this reading, separates from surrounding nature and society precisely *in order to* propose alternative versions; like any utopia, it exits history in order to return and accelerate it. The greenhouse is therefore a uniquely useful case because it does not let the analyst choose between the two readings. Both are simultaneously available, and neither is dispensable. For the question this dilemma is asking, the collective and the coercive are organized by the same structure.

Part 2: The Singing, Prayer or Mass Ritual?

For Muki, kibbutz singing originates not in the concert hall but in the most mundane and exposed of spaces. "Kibbutz singing was born in the shower, in the communal shower. There's no place where you're more embarrassed than in the communal shower, and when everyone is naked facing each other it's good to sing together." Nakedness, mutual vulnerability, and the need to cover embarrassment with noise generate an improvised practice that will later be formalized into choirs and festivals. What begins as a way of getting through an awkward daily situation becomes, over time, a central institution of kibbutz culture, and singing acquires a quasi-liturgical function. As Muki puts it, in the secular kibbutz world "singing replaced the synagogue. And to sing together is to pray." When he asked his first students to list the songs they sang that felt like prayer, each wrote down three, and most of the lists overlapped. The choirs institutionalized this language: each kibbutz movement maintained its own choir ("as if Marx sings differently," Muki adds with a smile), and they were integral to both holidays and political assemblies, providing the affective resonance that the ideologist's words on the podium could not by themselves supply.

Yet for me, the same practices mark the other side of the dilemma. In our dialogue I told Muki that the Gevatron[4] and similar mass-singing ensembles are almost unbearable to me. "I really have a problem with these events. For me, both the collective singing and the torchlight processions of the youth movements evoke connotations of Third Reich fascism and Hitlerjugend rituals. Raised in a German milieu without youth movements, singing evenings, or flags, I read these left-Zionist practices through the lens of fascist mass mobilization." What about Brecht and Weill, I asked, an alternative socialist aesthetic that is ironic, critical, and urban rather than pastoral, homogeneous, and collective? The unsettling proximity I was naming is one that an entire tradition of critical theory, from Walter Benjamin onward, has analyzed: left-Zionist and fascist mass aesthetics in the interwar period drew on the same reservoir of collective body rituals (marching, singing, torchlight, flags), and both sought to dissolve individual identity into collective energy. The crucial difference lies not in the form but in the political content and the experiential history the participant brings to it. Muki recognized this as a "clash of cultures" and observed that my tradition "is a leftist tradition, which has a lot of these things. They're stolen from this place. But it's interesting that from this you took the extreme liberal side, not the collectivist side." The same set of practices can be experienced as solidarity or as coercion, depending on whose traumatic memory they activate.

The Greenhouse and the singing are two registers of the same dilemma. One is spatial and institutional: collectivity organized into walls, schedules, supervised cucumbers, panoptic transparency. The other is affective and embodied: collectivity organized into rhythm, breath, voices in unison. Different registers, the same structure: a communal form that is simultaneously the substance of kibbutz solidarity and structurally available for coercive recuperation. The greenhouse will not let the analyst choose between Ofrat and Chinski; the choir will not let Muki and me resolve our disagreement into a single description. From inside, what is experienced as solidarity may be heard, by those whose biographical history primes them to hear it that way, as something closer to coercion; and there is no neutral standpoint from which to decide which hearing is the right one. The unresolvability *is* the dilemma.

4 The Gevatron is the iconic kibbutz folk-singing ensemble founded at Kibbutz Geva in 1948, long associated with the canonical "Land of Israel" song repertoire and a recognizable emblem of kibbutz musical culture.

Third Dilemma: Art as Protest

Art in the kibbutz has always been asked to do double work. It was supposed to help people get up in the morning to do "terrible jobs" for the collective, and it gradually became the place where doubts about that same collective could be voiced. In our conversations, Muki insisted that in the early decades work motivation could not be described in the language of "livelihood," a word that belonged to the Diaspora, where one has to "make a living" to protect a separate spiritual life (see Chapter 6 on the *livelihood discourse*). In the kibbutz, "the economy" was the only term in use; ideology "filled the motivation to work," and cultural events such as Seders, concerts, and festivals were not external to this economy but among its conditions of possibility. The third dilemma is what happens when these same cultural infrastructures begin to do the opposite work.

Muki captured the turn in a single moment. Every year the Israel Philharmonic Orchestra came to Ein Gev to perform a festival concert. Every year, he recalled, "everyone talks about the corrupt government." On the eve of the political upheaval in 1977, when the Likud Party came to power for the first time and ended Labor's long political dominance, the orchestra played Mozart's *Requiem*, and people in the audience murmured: "This is a requiem for the labor movement." A piece of high European liturgy, imported into a kibbutz festival, was suddenly heard as mourning music for the end of the movement's political hegemony. Culture here is no longer only motivating. It is diagnosing.

By the late 1960s the diagnostic register was no longer confined to a murmured remark at a concert. Around Muki Tsur, Yariv Ben-Aharon, and Avishai Grossman, a cluster of post–Six-Day War books took shape. *Siach Lohamim* (*The Seventh Day*), which recorded open conversations with kibbutz combatants; *Bein Tzeirim* ("Among Youth"), which called for unifying the kibbutz movements and breaking with the pro-Soviet orthodoxy of parts of the movement; and *Bedarkham* ("In Their Path"), conceived as a collective memorial that ultimately splintered along movement lines. The same cultural institutions that had once framed work as a redemptive act, publishing houses, youth-movement seminars, kibbutz libraries, became forums where the movement began to examine itself. The same impulse would later take overt visual form in the artists' group *Hameshutaf Kibbutz* ("The Common Kibbutz"), active between 1978 and 1988, which Tali Tamir describes as the "critical-political" fifth paradigm of kibbutz art. The project at the center of this dilemma, Metzer–Meiser in 1972, is situated between these two moments.

The road between Kibbutz Metzer and the Arab village of Meiser looked, at first glance, like any other strip of cultivated land in the "triangle" region.[5] Fields on both sides, a junction, a few scattered structures. On one side stood Kibbutz Metzer, founded in 1953 by Hashomer Hatzair immigrants from Argentina with a clear socialist-Zionist script in their heads. On the other side lay Meiser, a Palestinian village whose roots reached back to the late nineteenth century, long before the kibbutz members arrived. For decades, kibbutz education had spoken about coexistence as a principle; here, the principle was folded into daily routines, but also into suspicion and asymmetry. It was in this specific place that Micha Ullman, Avital Geva, Dov Or Ner, and Moshe Gershuni decided to stage what is now remembered as the first artistic project deliberately conceived in a shared Jewish–Arab space in Israel. The initiative came from Kibbutz Ein Shemer, Geva's home, where the idea of coexistence through work on the land still had real emotional weight, and it drew on a new language of conceptual art then emerging in Israel: art as action rather than object, intervention in space rather than picture on a wall.

The first scene was deceptively simple. Ullman gathered groups of young people from Metzer and Meiser and brought them to a point between the two settlements. He asked them to dig two rectangular pits facing each other. Once the pits were ready, the participants exchanged the soil: earth from the kibbutz side was carried over and poured into the pit on the village side, and earth from the village side was poured into the pit on the kibbutz side. There was no speech and no signboard, only bodies laboring together, the weight of soil in wheelbarrows or burlap sacks, the sound of shovels cutting into ground that until that afternoon had belonged to one community and not the other. In retrospect, the gesture came to stand for the entire project: a ritualized exchange of ground, a literal demonstration that what lies under one's feet need not be fixed forever.

The second scene unfolded through the circulation of words and objects. Or Ner prepared a short appeal, printed in both Hebrew and Arabic, and distributed it in Metzer and Meiser. The text asked residents to donate unused personal objects, things that had lost their immediate function but still carried some trace of a life: a cracked plate, a broken tool, an old toy, a book nobody read anymore. The objects were collected and brought to a shaft dug between the two communities, where Or Ner buried them together "as an archaeological deposit to be uncovered in the future." No one knew who would do the uncovering, or when. The shaft functioned as a time capsule but also as a quiet

5 The relationship between Metzer and Meiser is also discussed in Chapter 9 of this book.

challenge to the way official histories parcel out memory: the discarded fragments of two worlds were allowed to decompose and mingle without a clear hierarchy.

The third scene brought books to the junction. Geva secured access to volumes that had failed some commercial test and were destined to be pulped at the nearby Amir paper-recycling facility. Instead of disappearing into the machinery, they were scattered over the ground at the Metzer–Meiser crossroads. Passersby from both communities were invited to take them home, to leaf through them, to decide whether they wanted any of this printed matter in their houses. The image is hard to forget: heaps of books, exposed to sun and dust, waiting to be chosen or ignored. The gesture quietly inverted the familiar hierarchy of cultural distribution, in which centers send books outwards to the periphery; here, what the center had rejected was offered back to residents of a marginal space as a gift, or perhaps as a question.

Up to this point, the project could still be read as a set of experimental exercises in coexistence, consistent with the best version of kibbutz ideology: shared labor on shared land, the circulation of objects and words across community lines, the building of a minimal common archive. The fourth scene broke that comforting frame. Gershuni, looking at the same undivided fields that symbolized the kibbutz's collective ethos, drew invisible lines across them and mapped them as if they were a moshav or a suburban development. He parceled the land into family-sized plots and, at least for the duration of the project, granted "each kibbutz family its own share of land." On paper and in the imagination, the kibbutz's founding negation, no private property, no private field, was reversed. The reaction inside Metzer was immediate and furious. For many members, the act felt like a betrayal staged in their own backyard. The fields were not just an economic resource; they were the material basis of the collective, the place where the movement's rejection of private ownership had taken visible form. To divide them up, even symbolically, was to play out the dismantling of the kibbutz in advance. Years later, when curators looked back, they would call Gershuni's gesture "a prophetic act that anticipated the privatization process in the kibbutzim decades later." At the time, it felt more like an insult.

When I spoke with Muki about Metzer–Meiser, what he stressed most was not the Jewish–Arab dimension of the project but precisely this fourth scene. For Muki, the deepest provocation was not at the boundary between the kibbutz and its Arab neighbor but at the boundary between the kibbutz and its own future. Gershuni had used the tools of conceptual art (mapping, reframing, temporary fiction) to reveal a possibility that the kibbutz would only confront in earnest decades later: a future in which "the economy," understood as a collective category, would give way to "livelihood," with its individualized calculations (see Chapter 6). I confess that I had read Metzer–Meiser primarily through the coexistence lens; the Gershuni mapping was something I had registered only faintly until Muki pressed it. The omission was, I think, an unconscious bias on my side: my attention was tuned to the encounter between the kibbutz and its Arab neighbor, while Muki's was tuned to the encounter between the kibbutz and its own latent future. Both readings are correct, and Metzer–Meiser is what it is partly because it stages both encounters in a single afternoon.

Half a century later, when the curators Anat Lidror and Tali Tamir returned to the site for *Metzer–Meiser: Take 2* in 2025, the landscape had changed. The open strip between kibbutz and village was now marked by a "smart fence," erected after the 2002 terrorist attack on Metzer, and by layers of administrative and technological control that would have been hard to imagine in 1972. This time, the artists were not only Jewish; Arab artists from Meiser and the region worked alongside their Jewish counterparts. Ullman dug "Two Chairs," empty seats carved into the ground in front of the gallery. Geva installed "The Jewish Library in Concrete," books from the Zionist-Jewish canon immersed in a concrete swamp, an image, he said, of the petrification and moral corruption of texts that had once guided him. Saher Miari reopened Or Ner's old shaft, not by redigging it but by exposing the buried objects in a transparent column. Most strikingly, Abed Elsalam Sabia' painted the joint area as "two lungs," green and brown, breathing a single air but divided by a thin line.

The half-century interval is not a confirmation that art-as-protest endures unchanged; it registers how its conditions of possibility have been remade. In 1972 the four scenes could be staged on an open field because soil, objects, books, and the kibbutz's own collective fields were still continuous with the life they critiqued, the gesture and its referent shared a single ground. By 2025 that ground is bisected by a smart fence; the books are entombed in concrete rather than scattered for passersby; the chairs sit empty; the two lungs breathe a single air across a line they cannot cross. Each gesture in *Take 2* names something the 1972 project could still presume. The dilemma has therefore not been resolved but displaced: art-as-protest in the kibbutz tradition continues, but it no longer borrows its intelligibility from a confident collective infrastructure; the erosion of that infrastructure is now itself part of what the work has to register.

Conclusion

Read together, the three dilemmas of this chapter share a single structure. The artist in a working community could be neither freed from the demand of productive labor nor reduced to it. The communal forms that gave kibbutz art its distinctive shape, the greenhouse, the choir, the festival, were, at one and the same time, the substance of solidarity and the medium through which discipline could pass; the very feature that made them powerful made them coercive. And the cultural infrastructure that had been built to motivate work became, by an internal logic of the same arrangement, the place where the motivation itself could be questioned. None of these dilemmas resolves into a verdict. The Ofrat–Chinski exchange is the model case: not a debate to be won, but a structural ambivalence to be lived with. To name productivity as the axis of this chapter is to say that the kibbutz wrestled, in the field of art, with a question its founders had hoped to dissolve, namely the relation between making and meaning, and that this wrestling continues to take new institutional form.

These older cultural forms have not vanished; they continue to do new work. As Muki was careful to insist, the protest movements of the 2020s grow directly out of them. Many of the performances around the "black flags" protests and the demonstrations against judicial changes were produced in kibbutzim, and "lots of literature, and lots of paintings all have their origin in kibbutzim." At the demonstrations themselves, he observed, one often sees "people walking around one beside the other and having a kibbutz conversation basically. Not a demonstration against, but a kibbutz conversation." The protest space becomes an extension of kibbutz sociality rather than a purely antagonistic arena, and the cultural infrastructures that once underwrote the economy of collective labor now underwrite its critique. This continuity points beyond the cultural sphere. The kibbutz movement has long been involved in the political space of Israel, and it will need to remain so (see Chapter 10 on the post–October 7 moment). Its tradition of treating culture as a form of public reasoning, neither ornamental nor outside the economy of common life, equips it for precisely the kind of work that Israeli democracy now requires.

8. Whose Factory Is It?

Enterprise, Industry, and Innovation

The old Polyon factory and the new logistic center under construction, Kibbutz Barkai, 2026

Source: Alex Heilbrunn, photographer

Introduction

I remember the first time I visited the factory at Kibbutz Barkai. It was a plastic factory, Polyon, it was enormous, humming, immaculate and it occupied a place in the kibbutz's self-understanding that I found, as an outsider, unexpectedly thrilling. Members didn't just work there; they spoke about it with a quiet possessiveness I hadn't noticed in other contexts. "Shelanu", they would say. Ours. Thus, the factory was not a place of employment in the ordinary sense. It was a collective project, an extension of the community's spirit into the material world, something the kibbutz had built with its own hands and guarded with its own pride. Years later, I learned that the factory had passed into external ownership, and was then closed. The technical details of the transaction were complicated, as they always are in such cases. But the emotional texture of what had been lost was not complicated at all. A veteran member, someone who had spent decades on the factory floor, described it to me plainly: "When it belonged to us, every plastic roll that went out of the gate was something we made together. Now it's just a place some of our people happen to work in." Once the factory was closed for good, it became the location of businesses that have nothing to do with Kibbutz Barkai. They are just renting the place. The *shelanu* had gone out of it. And with it, something harder to explain: a sense that the kibbutz was not merely a community of shared consumption and solidarity, but a community of shared production, of collective authorship over something that existed in the world beyond itself. What was lost at Barkai was not only a factory but a particular way of tying work, ownership, and belonging together, precisely the nexus this chapter explores.

Chapter 6 examined the evolving relationship between the individual kibbutz member and their work. It discussed the origins of motivation, how a community rewards or recognizes contribution, and what happens when the ideology of collective purpose gives way to personal economic calculation. These are questions about the person in the workplace. In contrast, the current chapter asks something different: Who owns the enterprise? What is it for? What happens to communal identity when the factory, the field, or the start-up is no longer "ours?" This shift in level of analysis matters enormously. A member can lose faith in collective motivation and yet the kibbutz factory continues to operate. But when the factory itself passes out of communal ownership and hired workers replace kibbutz members on the floor, when the Swiss CEO replaces the elected production manager, when the movement's industrial wing dissolves and each kibbutz is left to negotiate alone with the global market, then the loss is of a different order altogether. It is not the individual's relationship to work that changes, but the community's relationship to what it makes and owns in the world, its means of production. This shift from the motivations of individual workers to the ownership and purpose of enterprises also echoes what Palgi, Sofer, and myself (2020) describe as a move "from work to livelihood" in the kibbutz, where employment and entrepreneurship increasingly become matters of assembling viable life strategies rather than simply fulfilling a collectively assigned role (Palgi, Sofer, & Heilbrunn, 2020). I have used this formulation in other academic articles to characterize the way kibbutz members come to experience their economic lives less as participation in a single communal project and more as the ongoing construction of an individual portfolio of jobs, ventures, and risks.

The kibbutz was born as an agrarian enterprise. It was small groups of pioneers breaking ground, draining swamps, planting fields and for decades the land and its cultivation remained the moral and practical center of communal life. Industry, when it came, was neither a natural extension of this ideal nor its straightforward negation. It arrived as an economic necessity, with its own controversies, its own competing visions, and its own pressures toward hierarchy and differentiation. As Muki puts it with characteristic precision, within kibbutz industry there were always two internal streams. One said "we made utopia in agriculture, now we need to make utopia in industry," and another that said "in agriculture we made utopias, in industry we'll make profit." These two voices were never fully reconciled. They simply traded places in dominance over time, and the tension between them shaped every major decision the kibbutz movement made about enterprise and economic life. This is where Muki locates the founding ambiguity that shadows everything that follows. "Already in the early 1920s," he notes, "there was a debate whether a kibbutz should be a village or should be a city. The large kibbutz was supposed to be a regional kibbutz of five thousand people... and if it's an alternative to the city, then there needs to be industry". The vision was synthetic, neither purely agrarian nor purely industrial and this tension was never resolved ideologically before it was resolved practically, often under conditions of crisis or external pressure. What complicates this further, I suggest to Muki, is that the first factories weren't built by individual kibbutzim acting entrepreneurially, rather they were assigned. "One of the things I wrote about a lot," I say, "is that the first factories established in kibbutzim were a kind of top-down entrepreneurship. Actually the movement decided who gets which factory at least in Hashomer Hatzair." Muki confirms this: the industrial wing of the movement allocated roles, mediated disputes, and initiated ventures. Kibbutz A was given plastics; Kibbutz B, food processing. The "entrepreneurship" was real, but it was collective and directed from above, and the individual kibbutz had limited say in what it made or owned. When that movement-level architecture later dissolved, each kibbutz was left to navigate the global market alone and many were not equipped to do so.

This chapter pursues three dilemmas that follow from this founding ambiguity. The first concerns ownership and the meaning of *shelanu*: what is at stake when a kibbutz sells the factory that once carried the community's name. The second concerns innovation and equality: whether a community committed to broad participation and bounded reward can also generate the kind of concentrated, high-risk entrepreneurship the modern economy rewards. The third concerns integration and transformation: whether the inherited formula of "capitalism outward, socialism inward" was ever a stable equilibrium, or always a generational compromise that would eventually become illegible to those born after it. None of the three is resolved in what follows. The chapter's claim is that they are best understood as continuing dilemmas rather than as settled questions.

Dilemma 1: Ownership and the Meaning of *Shelanu*

The first dilemma concerns ownership and identity and deals with what is at stake when a kibbutz sells its factory. Can the pragmatic security gained compensate for the communal coherence surrendered? From Degania's founding decision that the land would "never be their own," through decades in which kibbutz members were legally tenants of national institutions rather than private owners, collective control over the means of production was not a technical arrangement but a constitutive principle of the kibbutz experiment. In Nir Tsuk's (2005) terms, the early settlement pact between the collectivist groups and the Zionist institutions created a "positive-sum" configuration in which national bodies owned the land, but the group as a whole held the property and assets, and thereby fashioned itself as a working society whose cohesion rested on self-labor, common ownership, and mutual responsibility. However, when that ownership begins to migrate outward to banks, external investors, and multinational firms the question is not only who receives dividends, but what kind of social entity the kibbutz still is. One can see this concretely in kibbutzim that, under the weight of debt and market volatility, negotiate the sale of their factories to external corporations. Committees sit with lawyers and bank representatives, the community votes under the shadow of insolvency, and the moment the contract is signed, the factory that once appeared as *shelanu* becomes, in legal and practical terms, someone else's asset. The workers may remain; the buildings do not move. However, the meaning of the place changes entirely and dramatically. As I (Heilbrunn, 2005) argued in analyzing organizational change and entrepreneurship in community settings, shifts in organizational structure are never merely technical adjustments; they alter the field of initiative, responsibility, and identification within which members understand what belongs to them collectively and what no longer does. Muki's description of control over the kibbutz economy being "in an earthquake", and of the disappearance of the work coordinator, points to this deeper shift. In the classic cooperative model traced by Tsuk (2005), the member was simultaneously worker, owner, and citizen: work, home, and participation in the General Assembly were woven into a single fabric of everyday life. The industrialization of the kibbutz, with its gradual reliance on hired labor and outside management, already weakened that triangle, introducing a stratified structure in which members enjoyed rights and status that hired workers did not share. But the sale of factories marks another step: it severs the remaining link between collective self-labor and ownership, turning members from producers and owners into, at best, local stakeholders in enterprises whose strategic decisions are made elsewhere. Muki is precise about the emotional and psychological dynamic driving these sales. "I think this development, first of all, roots in social insecurity", he says. "It's a desire to be big, it's a desire to be influential... basically, a factor of insecurity about the kibbutz's very existence enters the kibbutz. And this insecurity seeks a capital solution. The attempt to acquire this security is done through selling the factories resulting in large capital gain, which is then partly turned into social insurance for the kibbutz members". The sale, in other words, is not simply a pragmatic business decision; it is a symptom of an existential anxiety, a conversion of shared productive identity into individual financial security. Sometimes the process is even less deliberate. "kibbutzim sometimes lose what I call 'losing self-knowledge of economics", he continues. "Either from extreme debt, or from a demographic situation... or if there are internal battles. Sometimes the internal arguments within the kibbutz create a situation where no one knows what's happening, because everything is in polemical, everything is in argument, and then no one knows what's happening and they simply sell. The kibbutz does not always consciously choose to sign away its *shelanu*; sometimes the *shelanu* simply slips through fingers occupied with other fights". I told Muki about the Nir Yaakov case which I find particularly instructive here. I had watched the negotiations between the kibbutz and factory management and the Swiss company closely. I remember being sceptical about all the promises made by the potential buyers. The factory will stay in Israel and in the kibbutz, kibbutz members will be employed for at least another twelve years, the factory management will remain in place. "I tell you Muki, this will not work. Because the kibbutz members from Nir Yaakov won't work under Swiss management, it won't work. The cultural incompatibility is not merely organizational; it is a collision between two entirely different assumptions about what a workplace is and who it belongs to". In an earlier article on entrepreneurship, social capital, and community development in the kibbutz, I argued that communal ownership mattered not only because it secured assets, but because it generated the dense networks of trust and mutual responsibility through which collective initiative became possible in the first place (Heilbrunn, 2005). Balberg's narrative helps us see the emotional and historical depth of what is lost here. The early halutzim deliberately refused private ownership of land, even inserting clauses into their contracts to prevent it, because they understood that direct proprietorship would pull them back toward "koulak" consciousness, toward thinking first of "my" plot, "my" inheritance, and "my" family. Their wager was that a community defined by shared ownership of land and tools could sustain a different kind of human being. A human being who experienced dignity not through accumulation, but through participation in a common project that spanned generations (Balberg, 2024). When contemporary kibbutzim, under conditions of debt and insecurity, sell their factories to Swiss or American corporations in order to create social insurance funds, they are inverting that founding gesture by using collective assets to secure individual and familial futures, rather than using individual sacrifices to secure the future of the collective, which was the vision of the founders. Seen through Tsuk's (2005) comparative lens, this is not a uniquely kibbutz story but a familiar trajectory of utopian enterprises under capitalist pressure. When the shareholder displaces the resident, the balance sheet displaces the founding covenant, and enterprise begins to live a life of its own. In the Garden Cities Tsuk analyses, the shift from limited-dividend, community-oriented companies to profit-maximizing property trusts signalled the quiet abandonment of Ebenezer Howard's cooperative commonwealth. Something analogous happens when kibbutz factories are sold. Ownership migrates outward, decision-making becomes opaque to residents, and the factory gate which was once a symbolic threshold between "inside" and "outside" no longer marks a clear boundary of *shelanu*.

What the sale of a factory actually reveals is therefore not what it first appears to be. Selling the factory does not move the factory; the building stays, the machines keep running, the workers may even keep their jobs. What the transaction moves is the community's relation to it. The asset that was *shelanu* becomes a workplace, and the loss is not the loss of an asset but the loss of the conditions under which an asset could be called *shelanu* in the first place. Ownership in the kibbutz tradition was never a legal designation that could be transferred and replaced with another; it was the medium through which a community of producers recognized itself as such. What was signed away at Nir Yaakov, what is increasingly signed away across the movement, is not so much the means of production as the form of belonging that had been built around them.

Dilemma 2: Innovation, Equality, and the Shape of Enterprise

The second dilemma concerns innovation and equality and we will discuss whether a community founded on the principle that all contribute and all share equally can also generate the kind of concentrated, high-risk, high-reward entrepreneurship that the contemporary economy rewards. Within kibbutz industry, as Muki notes, two internal streams were never fully reconciled: one that sought to "make utopia in industry" by extending egalitarian labor relations into the factory, and another that treated industry as the legitimate sphere in which to "make profit". In practice, this tension produced hybrid arrangements, "capitalism outward, socialism inward" that allowed kibbutzim to build substantial enterprises while attempting to preserve communal distribution. But as entrepreneurship took on more technological, capital-intensive, and globalized forms, the friction between egalitarian norms and the unequal rewards of innovation grew sharper. In an article I published in 2010 on entrepreneurial opportunities in changing communities, I suggested that periods of communal transition generate openings for innovation, but also unsettle the normative frameworks that determine who is permitted to seize those opportunities and under what moral conditions (Heilbrunn, 2010). Nir Tsuk's (2005) account helps to clarify why this friction was structurally hard to resolve. The original settlement pact between the collectivist groups and the national institutions assumed a non-capitalist model of development. National bodies would provide land and the initial means of production; the kibbutz would provide disciplined, ideologically committed labor; and the goal was a workers' economy that could, in principle, skip the classic capitalist phase (Tsuk, 2005). In this configuration, productivity and self-labor and not capital accumulation or speculative risk-taking were the primary virtues. Historically, as long as low-tech factories and agricultural branches dominated, it was still possible to combine modest surpluses with a relatively flat internal distribution, even as managerial hierarchies and stratification slowly emerged. But once the horizon shifted to hi-tech and high-risk ventures, however, the kibbutz's refusal to build large capital reserves and its suspicion of differential rewards placed it at a systemic disadvantage (Heilbrunn, 2005, 2010). This systemic disadvantage is something Muki articulates with characteristic directness. "Since the kibbutz believed in productivity, it didn't raise capital. And for industry, to develop industry, you need a large capital base. And this capital base didn't exist." The kibbutz's founding ethical commitment to labor and production rather than accumulation was also, in retrospect, a strategic constraint since it built enterprises without reserves capable of absorbing large losses. All this mattered little in the era of low-tech manufacturing, where modest surpluses and flat internal distribution could coexist. But the logic of hi-tech is different. "In hi-tech fields there are unusual successes," Muki observes, "but alongside all the unusual successes, there are unusual failures. The exceptional success of hi-tech is the success of distinct companies. These successes and the enormous financial capital they accumulated, covered the very large and numerous failures that exist alongside them. Something that in low-tech cannot exist." A movement that did not accumulate capital and did not build risk-absorption capacity was, almost by design, excluded from the sector that was to dominate the Israeli economy from the 1990s onward. I add here a further layer. Looking back at my doctoral research on kibbutz entrepreneurship, I found not only structural barriers but also human ones in people who were not trained for what they were asked to do. I saw that people who weren't skilled enough managed innovative enterprises. Suddenly they were supposed to manage, not that they were not talented enough, but they simply did not have the background. They didn't have enough experience, not enough training, not enough financial understanding, too much ego 'we know everything, no one will tell us what to do. The egalitarian culture that produced remarkable solidarity could also produce a resistance to outside expertise that was costly precisely when expertise mattered most. Following the same line of argumentation let me mention a research project in which we found that organizational change in the kibbutz altered not only the objective distribution of risk but also members' willingness to assume it. As kibbutz institutions sent mixed signals about equality and initiative, entrepreneurial risk-taking became both more attractive to some and more morally fraught for others (Davidovitch, Heilbrunn & Polovin, 2009).

Balberg's (2024) historical narrative shows that the aspiration to combine radical equality with economic dynamism is not new but was rather present already in Degania's effort to be both a profitable farm and a fully communal group. The early "table" discussions, in which every decision was debated collectively, embodied a faith that intensive participation and shared responsibility could substitute for the incentives and hierarchies of a conventional firm (Balberg, 2024). Over time, as Tsuk and others document, the growth of managerial elites, the introduction of hired labor, and the slow turning inward of kibbutz aspirations eroded that faith and normalized more unequal, expertise-based forms of authority. By the 1980s and 1990s, debates over differential management pay and the exodus of managers signaled that entrepreneurial skill and leadership were increasingly being framed as professions that deserved higher material reward, not as temporary roles within an egalitarian collective (Heilbrunn, 2010). As communal settings differentiate internally, entrepreneurial motivation shifts: members orient themselves less toward collective recognition and more toward hybrid measures of achievement that combine autonomy, market validation, and communal standing (Heilbrunn, 2010). When institutions send mixed signals, encouraging initiative rhetorically while preserving egalitarian suspicions of differential success, some members come to experience entrepreneurship as a moral risk as much as an economic one (Heilbrunn, Itzkovitch, & Weinberg, 2017).

Against this backdrop, the celebrated cases of mission-driven industry such as Netafim, or Be'eri's seed-improvement work in Africa and Asia, appear as both promise and problem. The story of the Netafim patent being entrusted to Hatzerim "because you're cooperative," with the contractual insistence that any future partner must also be a kibbutz, dramatizes the hope that cooperativeness can itself be an asset in building world-class innovation. Yet these examples are exceptional: their success depends on precisely the factors, strong managerial cores, technological expertise, access to capital, and willingness to absorb failures, that strain the egalitarian fabric elsewhere. They are rare cases in which local social capital and broader developmental goals temporarily reinforce one another, rather than a replicable model. The dilemma, then, is whether the kibbutz can devise a stable form of enterprise in which innovation does not inevitably generate new inequalities and distances between entrepreneurs and ordinary members or whether its most impressive ventures will remain heroic exceptions, standing somewhat uneasily atop an increasingly differentiated community (Heilbrunn, 2010; Palgi, Sofer, & Heilbrunn, 2020).

Muki offers what is, on the surface, a counterintuitive observation: "In the large kibbutz industries, there are industries that are really powerful, and one of the very interesting facts is that many of the kibbutzim with large and successful industries, are still very collective and implemented less substantial changes than others." He pushes the point further: "The richest kibbutzim of the movement didn't separate from the cooperative elements. Even if they introduced some changes, they perceive cooperation and collective features as fostering productivity of their industry." This is definitely not a minor footnote. It is a structural challenge to the dominant narrative of kibbutz decline. The dilemma of innovation and equality, as framed above, carries an implicit assumption, namely that entrepreneurial success and collective organization are structurally at odds, and that kibbutzim most exposed to global competition will inevitably drift toward privatization and differentiation. The empirical record is more complicated. Some of the wealthiest kibbutzim in Israel today, Ma'agan Michael with its global plastics firm Plasson, Mishmar HaEmek with its diversified portfolio of industrial enterprises, Baram with its advanced optics and defence technologies, and Be'eri with its printing industries and agricultural innovation are precisely kibbutzim that have held most tenaciously to collective organizational structures and communal culture. And one cannot describe them as marginal anomalies. Their factories employ hundreds of workers in Israel and abroad and generate revenues in the hundreds of millions of dollars yet they have not resolved the tension between innovation and equality by abandoning equality. Instead, they have, in varying ways, made collectivism itself into a competitive asset. Thus it seems that where dense social networks and collective institutions endure, they can reshape the terms under which communities enter markets and buffer them, at least partially, from the more corrosive effects of competition (Tsuk, 2005). In the prosperous collective kibbutzim, something is happening that neither pure market theory nor standard accounts of cooperative fragility capture well. It is the capacity of a stable, trust-dense, long-horizon collective to sustain the kind of patient investment in technology, talent, and institutional knowledge that short-term private capital cannot or will not make. Ma'agan Michael's Plasson is a case in point. It did not emerge from a lone heroic inventor backed by venture capital, but from a community that reinvested its surpluses collectively, tolerated long periods of modest returns, and retained skilled workers through non-monetary bonds of belonging, shared history, mutual responsibility, and a strong sense of *shelanu*. Strategic decisions about new product lines, export markets, and technological upgrades were taken not under the immediate pressure of shareholder value, but through collective deliberation in institutions answerable to the kibbutz as a whole. A similar pattern, in different registers, appears in Baram's optical precision industries and in Be'eri's industrial ventures: long-term commitments to specialized knowledge, heavy reinvestment of profits in productive capacity and community infrastructure, and a refusal, sometimes costly in the short run, to cash out communal ownership in favor of external control. What these kibbutzim demonstrate, against the prevailing logic, is that entrepreneurship can flourish not despite collectivist environments, but partly because of them. The very features often treated as weaknesses such as strong internal norms, egalitarian culture, embedded decision-making, and thick trust can, under certain conditions, become sources of patient capital, organizational resilience, and innovative capacity. The counter-narrative does not deny the tensions or the emerging inequalities inside these communities, but it insists that the relationship between innovation and equality is not given once and for all by abstract theory; it is worked out institutionally, in specific places like Ma'agan Michael, Mishmar HaEmek, Baram, and Be'eri, over decades of experiment.

What Ma'agan Michael, Mishmar HaEmek, Baram, and Be'eri tell us, taken together, is that the trade-off between innovation and equality has been mis-theorized. The trade-off is not structural but institutional; it is a feature of particular ownership arrangements and particular time horizons, not a feature of innovation as such. Where collective ownership combines with patient capital, mission-oriented production, and the absorption of risk across a long-horizon community, equality and innovation are not at war but mutually constitutive. The most enduring kibbutz industries have, in this sense, anticipated at the level of communal enterprise what Mariana Mazzucato now argues for at the level of the state (Mazzucato, 2013, 2021), namely that mission, patience, and shared risk-bearing are not residues of a pre-capitalist economy but conditions for the kinds of innovation that short-horizon private capital cannot finance. The dilemma of innovation and equality is therefore not resolved by these cases; it is reframed. The Plasson model does not prove that all kibbutzim can do what Ma'agan Michael has done. It proves that the standard pairing of equality with stagnation and inequality with innovation is itself a contingent ideological construction that the kibbutz, at its strongest, has worked institutionally to undo.

Dilemma 3: Integration, Transformation, and the Fate of "Capitalism Outward, Socialism Inward"

The third dilemma concerns integration and transformation and asks whether the famous kibbutz formula of "capitalism outward, socialism inward" was ever a stable equilibrium, or always a temporary compromise that would tilt, slowly but inexorably, in one direction. The generational fracture this produced is something Muki describes with particular care.

"You have to look, for example, at a kibbutz like Yagur that has a factory. And this factory was sold to an American company. Now, the American company doesn't know the kibbutz method. So what do they do? They make a list of employees with graded salaries, submit it to the American company, which pays all salaries and then the salaries are divided according to the needs of the kibbutz." The mechanism holds for a time. But then: "How do you manage with a factory in a completely different culture? And again, the problem deepened on one hand. On the other hand, the next generations already said: "Wait, what's this whole story? We don't understand this method. It does not make sense." The ingenuity of the redistribution cannot survive its own opacity; a generation that has grown up inside a market economy experiences the accounting mechanism not as an expression of social solidarity but as an inexplicable anomaly. Integration with global industry, in other words, does not only change wage tables or management charts; it destabilizes the very categories through which members understand what the kibbutz is as an economic entity. In an article I published in 2005 on the impact of organizational change on entrepreneurship in community settings, I argued that integration into wider markets often proceeds through incremental organizational adjustments whose cumulative effect is to transform the community's own understanding of its boundaries and purposes (Heilbrunn, 2005). Nir Tsuk's (2005) wider analysis of the kibbutz as an applied utopia embedded in a changing political-economic environment helps explain why this compromise is so fragile. From the outset, the kibbutz depended on a settlement pact in which national institutions owned the land, provided capital and guarantees, and in return relied on collectivist groups to carry out high-risk tasks of settlement and nation-building (Tsuk, 2005). In that configuration, the kibbutz could function as a protected enclave, with strong fences between its internal regime of self-labor, common ownership, and direct democracy, and an external environment dominated by private capital and state policy. As Tsuk shows, however, the expansion of the Israeli state, the growth of a centralized welfare and planning apparatus, and the gradual shift from a labor-socialist to a more capitalist political economy pulled the kibbutz into denser webs of regulation, subsidy, and market exposure (Tsuk, 2005). The result is a long process in which the utopian enclave becomes less autonomous and more thoroughly integrated into the national and global rules of the game, even as it continues to describe itself in the language of separation and distinctiveness. In later work on communities in processes of change and on the move from work to livelihood, I traced how such macro-transformations enter the everyday life of the kibbutz through changing livelihood strategies, shifting forms of entrepreneurial motivation, and a growing dependence on mixed economic repertoires rather than a single coherent communal economy (Heilbrunn, 2010; Palgi, Sofer, & Heilbrunn, 2020). In this context, Muki's description of a shrinking own economy, of outside work becoming "very, very important," and of the abolition of the work coordinator marks a tipping point. When most members earn their income in external labor markets, when factories are sold to multinational firms, and when kibbutz services are increasingly privatized or outsourced, the inside/outside distinction that once underwrote the slogan "capitalism outward, socialism inward" becomes hard to maintain empirically. Tsuk (2005) captures this as a change not only within but of the system, stating that the kibbutz moves from being a holistic alternative society, with its own modes of production, distribution, and governance, to being one sector among others within a liberal-capitalist state, distinguished by degree but no longer clearly by kind. The emergence of "new" and "communal" streams, the partial privatization of income and housing, and the reliance on progressive taxation and minimal mutual-aid guarantees represent attempts to salvage a core of reciprocity and mutual responsibility within a framework that now assumes individual property and market-based careers as normal (Heilbrunn, 2008; Tsuk, 2005).

In my 2007 article on entrepreneurship, social capital, and community development in the Kibbutz, I suggested that once communal integration weakens, entrepreneurial energy does not disappear; rather, it is redistributed into smaller-scale and more locally contingent forms of association (Heilbrunn, 2008). The rise of urban kibbutzim, mission-driven enterprises, and renewed interest in study circles and secular Jewish learning suggests a different pattern: instead of a single, movement-wide formula balancing capitalism and socialism, we see multiple, smaller experiments that accept full immersion in a capitalist and statist context while insisting on pockets of intensified communality and commitment (Balberg, 2024). In this sense, the dilemma of integration and transformation is not only about whether "capitalism outward, socialism inward" can be stabilized; it is about whether the kibbutz can reinvent itself as a family of applied utopias that live self-consciously inside a market society without either dissolving into it entirely or retreating into nostalgic self-enclosure (Tsuk, 2005).

The Yagur vignette names what the formula was always vulnerable to. "Capitalism outward, socialism inward" was never a stable equilibrium; it was a generational arrangement. It held as long as the generation in question remembered why the redistribution mechanism existed and what it was protecting. Once that intelligibility fell below a threshold, the formula did not collapse outright. It became opaque. The grandchildren of the founders did not refute the mechanism; they failed to recognize it. They asked, as Muki recalls, "What is this method? We don't understand." Opacity is a slower kind of failure than collapse. A collapsing institution announces itself; an opaque institution simply stops being legible to those who would otherwise inherit it, and the question of whether it is worth inheriting therefore never arrives in a form that can be answered. This, rather than market pressure as such, is the deepest threat that integration carries: not the visible loss of the kibbutz's enterprises, which the founders foresaw and accepted as a risk, but the moment when the kibbutz's own arrangements become unreadable to the kibbutz's own next generation.

Conclusion

The trajectories traced in this Chapter suggest that the fate of kibbutz enterprise cannot be reduced either to a simple story of decline under global capitalism or to a romantic tale of heroic collective resilience. What emerges instead is a more paradoxical and diverse picture. The very processes that hollowed out the classical model of self-labor, common ownership, and an integrated "own economy" have also generated new configurations in which collective structures and innovative enterprise sometimes reinforce rather than cancel one another. The factory gate, which once marked a clear boundary between "inside" and "outside", now often opens onto Swiss-owned plants, multinational partnerships, and start-ups oriented to global markets; yet in some kibbutzim it still functions as an institutional hinge between shared mission and technological ambition.

Put more simply, three shifts stand out. First, enterprise and ownership have changed from a relatively unified kibbutz "own economy", where members were workers, owners, and citizens in a single system to a landscape in which many kibbutzim rely on external employment, sold or partially privatized factories, and mixed ownership forms, while a minority maintain large, collectively owned enterprises. Second, the relationship between innovation and equality has proven not to be a simple zero-sum trade-off: in some cases, communal arrangements have underpinned patient, high-risk innovation, making collectivism a competitive advantage rather than an obstacle. Third, the old formula of "capitalism outward, socialism inward" has fragmented into a variety of hybrid arrangements, from partially privatized kibbutzim with residual mutual-aid mechanisms to urban kibbutzim and mission-driven enterprises that live fully inside markets while cultivating pockets of intensified communality.

The unnamed loss with which the chapter opens, the fading of *shelanu* from the factory floor in Barkai is indeed real and irreducible. Something has indeed been signed away: the confidence that a community could be constituted, in a straightforward manner, by its shared control over the means of production. Yet the materials assembled here also point to another possibility. A renegotiation of the meaning of *shelanu*, shifting from a singular, movement-wide structure of agrarian and industrial communality to a more plural field of applied utopias, each experimenting with different ways of tying work, ownership, and innovation to belonging and responsibility (Tsuk, 2005; Balberg, 2024). Whether these experiments will amount to a new phase in the history of the kibbutz, or merely mark its prolonged transformation into a set of interesting but marginal niches within a liberal-capitalist society, remains an open question. What can be said, at this point in the book, is that the kibbutz continues to matter not only as a chapter in Israeli social history, but as a site in which some of the central contradictions of contemporary capitalism, between innovation and equality, risk and security, global integration and local cohesion are being worked through in unusually explicit and institutionally visible ways.

9. What Do We Know and Refuse to Know?

Land and the Kibbutz

Kibbutz Metzer (on the right) and Meiser (on the left) from above, 2026

Source: Alex Heilbrunn, photographer

Introduction

When the planning for this book began, it was clear that there would have to be a chapter on land, and equally clear, almost from the beginning, that it would be the hardest chapter to write. In the working outline there was a simple placeholder: "Land and inequality." For months it remained only a heading, not because the material was lacking, but because each time the conversation approached it, something in it tightened and withdrew. At one point I asked

Muki, half in jest and half in desperation, what his introductory note to this chapter might say. He thought for a moment and answered: "My note? That I don't really want to talk about it." That answer was honest, and it named more than a personal reluctance. It pointed to something structural, namely the difficulty, for those who built and inhabited the kibbutz story from within, of looking steadily at the ground beneath their own feet.

Because Muki's hesitation and my own belatedness in formulating these questions could not carry the chapter on their own, I invited another voice to enter the conversation. Shuli Dichter, member of Kibbutz Ma'anit and a long-standing acquaintance, is a civil society activist and long-time practitioner and thinker of Jewish–Arab partnership within Israel. He served for a decade as co-executive director of *Sikkuy*, working to advance equality through policy change, municipal cooperation, and public advocacy; he later led '*Hand in Hand*', the bilingual school network that aimed to enact institutionally the possibility of a more equal Jewish–Arab civic life. His book *Sharing the Promised Land* is one of the most sustained recent efforts to think seriously about equality in a state defined as Jewish. In our conversation, Dichter offered a concept that captures nicely Muki's reluctance to talk about the subject and the impression I got often when starting a conversation about it: *latent ignorance*. Jews on kibbutzim, he suggested, live in a condition of knowing and not-knowing at the same time. They know that the land on which they built their communities has a prior Palestinian history that the Arab house did not get there by accident, that the orchard at the edge of the fields has roots deeper than the kibbutz. Yet that knowledge is held at bay, because to admit it fully would unsettle not only the national story of liberation, but also the kibbutz's story about itself as a community founded on justice and equality.

The Arab house at Barkai stands at the very top of the kibbutz grounds, sturdy and enduring. When I first arrived there as a young volunteer in the late 1970s, I did not see it. Or rather, I saw it but did not know to ask what it was. What I saw were the fields, the communal dining hall, and the children running between the houses, in short an experiment in human solidarity that seemed, from the outside, genuinely extraordinary. Back then, I was truly ignorant and did not ask about the Arab house at the top of the hill next to the swimming pool. However, those who have grown up in the shadow of that house have learned, across generations, the art of not quite looking. This chapter is also about that art, about what it costs, what it protects, and what it forecloses. Several tensions run through what follows. Whether a community committed to internal justice can sustain that commitment while remaining silent about the injustice on which it rests. By whose moral standards historical events should be judged, when the logic of those events has not ended but merely shifted location. How memory and forgetting collaborate in the stories communities tell about themselves. And what it means that land once allocated through dispossession has become, across generations, a form of inherited wealth. These are the questions the chapter carries, not as propositions to be argued and resolved, but as openings through which to look at a history the kibbutz movement has rarely looked at directly. In what follows, the c approaches these questions in three steps: first, through a historical account of how kibbutzim came to occupy their land; second, through moments of awareness and denial within the movement; and third, through the contemporary economic and political legacies of those earlier choices.

Three Phases, Five Cases

The relationship between the kibbutz movement and the land of Palestine did not begin with the events of 1948, nor did it end there. It unfolded across several decades, in three distinct but interconnected phases, each governed by different means but animated by the same underlying logic; the transformation of the land into the foundation of a new society. In the earliest phase, from the first waves of Zionist immigration through the 1930s and into the 1940s, land was acquired primarily through purchase. The Jewish National Fund and the agents of the Rothschild network operated within the legal framework of Ottoman and then British Mandate law, buying tracts from often absentee landlords in Damascus or Beirut at prices that reflected the buyers' need and the sellers' willingness. The process was not without tensions. British Mandate law held, as Dichter told, that even legal purchase did not entitle new owners to expel those who worked the land; the Arab tenant farmers and sharecroppers who found themselves displaced had not sold anything and had nowhere to go. From the kibbutz movement's side, there was awareness of this friction, but it was rarely allowed to slow the pace of settlement. The Zionist task came increasingly to overshadow the socialist one, and the acquisition of land was its most essential expression. Tower-and-stockade settlements (*Homa u-Migdal*) were raised overnight, secured against attack, and declared facts. The question of who had previously worked those fields was answered, implicitly, by the urgency of the national project. The second and most convulsive phase arrived with the war of 1948. This was the War of Independence for the Jewish side, and the *Nakba*, the catastrophe, for the Palestinians. By the time the fighting ended, approximately 700,000 Palestinians had fled or been expelled, and some 400 villages had been depopulated. The moral complexity of that moment was not entirely invisible to those living through it. Mira Balberg's account records what many kibbutz members knew and chose not to fully absorb: that the families who had lived in the houses they now occupied had not simply departed, that the orchards they tended had been planted by others, that the wells they drew from had been dug by hands they would never shake. The third phase was legal and administrative, and in some ways the most consequential for the long term. The abandoned land was declared government property, sold to the Jewish National Fund, and then leased to existing and new settlements. The Absentee Property laws, passed in the early 1950s, provided the legislative architecture for a massive permanent transfer of Palestinian land into Jewish Israeli hands. Kibbutzim that had been starved for land for years seized the opportunity to expand their holdings, often after competitive maneuvering with neighboring settlements. The Ministry of Agriculture actively encouraged kibbutzim and moshavim to harvest the crops of abandoned villages, framing it as a contribution to the war effort; the produce, and later the land itself, passed into the new state's hands. Nir Tsuk's account notes that some commentators have argued the government deliberately used this land distribution to compensate the Kibbutz movement for having been sidelined from the centers of political decision-making, a transaction in which moral accountability was exchanged for agricultural acreage. (Tsuk, 2005; Absentees' Property Law, 5710–1950) Indeed, by the early 1950s, the pattern became clear. The kibbutz population represented only a small percentage of Israel's citizens, but it controlled a third of the cultivated land and supplied a disproportionate share of the country's agricultural output. That productivity was real, and it was achieved through genuine labor and sacrifice. But its foundations rested, in many cases, on a prior dispossession that the movement had not sought to examine, and whose human consequences namely the Palestinian refugees, the destroyed villages, the severed community life, remained beyond the fence, out of view, and by and large out of conversation. The following, five cases, drawn from different parts of the country and different moments, illuminate the range of circumstances under which kibbutzim came to occupy their land and the range of responses that followed.

The pre-1948 pattern is perhaps most vividly illustrated by what happened in the Jezreel Valley in 1920, when the Jewish National Fund accomplished what was then its largest single land acquisition. Some 50,000 dunam were purchased from the Sursock family, wealthy absentee landowners based in Beirut. For the approximately five hundred Arab tenant families who lived and worked those lands, it was the beginning of a catastrophe. They did not own the land in any legal sense, since the Ottoman system of land registration had left most tenant farmers without title deeds, but they had farmed it for generations. When Yehoshua Hankin, who had orchestrated the purchase, came to prepare the ground for the arrival of the Work Battalion (*Gdud HaAvoda*), the tenants received notice roughly two hours before the settlers appeared, announcing that they were not to interfere, they were strongly encouraged to leave, and those who did so would receive some compensation. The people of Nuris tried to argue, but eventually complied. Some years later, from that same valley, several of the most ideologically committed kibbutzim in the country would emerge. One example is Beit Alfa (1922), founded by Hashomer Hatzair, a movement whose platform explicitly championed Jewish–Arab partnership and opposed Palestinian dispossession. Balberg's account captures the contradiction plainly: almost every kibbutz of Hashomer Hatzair, the most universalist and progressive of the kibbutz streams, was built on land from which Arab Palestinians had been removed. The geographer Arnon Golan's formulation, quoted in her account, is blunt: "You can think of it in terms of removing rocks from the ground before you plow it. Once you've set the rocks aside, you don't think about them anymore." (Balberg, 2024).

Against this pattern, a handful of kibbutzim offered acts of acknowledgment or resistance. According to accounts preserved in the kibbutz archives, when Kibbutz Manara was established in the upper Galilee in 1943 and was strongly encouraged by the authorities to rename the site with a Hebrew designation, its members refused, insisting they would not erase the history of the place and the people who had given it its name. It is a small detail, and a revealing one, and not to forget that such acts of acknowledgment were the exception rather than the rule. Kibbutz Bar'am represents the sharpest and most documented moment of moral resistance within the movement. In October 1948, Israeli forces took the village of Bir'im, a Maronite Christian community in the upper Galilee. The villagers surrendered peacefully and were told to leave for two weeks while military arrangements were made. In fact they were never permitted to return. Three Hashomer Hatzair groups were sent to settle on the village's land. When they arrived and understood what had happened, they refused to settle inside the village. Their representative went to the government office responsible for land allocation and was told: "No one is asking you. If you don't like it, you can leave; I'll just bring another group that won't cause so many problems." The founders of Bar'am established their kibbutz on the adjacent hill. They spent years supporting the Bir'im families' legal struggle, which reached the Supreme Court in 1951 and resulted in a ruling in the refugees' favor but which was never implemented (HCJ 64/51 Habib v. Minister of Defense; Jiryis, 1979; Forman & Kedar, 2004). In 1953 the village was bombed. Bar'am remains, to this day, the only kibbutz on Israel's northern border that does not occupy a former Palestinian village. The episode shows both that awareness was possible and resistance attempted and also illustrates, that the structural forces at work were larger than any individual community's conscience.

Kibbutz Zikim, established in 1949 on the southern coast near Gaza, represents the more typical post-1948 pattern. It was built on the lands of Hiribya, a Palestinian village depopulated during the war. There was no founding drama, no act of refusal or protest recorded. The land was simply allocated through the state machinery of the Absentee Property laws and the Jewish National Fund, and a new community took root where another had existed. The name Hiribya largely disappeared from public consciousness, as happened in hundreds of cases across the country (Khalidi, 1992; Benvenisti, 2000). The Gaza-area kibbutzim, among them Nir Oz, Re'im, Ein HaShlosha, Kisufim, and Magen were established on the lands and orchards of Ma'in Abu Sitta and the clans of the Tarabin tribe. Oral histories and land records document that the wheat fields, barley crops, and school grounds of these Palestinian communities became the agricultural base of the new kibbutzim after 1948. These are also the communities that were attacked on October 7, 2023, a fact that has layered new grief and new complexity onto a history already dense with unresolved claims. To hold both truths simultaneously, the genuine rootedness and the genuine loss on which it rests, is among the most difficult things this Chapter asks of its readers. Legal purchase with tenant displacement (Jezreel Valley, 1920), respectful acknowledgment without restitution (Manara, 1943), principled resistance overruled by state power (Bar'am, 1948), silent absorption through legal mechanism (Zikim, 1949), and the contemporary entanglement of past and present (the Gaza-area Kibbutzim) are all reflected in these five cases. Taken together, they sketch the moral landscape within which the later dilemmas of memory, ignorance, and inequality take shape.

Dilemma 1: "They Know but Don't Want to Know": Latent Ignorance and the Zionist Memory Machine

The Zionist narrative, as Dichter framed it in our conversation, is not a simple lie but something much more complex. "It is a system that is simultaneously a factory of memory and of forgetting." It remembers with extraordinary intensity the sacrifices of the pioneers, the hardships of the early settlements, the fallen in the wars, the children of Degania, and the names of the kibbutz founders engraved in stone. But it forgets, with equal systematicity, the names of the villages that preceded those settlements, the families who farmed the fields before the kibbutz was established, and the human texture of the communities that were erased. Memory and forgetting are not opposites in this system; they are partners, each enabling the other. Dichter (2022, ch. 2) traces this dynamic in his account of a kibbutz in the Beit She'an Valley whose second generation preserved a founding legend of settling desolate ground, until the founder's own archived testimony, written for the kibbutz newsletter on the tenth and twentieth anniversaries, turned up and described arriving in April 1948 to find a two-thousand-dunam field of tall wheat cultivated by Arab farmers, with irrigation water running through it. The family, reading the old pages, looked at one another in astonishment, since the kibbutz had preserved the opposite of the story its founder had told. Dichter frames the question this chapter is also asking: was it "innocent ignorance, or an effort to ignore what is known?" (Dichter 2022, p. 40). This practice is not, Dichter emphasized, unique to the kibbutz or to Israel. Every colonial society develops its version of this architecture. The difference is that in most cases, the distance of time eventually makes the reckoning easier. The dispossession becomes historical, settled and available for retrospective acknowledgment without threatening the present. In the Israeli–Palestinian case, that distance has never been possible, because the process has never ended. What happened in 1948 continued, in a different register, after 1967, and continues today in the West Bank. This is Dichter's most uncomfortable argument. He states that the reason 1948 cannot be honestly examined is precisely that its logic is still being applied in the present tense; to condemn the past would be to condemn the present, and so the past must remain latent, known but not known, present but unacknowledged.

Mira Balberg's account of her own coming-to-knowledge offers a striking personal parallel. Growing up in Israel, she writes, she was told that the Palestinian villagers of 1948 had simply "left", a formulation that removed agency and responsibility from the act of displacement in a single passive verb. It was only in her twenties, at university, that she began to understand what had actually occurred. Some Palestinians had been forcibly expelled, some had been killed, and the daily realities of life under military rule were nothing like the story she had been given. "It was striking," she writes, "to realize just how much I didn't know for the first two decades of my life about the place where I lived" (Balberg, 2024). The phrase captures the texture of *latent ignorance* precisely. It is socially produced, transmitted through education, song, and the stories families tell themselves. The not-knowing requires effort, but not the effort of active suppression, but the sustained, collective effort of simply not asking certain questions, not following certain threads, not walking to the top of the kibbutz to look at the Arab house too closely. What makes this particularly acute in the kibbutz context is the contradiction it creates with everything the movement claimed to stand for. The kibbutz was built on ideals of honesty, of facing reality without illusion, of the "new Jew" who would not flinch from hard truths. It was the incubator of Israel's most progressive social and political thought, the peace movement, the civil rights activists, the writers and intellectuals who, from the 1960s onward, began to examine Zionism critically from within. And yet it was precisely the most ideologically committed wing of the movement, Hashomer Hatzair, that established almost all of its kibbutzim on land from which Arab Palestinians had been removed, beginning with Beit Alfa in 1922. The contradiction was visible from the start and was never resolved. Rather, it was managed, through the mechanism Dichter describes, by keeping the progressive ideal and the dispossessing reality in separate compartments of consciousness. Muki approaches this question from another angle. He is deeply attentive to the psychological and political pressures that produce silence. The fear of providing ammunition to those who want total war, the sense that certain kinds of self-criticism are weaponised by adversaries who have no corresponding willingness to reflect. "People who were deeply educated," he said, "have deep inhibitions. It comes from politics that says: 'Shut up.' It's forbidden to speak because we're fighting, or it's forbidden to speak because we were defeated morally." This is a genuine insight, and it deserves to be taken seriously. The silencing of self-criticism in a society under existential pressure is a real and complicated phenomenon, not simply a bad-faith maneuver. And yet Dichter's counter-argument is equally compelling: the inhibitions that prevent honest accounting of the past are not simply imposed from outside, they are internally generated and actively maintained, because they protect something the community is not yet ready to release, which is the story of its own innocence. The Brecht song sung in many kibbutzim in the years after 1948 exemplified this well. The song states that the land belongs to those who care for it, who water it, who make it bear fruit. This song is perhaps the most eloquent expression of how *latent ignorance* becomes ideology. It is a beautiful sentiment. It is also, in this context, a mechanism for converting dispossession into virtue. Therefore, those who cultivate the land deserve it by virtue of their labor, and the question of what happened to those who cultivated it before is dissolved in the beauty of the agricultural vision. The kibbutz, in singing that song, was not lying to itself in any simple sense. It genuinely believed in the redemptive power of labor on the land. But that belief functioned, simultaneously, as a way of not seeing who else had labored there, and what had been done to ensure they could no longer do so. None of this implies that kibbutz members were, in any simple sense, bad people. By any ordinary measure they were unusually generous, idealistic, and willing to sacrifice comfort for a collective project they believed in. Precisely for that reason, however, the dissonance between their ethical self-understanding and the structural conditions that made their communities possible is so hard to face. The point is not to indict individual biographies, but to ask how a movement so committed to justice could coexist for so long with a history it preferred not to see.

The Brecht song shows the move in slow motion: a community that genuinely believes in the redemptive power of agricultural labor sings, in the dining hall, the precise sentence that converts its inheritance of a dispossession into a moral entitlement, and does so without anyone having to lie. This is the system-level operation of *latent ignorance*, and it is what makes the dissonance so hard to face. It is not a personal failing of individual kibbutz members, who were by any ordinary measure unusually generous and idealistic, but a feature of the way the kibbutz's ethical self-understanding and the structural conditions that made its communities possible were stitched together at the start. The challenge the chapter places before its readers is therefore not to render a verdict on individual biographies but to hold the two compartments – the genuine beauty of the project and the genuine cost at which it was built – open at the same time, and to ask what internal solidarity, communal generosity, and a commitment to honesty mean if they are systematically bounded at the kibbutz fence.

Dilemma 2: Moments of Awareness

Latent ignorance is not all encompassing and it is not permanent. Alongside the dominant pattern of not-looking, there have been, across the history of the kibbutz movement, moments, if so rare, often fragile and sometimes extinguished before they could take root, when individual communities or educators chose to look directly at what lay beneath their feet. These moments are worth examining not because they redeem the larger pattern, but because they illuminate what awareness, when it does emerge, actually looks like and what it demands. One of the most significant of these initiatives, mentioned by Dichter in our conversation, was an educational project undertaken in a number of kibbutzim, among them those associated with some educators in highschools, to map and teach the history of the Palestinian villages on whose land the kibbutz stands. The idea was straightforward and, in context, radical. Children growing up on that land should know its full name and full history. Not only the Hebrew name given to the kibbutz or the surrounding landscape, but the Arabic name that preceded it, the families who had lived there, the wells and schools and olive groves that had belonged to a community before theirs. The project was not framed as an exercise in guilt or political instruction, but as an act of historical honesty. If the kibbutz movement had always understood itself as a community that faced reality without flinching, then the history of the land it stood on was part of that reality. To teach it was to be faithful to the movement's own best instincts. That this kind of education remained exceptional rather than standard is itself a measure of the difficulty. Dichter noted that the project depended on specific individuals whose personal commitments drove it forward. Figures like Avishai Grossman, whose name runs through the educational and intellectual history of the kibbutz movement and to whom this book is dedicated. The fact that such initiatives depended on individual conscience rather than institutional policy meant they were always vulnerable to changing leadership, to political climate, to the ordinary attrition of institutional memory.

Grossman's place in this chapter is more than incidental. He was one of the small number of educators who, across decades, treated the history of the land as part of the kibbutz movement's own moral curriculum rather than as a topic to be handed off to others. The fact that this work depended on him, and on a handful of figures like him, rather than on an institutional mandate, is itself the chapter's diagnostic point. The Conclusion of this book is dedicated to his memory, and the reader will find the argument there returning, in a different register, to what he made possible while he was here.

The relationship between Kibbutz Metzer and its Arab neighbor Kafr Meiser offers a different kind of example. The connection between these two communities is not a historical reckoning but a living, daily proximity that has, over time, produced something unusual. Two communities physically close enough that one turns right for the Kibbutz and left for the village at the same junction, yet separated by all the usual fault lines of Israeli society. What makes Metzer distinctive is that those fault lines have, at least in certain respects, been partially bridged. The education system there has developed to include not merely Meiser's employees in auxiliary roles but leading educators and kindergarten teachers are working as full pedagogical partners in the kibbutz's education system. Read alongside Chapter 7's account of the 1972 Metzer–Meiser conceptual-art project and its 2025 curatorial return, the educational partnership Sibylle describes here is its institutional sibling: what the artists were trying to image at the junction, and what the later curators returned to register as changed, the educators have, in a quieter idiom, made into a daily practice. Not every moment of awareness arrives so fully formed. Sometimes recognition and denial sit side by side within a single community, and it is not always clear which is which. I recalled that at Kibbutz Barkai there was an old orchard planted by the Palestinians who had lived on the land, next to the Arab House. Around the same time that this orchard was being rediscovered, one of the kibbutz members decided to establish a new orchard, with strikingly similar trees but now at the entrance to the kibbutz. I don't believe this was a conscious decision. It was, I think, a denial of what was already there. Dichter (2022, ch. 3) describes an almost identical episode at his own Kibbutz Ma'anit, where the second generation planted fig trees, pomegranates, sabra hedges, and olive trees on the slopes of Tel Narbata in the 1980s – a grove that any passing visitor would naturally read as the trace of a Palestinian village, even though no Palestinian village had stood on that hill. When asked about his motives, the kibbutz member who led the planting spoke of wanting "local fruit trees" drawn from the biblical Seven Species. Dichter reads this as a form of unconscious scenery-making: the construction of the signature of Palestinian presence in order to ratify a sense of inheritance, even in places where there is nothing concrete to inherit. The new orchard at Barkai belongs, I suspect, to that same family of gestures.

What the educational projects, the Metzer–Meiser partnership, and the orchard at the entrance of Barkai together show is that awareness in the kibbutz movement has been real but episodic. It has arrived, when it has arrived, through the conscience of particular educators, the daily proximity of particular neighbors, and the chance encounter of a member with what was already standing on the hill. What it has not arrived through is institutional architecture. The movement built dense institutional architecture for almost everything else it cared about, assemblies, committees, festival cycles, education systems, archives. It did not build a corresponding architecture for the question of how it came to be on the land it occupies, and the result is that awareness, where it appears, has remained dependent on individual conscience and therefore vulnerable to the ordinary attrition that conscience suffers across generations.

Dilemma 3: Land as Capital: The Compounded Inequality

There is a further dimension to this story that has received little attention, namely the transformation of the land question from a moral and historical issue into an economic one. The land on which kibbutzim were established, much of it acquired through the processes described above, did over time not remain simply agricultural. Over the course of the 1990s and into the twenty-first century, it became capital. The distribution of that capital has generated a new layer of inequality, one that compounds the original injustice with a contemporary one that the kibbutz movement has been equally reluctant to examine. To understand how this happened, it is necessary to recall the economic crisis of the 1980s, described in Chapter 8. By the mid-1980s, the collective debt of the kibbutz movement had reached staggering proportions, eventually climbing to twelve billion shekels by 1989, and the only asset that stood between many kibbutzim and effective bankruptcy was their land. Balberg (2024) describes the atmosphere very well, panic was rising, members prepared to have their furniture and cars auctioned, and "the only thing they had that was really valuable was their land." (Russell, Hanneman, & Getz, 2013; Yiftachel, 2006). The crisis forced the movement, the banks, and the government into a complex set of negotiations whose resolution permanently altered the relationship between the kibbutz and its land. The crucial shift came through a series of decisions by Israel's National Land Authority beginning in the early 1990s. Agricultural land, which until that point had been treated purely as a means of production, leased from the state for farming purposes and carrying no market value, was reclassified in a way that allowed it to be used for residential and commercial development. Almost overnight, land that had been an agricultural tool became a real estate asset. Muki articulated the significance of this moment with characteristic precision: "The big debt of the kibbutz movement will be paid by land having a price. Agricultural land. Until then agricultural land had no price. And at the same moment they gave land a price, the regional councils in the centre became real estate in an extreme way." Further decisions enabled kibbutzim to develop parts of their holdings as communal neighborhoods where non-members could purchase homes, with a portion of the proceeds flowing to the kibbutz. The debt-restructuring agreements explicitly incorporated land as collateral and, eventually, as a vehicle for repayment. The consequences of these developments were profound and deeply unequal. Kibbutzim located near Israel's urban centers such as the Sharon plain, the Jezreel Valley, the coastal strip suddenly found themselves sitting on land worth hundreds of millions of shekels. kibbutzim in peripheral regions, where the same agricultural land had no development potential, had no equivalent windfall. As Tsuk notes, this ability to sell land as valuable real estate did not exist for peripheral kibbutzim, a fact that enlarged the economic gaps between them. What had begun as a relatively uniform movement, structured around collective principles that were supposed to override geographic and economic difference, fractured along lines determined entirely by the accident of location. And that location was, in many cases, the direct product of the state's post-1948 settlement policy, the same policy that had allocated land from depopulated Palestinian villages to new and expanding kibbutzim.

The irony runs deep. Land allocated to kibbutzim in the late 1940s and early 1950s, often the fields and orchards of Palestinian communities was originally understood primarily as agricultural resource and its moral origins suppressed or rationalized. Decades later, when that same land acquired extraordinary monetary value, the kibbutzim that held it found themselves endowed with a capital windfall that bore no relationship to their members' labor or virtue. It was based only onaccident of location their historical position within a system of allocation that was itself the product of dispossession. Those who were dispossessed, meanwhile, received nothing. Their claims were not revisited when the land acquired its new value; the Absentee Property laws remained in force; and the Palestinians whose families had farmed those fields remained in refugee camps or in Arab towns and villages where land scarcity and planning restrictions had produced the exact opposite of a windfall. This is the dimension Muki had in mind when he observed that "the kibbutzim in the center have alternative capital which is the land." He was speaking about a structural feature of contemporary kibbutz inequality. But the observation names that original acquisition of land has compounded itself across time into a form of inherited wealth whose origins remain unacknowledged. A community that devoted a century to the critique of inherited privilege, that built its entire ethical architecture on the principle that no one should benefit from what they did not earn, has, in many cases, become the beneficiary of precisely such a privilege, rooted in a history it has not found the language to confront. Kibbutz Barkai, where I lived many years, is located in the Menashe Hills, in the Wadi Ara area. It is close enough to Israel's center and newly built infrastructure that its land has acquired real value. It is however surrounded by Arab towns and villages that have long faced severe planning restrictions and chronic land scarcity. Dichter (2022, ch. 6) documents this geography in detail. The Menashe Regional Council to the south and the Megiddo Regional Council to the north enclose Wadi Ara from both sides, so that the city of Umm al-Fahm and the surrounding Arab villages are compressed between mountain ridges under Jewish regional-council jurisdiction. The shortage of living space has pushed construction in the villages to four and even eight stories, while small Jewish settlements along the ridge enjoy generous allotments for expansion and attract state incentives to continue growing. The contrast between Barkai and its neighbours is therefore not an accident of topography; it is the local expression of a statewide structure in which land confiscated after 1948, channeled almost exclusively to kibbutzim and Jewish development towns, continues to determine who can build, where, and at what density. The contrast is not incidental. It is the contemporary expression of a historical arrangement that allocated land, development rights, and economic possibility along lines drawn in 1948. When I first knew Barkai in the late 1970s, none of this was visible. The kibbutz seemed simply like a remarkable human experiment, poor in material terms but rich in solidarity and purpose. Only with the perspective of decades does the landscape tell the story of an experiment that was made possible, from the beginning, by conditions whose costs were borne by others, and that those costs have never been reckoned with or repaid.

The structural claim of Dilemma 3 can now be stated plainly. A community whose founding ethical commitment was the refusal to benefit from inherited privilege has, through no individual act of bad faith and through the slow operation of policy and time, become a major beneficiary of exactly such a privilege. The wealth in question is not the wealth members earned by working the land; it is the wealth they hold because the land they happened to be allocated turned out to lie in the path of the country's growth. That allocation was itself the residue of 1948. The language for noticing this, the language of inherited privilege, of unearned advantage, of the asymmetry between those who work and those who inherit, is precisely the language the kibbutz movement spent a century developing in critique of others. What Dilemma 3 asks is whether the movement can yet turn that language back on itself.

Conclusion: The Hidden Question, Revisited

But the continuity is not only material. What persists is not only the inherited land value, but the logic that made its acquisition possible in the first place. And that logic, Dichter argues, has never stopped operating. Dichter's argument is precisely that the kibbutz left's self-understanding as a progressive counterforce to the settlement enterprise, supposedly innocent of the dispossession happening in the West Bank, is complicated by the continuity between the earlier dispossession and the later one. Not because individual kibbutz members bear personal responsibility for what settlers and the Israeli Army are doing in Hebron or Nablus, but because the structural logic is the same. The logic claims that Jewish settlement creates facts that cannot be reversed, that the land belongs to those who plant roots in it, that the religious or national imperative outweighs the rights of those displaced. For Palestinians, this has been the underlying operating system of 1948, namely Jewish settlement creates facts that cannot be reversed, and the rights of those displaced are subordinated to a higher national claim. It remains the operating system of the West Bank settlement project today, even if articulated in a different idiom. The kibbutz movement largely opposes the latter while having benefited from the former. A major dilemma exists at this junction, since it is impossible to coherently invoke the moral bankruptcy of the West Bank settlement enterprise while refusing to examine the conditions that made one's own community possible. The structural thread that connects them has to be acknowledged. Dichter raised a further point with particular sharpness. The well-known standard retrospective defense, judge us by the values of our time, which has some validity when applied to the founding generation of the 1930s and 1940s, collapses entirely when the same actions are being performed now, in the twenty-first century, by settlers and the Israeli Army who justify displacement with explicit reference to biblical entitlement. In the West Bank, the values being invoked are not the progressive socialist nationalism of the Second and Third Aliyahs; they are explicitly pre-modern, drawing on the very sources of the Bible, the covenant, divine promise. The original kibbutz founders largely rejected these sources in their secular, socialist self-understanding. This is, Dichter suggested, one reason that 1948 has become harder rather than easier to examine as the occupation has deepened: because the explicit religious justification now offered for West Bank settlement throws retrospective light on what was also, at some level, happening in 1948, even if articulated differently at the time.

How does the kibbutz movement today position itself within this landscape? In a recent interview, Muki articulated a vision that has remained consistent across his long public life: that the task of those who believe in peace is not to wait for the right political conditions but to remain ready. To ensure that when someone on the Palestinian side reaches out, there will be a voice on the Israeli side capable of hearing it. "We've been entrusted not to lose our attentiveness to that voice when it comes." To me it seems, that the statement could be reversed to those at the Palestinian side, who believes in peace and whose task it is to wait for the right political circumstances on the Israeli side.

This is not, finally, an argument that the kibbutz movement is morally equivalent to the settler movement it has consistently opposed. It is not. The distinction between those who seek to dispossess Palestinians further and those who have sought coexistence, dialogue, and a negotiated peace is real and important. But the past cannot be safely bracketed as "then" while its logic continues in the present. The Arab house at Barkai, the orchards of the Jezreel Valley, the village of Bir'im that was never restored and these are not only matters of historical record. They are the foundation on which the present stands, and the present cannot be fully honest about itself without acknowledging them.

Yitzhak Epstein's 1907 essay "The Hidden Question" asked, more than forty years before 1948, how Zionism would confront the fact that the land it sought to redeem was already inhabited. For decades, that question was treated as marginal, even subversive, within the Zionist conversation. In the kibbutz movement, it was answered implicitly rather than explicitly, through settlement practices, legal frameworks, songs sung in the dining hall, and the quiet decision to treat the Arab house at the edge of the fields as part of the scenery rather than part of the story.

This chapter has tried to show that the question never disappeared. It simply migrated into different registers: into the *latent ignorance* Dichter describes, and into the structural inequalities produced when land became capital. The hidden question, namely what it means to build a just society on land taken from others, has remained unasked in public yet present in the landscape, in the archives, and in the quiet hesitations of people like Muki who "prefer not to talk about it." What would it mean to talk about it now? Not in order to undo what cannot be undone, and not to indulge a paralyzing guilt that leads nowhere, but to sketch a horizon of questions and possibilities through which such a conversation might proceed.

It would mean, first, epistemic honesty: naming the villages whose lands became kibbutz fields, teaching their histories alongside those of the kibbutzim, and acknowledging that the story of Jewish return unfolded in intimate entanglement with Palestinian loss. It would mean recognizing that the economic windfalls of recent decades did not appear from nowhere; they are the compounded outcome of earlier acts of allocation and exclusion. Symbolic forms of acknowledgment have been proposed in various contexts such as joint commemorations, shared curricula, bilingual place-names, archives that catalogue not only kibbutz founders but also the Palestinian communities that preceded them. Material forms might include revenue-sharing arrangements, land-use agreements, or joint development projects that begin to address the stark asymmetries between kibbutzim with development rights and neighboring Arab localities facing chronic land scarcity. Parallel initiatives in mixed or neighboring Jewish–Arab localities have been documented elsewhere (Rabinowitz, 1997; Yacobi, 2009).

Dichter (2022, ch. 6) has argued, more boldly, for a large-scale redistribution of jurisdictional land from the Jewish regional councils to the Arab local authorities they currently encircle, enough to accommodate genuine Arab urban development through the middle of this century. His proposal is honest about what it would cost. Jews would have to relinquish land from which they have unjustly benefited, and Arabs would receive a form of collective historical compensation rather than individual restitution of ancestral plots. Whether or not one follows him all the way there, the proposal names the scale at which repair would have to operate if it were to be more than symbolic. In the final chapter of *Sharing the Promised Land*, Dichter offers a broader framing he calls "*Civic Zionism*" (2022, ch. 17): a reformulation of the Zionist project that retains Jewish collective life in the land but grounds it in equal, shared citizenship with the Palestinian citizens of the state, including a fair redistribution of land and resources. None of these proposals would amount to a full "solution" to the land question. Each would mark a shift from *latent ignorance* to acknowledgment.

For such a shift to occur, the kibbutz movement would have to apply to its own foundations the same ethical seriousness it has long brought to questions of internal equity and democracy. It would have to extend its critique of inherited privilege to include the privilege of holding land whose value derives from a history of dispossession. It would have to accept that the virtues on which it prides itself, solidarity, generosity, a culture of self-criticism, are incomplete if they stop at the kibbutz fence. Muki once said that the task of the peace camp is "not to lose our attentiveness to the voice that may one day come from the other side." The argument of this chapter has been that attentiveness also has a backward-looking dimension, a willingness to hear the voices that did come, and were not answered, from the villages on whose land the kibbutzim were built. Between Epstein's hidden question and the Arab house at Barkai lies a century of choices about what to see and what not to see. As long as the logic first enacted in 1948 continues to operate in the present, the temptation to leave that past latent, to keep it known but not known, will persist. The possibility of repair, if it exists, begins with a different choice. To look directly, to allow what has been known only latently to become known plainly, and to let that knowledge reshape what the kibbutz means when it speaks in the name of justice. Whether and how such acknowledgment will emerge is not a question this chapter can answer. It belongs to the communities who live with the Arab houses in their fields and in their memories.

10. Can Solidarity Be Initiated?

The Kibbutz Movement after October 7

Caravan houses transported for the people of Kibbutz Nahal Oz to Kibbutz Mishmar HaEmek after October 7, 2023

Source: Archives Kibbutz Mishmar HaEmek, Ronit Agiv

A Personal Entry Point: Continuing After

On the morning of October 7, I did not really understand what was happening. Our four small grandsons were playing around the house, and so we did not switch on the television. Rumors reached us in fragments, and for a while I held them at the edge of comprehension. My first call was with my friend Zohar, Muki's daughter, who knew more by then than I did and told me, in pieces, what could be told. At noon my secretary called: both of her children had been at the Nova festival and were on their way home to Kibbutz Kinneret, alive. Neither of us, in that moment, knew how lucky they were. The rest, the murders, the abductions, the running through fields under fire, would arrive in the days that followed, in the slow accumulation of names. I do not remember when I first heard that Vivian Silver was missing. For some weeks she was thought to be among the hostages, and that hope was, for me and many who knew her, one of the few things to hold on to. When the news came that she had not been taken but had been killed in her home in Kibbutz Be'eri, it was the loss that crystallized, for me, the moral catastrophe of that day. Vivian had spoken to our students for three years running, alongside her Palestinian partner from Gaza, about the patient and unfashionable work of building peace from below. She was the ultimate tragedy of the terrible events. Not because her loss was greater than any other, but because what she stood for was precisely what was being murdered alongside her. In spite of all, her son, Jonathan, has continued her legacy of not turning away, but continuing the path of peace.

The chapter moves through four parts: this personal entry; an account of what October 7 asked of the kibbutz movement; an empirical record of the eighteen months that followed, drawn from the parallel research that Zeevik Greenberg and I conducted and published in an academic article (Greenberg & Heilbrunn, 2026); and three interpretive dilemmas that have stayed with me from our data.

October 7: The Scale for the Kibbutz Movement

Beyond the small unfolding of that Saturday morning in our house, the events of the day were redrawing the geography of communal life in Israel. Hamas men had broken through the perimeter of the Gaza envelope kibbutzim in the dawn hours and moved through the homes, the safe rooms, the kindergartens. They murdered, mutilated, raped, and abducted members and their families. They burned the houses and destroyed communities that had lived along that border for generations. Among the most heavily attacked were the Gaza-envelope kibbutzim discussed in Chapter 9, namely Nir Oz, Re'im, Ein HaShlosha, Kisufim, and Magen, whose earlier layering of presence and absence now carried a new weight. Within days, the kibbutzim along the Lebanese border in the north were evacuated as well, against the prospect that the same pattern would repeat there.

The figures alone speak to the scale of what was asked and given. By the time the kibbutz movement issued its first formal status report[1], in November 2023, more than fifty kibbutzim from the southern and northern frontiers had been evacuated, roughly a fifth of the movement's total membership displaced from their homes. Approximately one hundred kibbutzim had established themselves as host communities. Some fifty thousand displaced people, kibbutz members and others, were being absorbed into kibbutz dwellings and guest houses across the country. Fourteen temporary educational centers had been set up adjacent to the host sites. The kibbutz movement's emergency call center had handled more than a thousand requests for assistance in its first weeks, and more than twenty kibbutz movement representatives were embedded full-time with evacuated communities.

Behind these aggregate figures lies a labor of coordination that, on October 6, no one would have predicted the movement still capable of performing. What follows is the story of how that capacity was assembled, kibbutz by kibbutz, room by room, decision by decision, across the eighteen months that began that day. It is the story of what Zeevik Greenberg and I came to call *facilitated solidarity*, and the section that follows traces how it took shape.

From Late 2023 to Mid-2025: What Was Done

The months that followed October 7 produced a record of communal action whose scale and coordination surprised nearly everyone who studied

1 These figures are drawn from the kibbutz movement's November 2023 status report to the ICETT Plenary, Cooperative Resilience: Kibbutz Movement Update, supplemented by the movement's internal coordinating documents and our own fieldwork. The full picture of human loss is heavier than these aggregate numbers can carry. According to the same report, 302 kibbutz members were murdered on or in the days following October 7, many while defending their kibbutzim and families; an additional twenty-eight foreign agricultural workers were killed; and of the 240 people taken hostage to Gaza in the initial attack, 140 were abducted from kibbutz communities, ranging in age from nine months to eighty-six years, of whom thirty-eight were children. The displacement and absorption figures cited above describe the response capacity that materialized within the first month and continued to expand through 2024. The chapter is concerned with how that capacity was assembled and what it means; the figures, here, mark only the arithmetic of what was done.

it, including, in many cases, those who did the acting. In late 2023, my colleague Zeevik Greenberg, who has been studying kibbutz life and resilience for many years from his Galilee base Tel Hai, suggested that we ought to document what was happening before its forms dissipated[2]. From late 2023 to mid-2025, we conducted forty-six in-depth interviews across more than thirty kibbutzim, supplemented by movement newsletters, internal questionnaires, and the kibbutz movement's own coordinating documents. Our sample reached host communities and evacuated communities, regional councils and movement officials, members at every position in the work of receiving and being received. The methodology was deliberately open: we did not arrive with a hypothesis about what we would find. What follows is what we found, drawn from those materials and from one parallel case, Kibbutz Nahal Oz, documented from inside the experience by Ayelet Glass, which we have set alongside our own data because it sharpens what the data already showed.

The infrastructure that activated on October 7 had not been built for that day. It had been built across a century of kibbutz federation, refined through earlier wars and emergencies, and exercised in small ways, repeatedly, in the years immediately preceding the attack. In one of our conversations, Zeevik told me that in August 2023, two months before the attack, the secretariats of Kibbutz Yiftach in the Upper Galilee and Kibbutz Magal in the Sharon plain met to make sure their evacuation arrangements were in order. They were preparing for a northern war that did not, in the event, happen on October 7. But what they were rehearsing in August was what would be called upon, six weeks later, in the south. Each previous activation had been partial, the plans never quite materializing as intended. The framework had nonetheless persisted as dormant institutional knowledge, carried forward by people whose job it was to remember.

Within hours of the news on October 7, kibbutzim across the country began to do what no one had instructed them to do. One interviewee from a host community described the Saturday the terrible news arrived: "We mapped vacant rooms, and built a team of 150 volunteers. The entire kibbutz worked that day cleaning the rooms, moving furniture, and preparing the rooms to accommodate the evacuees." By the evening, families who had fled the south that

2 What follows is based on the data Zeevik Greenberg and I gathered for our academic article. Greenberg, Z., & Heilbrunn, S. (2026). Multi-level solidarity in crisis response: insights from Israeli kibbutz communities following 7 October 2023. Israel Affairs, 1–31.

morning had keys to rooms with their names on the door. Another respondent put the underlying logic plainly: "We cleared empty rooms and temporary apartments for young people and invited them here. Why stay in a hotel when we can arrange a small apartment? A home?" In the same first week, two volunteers from one of our host kibbutzim reported to the educational institution, which had been turned into an emergency reception center for residents of the Gaza envelope, and took on the running of the center itself. Multiplied across dozens of host kibbutzim in the same forty-eight hours, the pattern was unmistakable: not centrally directed, but everywhere doing roughly the same thing, on roughly the same logic, at roughly the same time. These earliest acts were direct and uncoordinated. A member calling a friend on another kibbutz to say *come, we have rooms*. A youth movement clearing its own dormitories on a Saturday afternoon. An art instructor on one kibbutz opening a mosaic class for elderly evacuees newly arrived in her community. A member of another kibbutz providing emergency financial consulting to displaced families and helping them obtain interest-free loans. An individual taking on the role of unofficial liaison between two communities. The pattern of the first month was overwhelmingly one-sided. The host kibbutzim received evacuees, opened rooms, supplied food and clothing and emotional attention, and asked nothing in return.

Already by the third month, the picture had changed. Reciprocity had begun to emerge. Evacuees were teaching in their host kibbutzim's schools, helping with elderly care, contributing to agricultural and cultural work. One member of an evacuated community told us: "I volunteered to help elementary school students in Kibbutz Kinneret, where our evacuated children studied. The assistance was mainly educational, but there was also emotional support." Joint secretariats had been established between specific host-evacuee pairs, coordinating bodies in which decisions about housing, education, work, and absorption were made together. One organizer described the arrangement plainly: "We built a joint secretariat for the large settlement of the kibbutzim, and there was constant contact, we checked what was needed, what was required to bring, we activated volunteers in every area. But we let them manage themselves independently." It was the joint secretariat that allowed personal intimacy at the level of households to coexist with movement-wide coordination at the level of federations. By about six months, the kibbutz movement had set up a coordinated assistance command and control center in collaboration with the Regional Councils Centre and the Religious Kibbutz Movement. The KAMEA fund, together with the Negev Farms Organization, issued interest-free guarantees totaling NIS 35 million in favor of the affected kibbutzim, a financial instrument that did not exist on October 6, and to which Bank Mercantile and other commercial banks soon added their own guarantees. Agricultural labor was redistributed across the country through what came to be called the Nomadic Kibbutz program: members of evacuated communities continued their work, crop tending, fish farming, cattle care, at host sites that absorbed both the people and their professions. Hundreds of veteran members from Kibbutzim Kinneret, Degania, Beit HaShita, Geva and elsewhere worked the agricultural shifts of evacuated kibbutzim along the northern border, heading out every morning before sunrise. A new program brought roughly forty young men and women aged twenty to thirty from the Western Negev and the Galilee to assist with seasonal harvesting in kibbutzim whose own communities had been evacuated. The 'Kibbutz Embracing Kibbutz' initiative established clusters of host kibbutzim that mobilized over the long term to assist a single evacuated community of the western and northern frontiers. By mid-2024, joint Hanukkah celebrations in which children from host and evacuated communities performed together had become normal small ceremonies in which the question of who was helping whom had become uninteresting.

A parallel story, documented from inside the experience by Glass (2025), followed, they rehabilitated the cowshed on the kibbutz, erected a Nahal Oz tent in Hostages Square in Tel Aviv, organized a tractor convoy from Kibbutz Carmim and Mishmar HaEmek to Hostages Square, held *Kabbalat Shabbat* gatherings, put up signs on the granary and the dining hall, and mobilized resources, marches, and rallies. They held the historical narrative of the place, what Glass describes as the memory of what the kibbutz had been in its former years, and offered it back to a core community whose ability to carry that narrative had been suspended by trauma and dispersal. The pattern Glass describes echoes what Zeevik and I were finding across our thirty kibbutzim: the same widening of who counts as participating in a community's life, the same readiness of dispersed connections to coalesce into a working organizational body when the need arose. The case returns in Dilemma 3, where its outward extension takes on a particular weight.

These, then, are the materials. What they mean, about whether the kibbutz ethos was reactivated or revived, about whether what worked was spontaneity or infrastructure, and about whether the walls that fell extended outward or held within familiar lines, is the work of the next part.

The Meaning of It

Dilemma 1: Reactivation or Revival?

For at least two decades before October 7, the question of whether the kibbutz still possessed a living ethos of solidarity had been answered, by most observers and by many members themselves, in the negative. The financial collapse of the 1980s, the privatization processes of the 1990s, the steady demographic shrinkage from roughly 3.5 percent of Israel's Jewish population to half that, and the departure of much of the third generation immediately after their military service had together produced a story of long retreat. Articles, documentaries, and op-eds carried titles like "A Eulogy for the Kibbutz." The communal dining halls had emptied. The children's houses had closed. The principle of "from each according to their abilities and to each according to their needs" had been formally dismantled in most kibbutzim through differential salary models. What remained, the dominant narrative held, were villages with kibbutz-shaped histories and increasingly conventional economic logics.

Then, within hours of the attack on October 7, that dormant architecture activated, and not as an isolated gesture by a handful of veteran ideologues, but as a movement-wide pattern. The first dilemma asks whether what we observed should be understood as a revival, the genuine return of a living tradition that had merely been hidden, or as a reactivation in the more limited sense, a temporary mobilization under crisis conditions that drew on residual habit but might not survive the return of normal time. In our July 2025 conversation, Muki offered a framing that has stayed with me. The catastrophe, he writes in his essay *The Kibbutz After October 7*, "reawakened several elements of what might be called the genetic code of the kibbutz. Both the communal element and the missionary element. Both the practice of dialogue and the bond of fellowship, and the need to volunteer for action in the wider circle." The image of a genetic code matters because it concedes what the long retreat had taken, the surface practices, the daily textures of mutual life, while insisting on what it had not. Some patterns of response, Muki suggests, are encoded deeper than the institutions that visibly carry them. They are encoded in education, in shared memory, in the architecture of the community even when its functions have been privatized. A genetic code can lie unexpressed for long periods. It can also be activated quickly when conditions demand.

Evidence that the code activates across the spectrum of kibbutz forms, including the ones that explicitly broke from the traditional model, came from a development Muki was careful to flag. In recent years, urban kibbutzim have come into being. Unlike kibbutzim based on agriculture and industry, the main occupation of these communities is education. They had been founded, in many cases, in critical relation to the traditional kibbutz: their members sought to be small, liberal, and engaged, graduates of youth movements and children of kibbutzim looking for deep and intimate involvement with the society around them. After October 7, members of the urban kibbutzim mobilized to help with educational activities in the kibbutzim that had been attacked. The form had changed, sometimes pointedly. The response did not require the form to be the same.

In the language of our article, this corresponds to what Zeevik and I came to describe as the *reactivation of foundational principles* alongside the *adaptation of traditional mechanisms*. What we observed was not the reproduction of the historical kibbutz but rather new forms. The KAMEA fund and the Negev Farms Organization issuing NIS 35 million in interest-free guarantees is paradigmatic: a financial instrument that did not exist on October 6, but whose logic, namely communal pooling of risk, the federation standing behind the local kibbutz, is rooted directly in the founding ethos. Joint secretariats drawing upon traditional kibbutz democracy; the intergenerational transmission visible in the youth movement clearing dormitories on the first Saturday and in younger members socialized into solidarity practice through their participation in the work; the immediate provision of shelter and pooling of resources as direct echoes of the movement's mutual-aid origins, across all of these, the empirical pattern was the same. Historical principles, reactivated. Modern instruments, adapted from them. Zeevik's account of the August 2023 meeting between the secretariats of Yiftach and Magal sharpens the point. Two months before the attack, knowing nothing specific about what was coming, organizers from Yiftach met with Magal to make sure their evacuation arrangements were in order. They were preparing for a northern war that did not, in the event, happen on October 7. But the capacity they were rehearsing in August was the same capacity that mobilized, six weeks later, in the south. This suggests that the reactivation/revival framing is poorly posed if held as a strict binary. Both can be true at once: the infrastructure was real, and the practice of drawing on it was always there.

And yet the dilemma does not close. Muki himself is clear that none of this guarantees survival of the ethos beyond the crisis that summoned it. He warned:

> "There's always a danger of a rapid decrease in the level of solidarity at tremendous speed after a war. The war ends, and people don't hitchhike anymore, and don't help each other anymore, because they exhausted everything during wartime. Crisis creates solidarity, but there's always a risk that when the crisis passes, in people's desire to escape from what was, the level of solidarity decreases". He paused on the formulation, then added: "This hasn't happened yet, because the crisis hasn't passed yet."

The honest answer is therefore that we do not yet know. What we can say is that the response was not the temporary mobilization of a community whose communal ethos had genuinely died. It was the activation of a code that had remained latent, carried forward by infrastructure and education and the long memory of those whose work it had been to keep it ready. Whether activation becomes durable revival, whether the post-crisis kibbutz looks more like the post-1985 kibbutz with mutual aid quietly re-eroding once urgency passes, or whether something has shifted in the movement's understanding of what it still is, is a question this chapter cannot answer. It can only frame it precisely.

Dilemma 2: Spontaneity or Infrastructure?

If the first dilemma left us with a code that activated, the second is the mechanical question that follows: how, exactly. To say that something was "encoded" in the kibbutz is suggestive but not yet explanatory. Codes do not act on their own. Something and someone has to read them and translate them into rooms cleared, volunteers mobilized, financial guarantees written, children received. In studying what happened across the kibbutz movement from late 2023 to mid-2025, Zeevik and I were trying to understand that translation. The most honest answer we can give is that the response was neither spontaneous nor institutional in the senses those words usually carry. It was something else, for which the existing literature on solidarity does not have a clean name. We have come to call it *facilitated solidarity*.

The framework Zeevik and I used to analyze our empirical data comes from the Dutch sociologists Paul de Beer and Ferry Koster (2009) whose 2009 multidimensional model proposed that solidarity in any setting can be analyzed along five dimensions: reciprocity (one-sided giving versus mutual exchange), organization (informal versus formal), voluntariness (compulsory versus voluntary), scope (local versus broad), and form (material, financial, temporal, symbolic). Their typology was designed for static comparison, for asking whether the solidarity in one welfare state differs from another, or whether mutual aid in one community looks different from another. It was not designed to track change. What Zeevik and I found, looking across newsletters, interviews, and questionnaires from more than thirty kibbutzim, was that all five dimensions moved together, and that they moved in a particular direction.

In the first weeks, solidarity was overwhelmingly one-sided: host kibbutzim received evacuees, opened rooms, supplied food and clothing and emotional attention, and asked nothing in return. By roughly the third month, reciprocity had begun to emerge. Across the same months, organization moved from informal to formal, from a member calling a friend on another kibbutz to say *come, we have rooms*, to joint secretariats with constituted authority and a movement-wide command-and-control infrastructure. Voluntariness also shifted, from individual initiative to coordinated expectation while preserving choice at the personal level, what the article calls the maintenance of voluntary participation within institutional frameworks that create collective expectations. Scope expanded from bilateral kibbutz-to-kibbutz arrangements to regional networks and finally to movement-wide coordination involving multiple federations. Form diversified: what began as material support broadened to include financial instruments, sustained labor contributions, and symbolic acts. The five dimensions did not move in parallel, like five separate tracks. They moved together, in coordinated transformation, as if responding to a single underlying pressure: the recognition that emergency response and prolonged displacement require different forms of collective life, and that one must evolve into the other without breaking the thread.

What Zeevik and I came to see was that this coordinated transformation could not have happened through pure spontaneity, because the coordinative structures it required, such as joint secretariats, financial instruments, agricultural redistribution programs, are not built in weeks. Nor could it have happened through pure institutional action, because the relational fabric it depended on, the willingness to clear a room for a stranger, to teach in a school you did not choose, to celebrate a holiday with children whose parents you had never met, cannot be issued by command. It happened because the institutional infrastructure was already there, latent, and because the relational fabric was, when activated, denser than two decades of demographic pessimism had suggested. Each made the other possible. This is what we mean by facilitated solidarity: solidarity enabled by pre-existing communal infrastructure and collective memory, neither purely spontaneous (informal/voluntary/personal) nor purely institutional (formal/compulsory/structural), but a third form distinct from both. Our academic article frames this as an extension of de Beer and Koster's framework on three points. First, the framework treats solidarity dimensions as static categories applicable at a single point in time; our data show they evolve interdependently across the duration of a prolonged crisis, transforming from spontaneous/informal/local toward formalized/coordinated/movement-wide while preserving the relational fabric of the earlier phases. Second, the framework treats organizational levels, what we called *micro* (interpersonal), *meso* (community), and *macro* (movement-wide), as separate analytical units. Our data show that effective crisis solidarity depends on integration *across* these scales, with institutional scaffolding enabling coordination while preserving local autonomy. The joint secretariats Zeevik and I documented again and again were the paradigmatic cross-level coordination mechanism, bridging individual relationships with movement-wide infrastructure, allowing personal intimacy at the level of households to coexist with federation-level resource flows. Third, the framework does not adequately specify the role of historical tradition and institutional infrastructure as moderating factors. Facilitated solidarity, as a category, names that role explicitly.

The clearest illustration of what facilitation makes possible, and what it cannot substitute for, came from a comparison Muki drew about the early weeks of the displacement. Kibbutzim and development towns from the Gaza envelope had often ended up evacuated to the same hotels. The communities had suffered the same losses, often the very same attack. They lived in the same corridors, ate at the same buffets. And yet the trajectories of the two communities, in those hotels, were not the same. Muki put it plainly:

> "It didn't work because solidarity needs to grow, and people arrived at the same hotel when on one hand each one worries about himself, and needs to go through a process to understand that he lives in a fateful group, and in the kibbutz next to this it goes at record speed".

The difference, he was careful to note, was not in goodness. "Unusual solidarity things were done in those towns," he insisted.

> "The difference was in speed. The kibbutz members did not have to become a community in the hotel. They already were what their situation demanded.

> The towns had to do that work from a colder start. Goodwill, both groups had. What only one of them had was the facilitating infrastructure: the federation behind them, the practice of cooperative governance, the institutional muscle of mutual care, and the collective memory of having been a community of this kind before".

The kibbutzim that worked best, in our data, were the ones where the institutional forms were inhabited by a relational discipline, where the secretariat met because people in it actually wanted to know what the other community needed, where the holiday celebrations happened because someone had thought about what would land for the children who had lost their homes. *Listening as method*, in Muki's phrase. He named it directly in one of our conversations:

> "One of the things that really happened in this period is that solidarity was organized also on the basis of personal conversations. Of interpersonal relationships. A method of listening. There was a method in this solidarity. People sat and heard, listened to each other".

The word *method* is interesting here. Listening is not usually thought of as a method; it sounds too soft for the word. But Muki uses it in something like its older sense, a discipline, a practice that can be taught and transmitted. What it looked like in practice was the kind of thing one host kibbutz member described after the first joint Hanukkah celebration with the children from the evacuated community: "We just celebrated Hanukkah together, which moved us to tears. The children from both kibbutzim put on a joint performance." The same pattern was visible in the Mishmar HaEmek case, where the work evolved across the months in striking ways. At first the task was absorption: rooms, supplies, the basic infrastructure of being received. Then, as some of the displaced began to return to their reconstructed kibbutz and others decided to remain, the support shifted: not absorption anymore, but support for transitions. The actions changed because the needs changed. This kind of flexibility was not in any plan. It came from watching, listening, and adjusting. The infrastructure had built the conditions; the institutions had set the meeting. But what happened in those halls was not infrastructural. It was the moment when scaffolding became shelter, when facilitated solidarity stopped being a sociological category and became, briefly and movingly, a community.

Dilemma 3: Inward or Outward?

The third dilemma asks whether what we have been describing was an essentially internal achievement of the kibbutz movement or whether something larger happened. In other words, whether the response to October 7 reshaped the relationship between the kibbutzim and the wider periphery of Israeli society. The question matters because the kibbutz movement has, for most of its history, been embedded in landscapes of difficulty it did not always meet generously. The development towns founded in the 1950s and 1960s for new immigrants from North Africa and the Middle East were positioned, often deliberately, near kibbutzim whose members had arrived a generation or two earlier from Europe. The relationship between these neighbors has been, throughout, asymmetrical, freighted with class and ethnic tension, and politically charged. Whether the period from late 2023 to mid-2025 changed any of that, and whether the solidarity Zeevik and I documented within the kibbutz movement extended outward into the surrounding communities or whether the walls between kibbutzim, moshavim, and development towns held, is a question on which the chapter's answer is more complicated than the previous two.

Muki, in his essay, offers a strong reading. "Walls that had been cultivated by political establishments, between development towns, moshavim, and kibbutzim, fell apart." The bonds among the forms of life in the frontier regions, he writes, tightened. The kibbutzim's organization in the face of catastrophe was swifter, "but the urban and rural communities followed in their footsteps." He is not saying the kibbutz movement absorbed the development towns into its own logic. He is saying that the political and social architecture which had kept these communities suspicious of one another lost some of its hold under the weight of shared catastrophe. People who had not previously seen each other as belonging to a common project began to act as if they did. Joint funeral processions. Shared makeshift kitchens. Volunteer networks that ignored municipal lines.

A second form of outward extension, sharper in its theoretical interest, is the Nahal Oz Community Across Generations described earlier in this chapter. This was not solidarity within a kibbutz; it was solidarity across the diaspora of a kibbutz, a redrawing of the geography of who counted as participating in a community's life. Several hundred former members, sons and daughters of the place, former workers and volunteers, found in a moment of catastrophe that their loose ties added up to an organizational identity. The body they formed acted on the kibbutz's behalf during months when the kibbutz itself could not. It is one of the most suggestive findings of our work, because it widens the unit of analysis: a community is not always coextensive with its physical site or its formal membership; under certain conditions, its dispersed connections can coalesce into something capable of carrying its narrative for it.

There is a third form of outward extension that is also, in another sense, an inward one. To open it, I want to give Muki the floor. In a note he sent me as I was working on this chapter, he sketched the historical context plainly:

> "Throughout the long history of the kibbutzim, which were always democratic societies, disputes erupted within them. Often the disputes saved the kibbutzim and opened new horizons for them, but not always. As in all cooperative societies, disputes sometimes split the community and led to schisms. Anyone who tracks the schisms in the kibbutzim discovers that they usually occurred during periods of crisis in the wider society, during economic crises, and after wars".

On October 7, the kibbutzim in two regions went through an extreme crisis, but here, of all things, what emerged was solidarity and sensitivity to the crisis. Gates were opened to non-kibbutz communities living in the same region. We don't know whether this phenomenon will continue, but it is worthy of note. One of the kibbutzim, where many were murdered and many abducted, went into exile in another kibbutz. When they sought to return to the kibbutz, it turned out that some of its members had decided that emotionally they could not return to the site of the trauma. Those who returned and those who did not did not go through a process of schism. Rather, they supported one another, community within community, in the new community that is about to be established. This is a deep test of solidarity. The empathy, the coping, the self-examination will accompany the kibbutz for a long time.

The historical resonance is important. The kibbutz movement is full of stories of bitter ideological splits, over Soviet politics, over religious practice, over family sleeping arrangements, over the privatization reforms of the 1990s, that left wounds which did not heal. What Muki names is a split that did not produce that wound. The members who stayed and those who left understood each other. The host kibbutz and the original kibbutz remained in dialogue. The boundaries of a community had been redrawn without the redrawing being experienced as betrayal. The wall that fell here was not between communities but within the practice of communal life: an institutional form taking, at its own moment of testing, a softer and more capacious shape than its history would have predicted.

So far, this section has drawn an optimistic picture: walls fell between kibbutz and neighbor, between kibbutz and its diaspora, between the kibbutz and its own internal differences. But the picture is incomplete.

As described earlier, in some cases two communities lived in the same building for weeks or months, kibbutz members and people from evacuated towns. They shared corridors and dining rooms and the dull misery of displacement. And the walls between them did not become much more porous. Kibbutz members organized among themselves, supported each other through their existing networks, and emerged from the displacement with their communal life. The development-town residents were doing the slower work of becoming a community for the first time, and their resources for doing so were thinner. The two groups passed each other in the lobby. They did not, by and large, become one community in the hotel. In our view, this is not a moral failure on either side. It is a structural fact about what facilitated solidarity makes possible and what it does not. The kibbutz response was efficient because it had the code of kibbutz members helping other members. Extending it to non-kibbutz neighbors required additional work, additional translation, additional patience, and in conditions of acute trauma, that work was often more than people had the capacity to do. Muki's claim about walls falling, read against the hotel evidence, has to be qualified. The walls fell in some places, between some people, under some conditions. They held in others. The geography of the falling and the holding is itself a question for further research, and not one this chapter can settle.

There is one further qualification, harder to flag, but the chapter is incomplete without it. In our June 2025 conversation, in a very different register, I asked Muki whether the kibbutz movement was doing enough with its public voice. The conversation had been about the moral catastrophe of the ongoing war in Gaza, about what happens to Palestinians in the West Bank, about the silencing of dissent in Israeli society, about the difficulty of speaking honestly under conditions of grief and fear. I asked him directly: don't you think that the kibbutz movement right now, in these days, needs to be more active in its political and social statement? The kibbutz movement had, historically, occupied a particular position in Israeli public life as a moral voice, sometimes self-righteous, often resented, but audible. In the months following October 7, that voice had been quieter. Muki did not give me a direct answer. He shifted, as he often does, to a longer view, to what conditions make moral speech possible, to his concerns about the silencing of dissent across Israeli society more broadly. The conversation moved on. But the question lingered, and it lingers in this chapter. The expansion of solidarity outward that this section has been tracing was largely an expansion of practical care: rooms, money, work, listening. It was not, on the whole, an expansion of political voice. The kibbutz movement that organized itself so impressively to receive its evacuees did not produce a corresponding public reckoning with the war being conducted in their name, or with the broader collapse of moral discourse around it. Whether this represented prudence, the recognition that a community in crisis cannot also be a political vanguard, or whether it represented a failure of the very mission Muki himself, in his essay, names as part of the kibbutz's reawakened genetic code, is a question we could not answer.

Concluding Thoughts: The Image of the Future

When I was writing this chapter, Muki sent me a short piece he had been working on. Before reaching for the larger frame, he flagged a concrete sign that the materials of communal life are not only enduring but generative:

> "In recent years, the kibbutzim have grown through young families with children, some of them children of kibbutzim. This had not been the way of the kibbutzim for many long years. Traditionally, kibbutzim were founded by groups of young people before they started families. After October 7, youth groups in their pre-family stage came back and arrived at the kibbutzim, especially the kibbutzim that had been attacked. The existence of such groups is an integral part of the rehabilitation process of the kibbutzim. Even kibbutzim that were not attacked are absorbing groups of young people before their military service. These phenomena may influence the future of the kibbutz. In other forms of communal life as well, youth groups have emerged with a lifestyle influenced by the kibbutz".

That observation is important to register before the larger frame, because it speaks to what the test of crisis has actually produced. The kibbutzim had been growing, in recent years, in a way the movement had not seen for decades; and after October 7, a different and older form, the pre-family youth group, returned. Neither pattern proves that the future is secure. Both indicate that the form, far from being exhausted, is generating new versions of itself even at the same moment that some of its sites are being destroyed.

The piece he sent then opened onto a larger frame: two utopian projects from 1939. The first was the New York World's Fair, intended to lift the United States out of the shadow of the Great Depression under the slogan "The Dawn of a New Day." A few months after it opened, the Second World War broke out. By 1940 the slogan had changed to "Peace and Progress," weaponry had been added to the exhibits, and some of its materials were eventually cast into ammunition. The second project was unfolding at the same moment in Moscow, where preparations were being made to place a giant statue of Lenin, meant to be the tallest in the world, atop the House of the Communist Party, even as residents of the building constructed for veteran party members were being arrested, exiled, and murdered under Stalin. With the Nazi attack on Russia, the metal intended for the statue was cast into materials for the defense of the city. After October 7, Muki writes, these two stories rose again in his memory. I felt how much, in our arguments and in our pride, we conceal, how much we forget the real challenges. Not always because of preserving nostalgia, but also because of a future dream, or because of a nightmare from which we are fleeing.

Two grand projects of the future, each transformed in the same way: their materials melted down into munitions when the world stopped allowing them to be merely dreams. What the pairing makes visible is that the question of the future is never settled at the level of the dream. It is settled at the level of what the materials become when crisis arrives. The fair's color and television, the statue's image of revolution, neither was false, exactly; neither was what its moment required. In each case the metal was put to a different use than the one its imaginers had envisioned, and the futures those projects proposed did not survive the test.

The kibbutz is differently placed. Its founding materials were not poured into a fair or cast into a statue. They were poured into a community, into the daily textures of mutual responsibility, into the capacity of one kibbutz to help another. For decades preceding October 7, that material had appeared, to many observers and to many kibbutz members themselves, to have grown thin. What the period from late 2023 to mid-2025 revealed was that it was substantial enough to do what the dreams of 1939 could not: to pass through the test of crisis without being melted into something else. The kibbutz response was not a utopia transmuted into munitions. It was a utopia tested in its own substance and found capable. This, perhaps, is the deepest answer the chapter can offer to its three dilemmas. Reactivation or revival is the question of whether the materials of communal life were still substantial enough to work when needed; they were. Spontaneity or infrastructure is the question of what those materials were made of; they were made of what Zeevik and I have called facilitated solidarity, neither grand spontaneity nor grand institution, but the practiced capacity of a community that knew how to be one. Inward or outward is the harder one: it is the question of what the substance, once tested, can be used for now. It is on this last question that Muki's reflection offers the clearest direction:

The meaning of these things, in the end, is that there is a change that comes because of crisis. The main point, after the description of the exhibitions, is that there is still an ability to create an image of the future. Not an oppositional image, not merely an anti-neo-liberal one, but one that still contains utopian foundations that have passed through the test of crisis. This image of the future requires us to take responsibility for the present as well. The kibbutz movement, in the months following October 7, demonstrated that it possessed a working image of the future: not a slogan, not a monument, but a community whose practice could be activated under the most demanding conditions a community is ever asked to face. That image is real, and it can, with care, be built elsewhere. But Muki's sentence insists that an image of the future, having survived the test, is not yet sufficient. It must be matched by responsibility for the present. The kibbutz movement has shown what it can do for its own. It has not yet shown, on the scale the moment requires, what it can offer to the wider society in which it sits: to the development towns it shared hotels with but did not become one community with, to the moshavim and urban communities of the periphery where the walls fell partially and held in others, to the Israeli public sphere where the moral voice of the kibbutz movement has been quieter than the question of the moment seems to warrant.

11. Can the Kibbutz Carry Its Unresolved Questions?

A Retrospective Synthesis

A general assembly at Kibbutz Barkai in 1985

Source: Riva Segel, photo collection

The present chapter is structured slightly differently from the former ones, since it attempts to address the different dilemmas that have shaped kibbutz life across the entire arc of the movement's history and have not been resolved at any single point of that history.

Each of these dilemmas has been examined elsewhere in the book, in the chronological and thematic chapters that precede this one, through different material. Chapter 7, on art and culture in the kibbutz, is especially relevant here, because it traces how several of these same dilemmas surface in the specific arena of artistic production: the artist's place in a working community, the question of when communal cultural practice becomes coercion, and the role of art as both motivation for and critique of the collective. Where the present chapter touches on questions Chapter 7 takes up at length, we cross-reference rather than recapitulate.

The chapter is therefore organized by dilemma rather than by chronology. Each of the five sections traces one dilemma across four historical periods: the years up to 1977, the period from the early 1980s through the early 2000s, the period of consolidation and expansion-neighborhood development from the early 2000s through October 2023, and the period that began on October 7 and is still unfolding. Within each period, each section offers a single anchor moment, namely a scene, a quotation, an episode through which the dilemma is illuminated. The argumentative work of the concluding part comes not from the historical detail of any one anchor but from the contrast between the four anchors of each section. The kibbutz idea has migrated across these anchors. It has been carried by different populations in different periods, and held by different generations in different forms. What we argue in the chapter is that, taken as a whole, the kibbutz movement's continuing life has consisted in the carrying of these dilemmas, not in their resolution.

Section 1. Who is a member? The shifting boundary of belonging

The question that gives this section its title is the kibbutz movement's most persistent and least settled. Every period of the movement's history has produced a different operational answer, and every answer has been undone by the period that followed. The line between *inside* and *outside* the kibbutz, between members and non-members, between workers in the kibbutz economy and laborers from elsewhere, between physical residents and absent kin who still consider themselves attached, has been redrawn at least four times across the past seventy-five years. Each redrawing preserved something the previous boundary had protected, and each lost something it had taken for granted. What this section traces is the migration of that boundary across the four periods, and the question that arises when, in the present, the boundary no longer corresponds to physical residence or to formal membership.

Period 1: The hired-labor controversy

The first redrawing took place under the pressure of mass immigration. Between 1948 and 1953 approximately 700,000 thousand new immigrants arrived in Israel; the total population of the kibbutzim was under fifty thousand, and fewer than four per cent of those immigrants joined kibbutzim (Gavron, 2000). David Ben-Gurion delivered the most famous attack on the movement's response from the Knesset podium in January 1950:

> "During the past two years I have been humiliated and shamed by the pioneering movement's failure: the greatest thing that has ever happened in its history has taken place, the exodus from Egypt has begun, the ingathering of the exiles has begun, and what have our pioneers done? Have the kibbutzim put themselves to the task?"

Ben-Gurion, Knesset speech, January 1950 (as cited in Shapira, 2010). Ben-Gurion's demand was that the kibbutzim absorb new immigrants as workers (that is, accept hired labor) to integrate the country's most exposed newcomers into the productive organs of the movement. The kibbutz movement refused. Shlomo Rozen, secretary-general of the Kibbutz Artzi Federation, gave the refusal its sharpest formulation: "Hired labor in the kibbutz economy means the destruction of the kibbutz economy, with its social and its Zionist-class values" (as cited in Shapira, 2010). The refusal held, ideologically, for roughly a decade. By the 1960s, when the kibbutzim had begun the rapid industrialization that would become their economic foundation (Palgi & Reinharz, 2011), the wall had quietly cracked. Factories required hired labor from the new development towns, where the immigrants Ben-Gurion had wanted absorbed had been settled instead (Tsuk, 2005). By the late 1970s the configuration was systematic: workers from the development towns, managers from the kibbutzim, two opposed classes inside a single regional economy, divided not only by employment but by ethnicity (Shapira, 2010). The formal boundary between member and non-member had not moved; the kibbutz still denied its hired workers membership, schools, swimming pools. But the kibbutz had become economically permeable in ways that the founding ideal of self-labor could no longer justify.

Period 2: The boundary moves on every front

By the 1990s the boundary had moved on every front simultaneously. Palgi and Reinharz (2011) summarize the redrawing as five concurrent regulatory changes: kibbutzim legitimated paid hired labor in both production and education; opened children's houses and schools to non-kibbutz children; legitimated and encouraged members to work outside the kibbutz; partnered with non-kibbutz investors in kibbutz enterprises; and rented apartments and built residential neighborhoods for non-members. Each of these had previously been a structural marker of what made the kibbutz the kibbutz. Each was now opened, in practice and increasingly in principle, to the surrounding society.

The most painful of these redrawings, for many older members, was the normalization of outside work. Through most of the kibbutz's history the member's working week had taken place inside the kibbutz; departure for outside employment was, when it occurred, a defection. By the 1990s paid outside employment had become an accepted route to the kibbutz's cash flow, and the proportion of members earning outside income rose steadily through the decade. The complementary movement, namely outside professionals coming in to manage failing kibbutz enterprises, eroded the formerly absolute correspondence between kibbutz member and manager of the kibbutz economy. Hired labor in kibbutz industries reached approximately sixty-seven per cent by 2000 (Manor, 2004), more than double the rate of a decade earlier. As Tsuk (2005) puts it, the introduction of hired labor into a setting whose entire ethical architecture had been built on self-labor was the "crucial turning point." The line between member and non-member, in operational terms, had become the line between those who held formal membership status and those who did not, with every other line that had once tracked it now running independently.

Period 3: The legal tiers

Period 3 codified what Period 2 had improvised. The Beit Oren case of 1999, in which eight members petitioned the High Court to strip the kibbutz of its legal classification on the grounds that differential salaries, the closed dining hall, and privatized education made it impossible to call the place a kibbutz under existing law, forced a public reckoning with what membership now meant. The Public Committee convened in 2002 returned its report in 2003, recommending two parallel legal classifications: *Kibbutz Shitufi* (Communal) and *Kibbutz Mitchadesh* (Renewed) (Manor, 2004). The Renewed Kibbutz definition explicitly permitted differential wages, allocation of apartments, and allocation of production means, provided that mutual guarantee and a basic safety net were preserved.

What this codification did was to multiply the number of recognized membership statuses. Manor (2004) typologized them: full members; candidates for membership; expansion-neighborhood residents (non-members purchasing homes on developed kibbutz land, paying community taxes, using kibbutz facilities, but with no voting rights and no claim on kibbutz assets); permanent non-member residents and renters; and "new membership," a category permitting people to build inside the kibbutz boundary without owning kibbutz assets but with the right to buy shares in the community's economic life. By the late 2010s, of the approximately 170,000 living in the 250 kibbutzim, only 60,000 were members (Balberg, 2024). The dilemma the multiplication produced is the one Manor flagged at the time: the appearance, on a single kibbutz, of two adjacent communities, "one with old houses and poor members, and the other with new, luxurious houses and upper middle-class residents" (Manor, 2004). The boundary had been drawn so many times in so many places that it no longer described a single circle.

Period 4: Membership without residence

The fourth iteration was prepared by the third but became visible only under catastrophe. In the months after October 7, 2023 the practical community that mobilized to support the evacuated kibbutzim included a population that no existing legal category accommodated: the kibbutz-born and kibbutz-raised who had left in earlier decades and built lives elsewhere, who had not been members for years, and who were nonetheless willing, and able, to act as members of the community in the emergency. Muki, in our July 2025 conversation, named the inversion directly:

> "Social networks did a huge thing. They managed to mobilize a community much broader than the community sitting in the kibbutz and needing to evacuate, because it's a community of all those who left the kibbutz. Suddenly the anxiety for kibbutzim became solidarity far beyond the concrete kibbutz we know."

What that broader community indicated was the inverse of every previous redrawing. The first three periods had drawn non-members *inside* the kibbutz boundary in widening numbers: hired workers in the factories, residents in the expansion neighborhoods, holders of new-membership shares, candidates and renters and tenants of every legal description. The fourth identified a population that was unambiguously *outside* the kibbutz boundary (geographically, legally, often generationally) and unambiguously inside the practical community at the moments when it counted. The kibbutz movement's November 2023 status report described, in aggregate, the visible work of that community: more than fifty kibbutzim evacuated, around fifty thousand displaced absorbed across roughly one hundred host kibbutzim, fourteen temporary educational centers established in weeks (Kibbutz Movement, 2023). Behind those figures lay a labor of coordination performed by people whose addresses were in Tel Aviv, Jerusalem, Berlin, New York, and whose claim on the kibbutz's identity could not be located on any membership register. Membership, in the autumn of 2023, had ceased to coincide with residence; the kibbutz's most operationally meaningful definition of itself, in that moment, was the one that required the fewest legal entries on a register.

Section 2. Vanguard or community? Where the kibbutz idea lives

Is the kibbutz a small, selective vanguard or an open, broader community? The question has been debated since the first *kvutzot* of the Second Aliyah, and every period of the movement's history has produced a different operational answer. None has settled the dilemma; each has redirected it. What this section traces is the migration of the kibbutz idea, the *where* of its meaning, across the four periods. Sometimes it has been carried by the mainstream of the movement, sometimes by a self-conscious margin, sometimes by people who had never set foot inside a kibbutz before and arrived only because they had been drawn to the principle. The dilemma has not been resolved by any of them. It has been kept alive by all of them.

Period 1: Three federations, three answers

The first formal articulation of the dilemma came in organization. In 1927 the kibbutz movement formed itself into two competing federations, each carrying a different answer to the question of what the idea most was. *HaKibbutz*

HaMeuhad, under Yitzhak Tabenkin, advocated big kibbutzim, open to absorbing newcomers, with diversified economies of agriculture and industry. *HaKibbutz HaArtzi*, under Meir Ya'ari and Yaakov Hazan, required *ideological collectivity* (a shared political-Marxist worldview as a condition of membership) and adhered to the most leftist orientation of the movements. Two years later, *Chever HaKvutzot* was founded around a third answer: small, intimate kibbutzim in the Degania tradition, modest in scale, refusing the urge to grow into national instruments at all (Palgi & Reinharz, 2011).

These three federations were not three implementations of a single idea but three rival theories of what the kibbutz was for, and the pedagogical institutions each built tracked the difference. HaKibbutz HaMeuhad built schools whose central premise was that students should remain in constant contact with the veteran pioneers and learn the kibbutz by living inside it. HaKibbutz HaArtzi built educational institutions "organized around the idea that the institution is another kibbutz," as Muki has described it: a vanguard inside a vanguard, designed to guarantee a permanent youth rebellion against adults, because constant rebellion was the engine of the project. Chever HaKvutzot opted for general humanistic education in regional schools and trusted the students to draw their own conclusions. Three educational systems for three theories of the same word. The dilemma was not adjudicated; it was institutionalized.

Period 2: "That man in the swimming pool"

By 1981 the kibbutz movement had become, by every visible measure, the symbolic property of the Israeli labor establishment: a small, productive, idealistic elite that had built the country and continued to provide its leadership. That self-image was, in the summer of 1981, weaponized against the movement in a single televised episode. After his electoral victory of June 1981, in a campaign in which Mizrahi resentment toward the Ashkenazi Labor establishment had been a central mobilizing force, Prime Minister Menachem Begin was asked on Israel Radio about his rhetorical strategy. He replied with a question: "Did you not see on television that man in the kibbutz sitting in his swimming pool like some American millionaire and talking with a great deal of contempt about the residents of the neighboring development town?"

Menachem Begin, Israel Radio, summer 1981 (as cited in Balberg, 2024). Begin was referring to a recently broadcast television segment in which a member of Kibbutz Manara, on the Lebanese border, had been interviewed about strained relations with neighboring Kiryat Shemona; the journalists had filmed the interview at the kibbutz pool. Within twenty-four hours *millionaires in swimming pools* had become a national sobriquet for kibbutz members (Balberg, 2024). The markers of the kibbutz movement's pride (its disproportionate share of the country's educated, talented, idealistic citizens; its pilots and philosophers and dancers) became, in Begin's framing, the markers of a leisured class living off the labor of immigrants it would not admit to its schools or its swimming pools. Muki traces the inversion directly: the overrepresentation that had been a source of pride "becomes a political weapon: you are up there, you are snobs." Shapira (2010) makes the structural point: by 1981 the kibbutzim had "found themselves at the center of a class and ethnic confrontation," and the swimming-pool episode was less the cause of their de-legitimization than its perfectly fitted symbol. The dilemma the movement now faced was the one Muki has named, in our conversations, as the master dilemma of the period: "do you respond by closing yourself off and becoming a sect, or do you respond 'let's bring many things into the kibbutz to adapt ourselves to the surrounding atmosphere'? So we won't be a sect, but maybe then we'll betray ourselves." The 1981 unification of TaKaM (the merger of HaKibbutz HaMeuhad and Ihud HaKvutzot VeHaKibbutzim, in the same year as Begin's broadcast) can be read as a defensive consolidation against an environment that no longer underwrote the federations' separate identities.

Period 3: The urban kibbutzim

If Period 2 ended with the kibbutz mainstream's political and economic delegitimization, Period 3 saw the kibbutz idea quietly migrate to a small, mission-driven margin while the mainstream became suburban. The first urban kibbutz, Reshit, was founded in 1979 in Kiryat Menahem, a Jerusalem neighborhood with high crime and poverty, by graduates of the kibbutz youth movements who had concluded that the original kibbutz form had drifted from its social vocation. Three more followed: Migvan in Sderot in 1987, Tamuz in Beit Shemesh in 1987, Beit Israel in Gilo in 1992. Their combined membership has remained small, roughly 1,500 to 2,000 individuals across all of them and the educators' kibbutzim associated with the same movement (Balberg, 2024; Palgi & Reinharz, 2011).

What is striking about these communities is the deliberate avoidance of past mistakes (Balberg, 2024). Children live with parents. Privacy is protected. Each member exercises discretion over distributed funds. Their work is in education, sustainability, welfare, public health, and housing: direct engagement with Israel's social fractures rather than autonomous agricultural-industrial production. Two thousand members against a contemporary kibbutz population of roughly 70,000 is a margin within a margin, but the structural significance is greater than the numbers suggest. While the rural mainstream had settled into the demographic profile of a desirable suburban consumer good (green lawns, safe childhoods, a house with a garden at a price the cities could not match), the urban kibbutzim were carrying the line of vocation that the mainstream had quietly relinquished. As Muki put the contrast in our June 2025 conversation, what these small urban communities were doing was the "inspiration of the kibbutz idea on urban society": form adapted, scale reduced, assets redistributed, but the underlying intention to live in a way that demonstrates something to the larger society preserved.

Period 4: The flow of new people

October 7, 2023 produced a development neither the urban-kibbutz movement nor the rural mainstream could quite have predicted. As host kibbutzim across the country received evacuated communities from the Gaza envelope and the northern border, a third population began to arrive: groups of young people, many from pre-army programs and youth-movement frameworks, who had no biographical connection to the kibbutzim being evacuated and no family ties to the host communities receiving them. They came because they had been drawn, through their own training and their own moral formation, to the kibbutz idea. Muki, who teaches in several of these programs, named the phenomenon directly: "Solidarity is expressed in the flow of new people into the story. Groups of young people come to these places, they're not connected to the place, but they're connected to the principle, to the principle of solidarity. And they come to the place without knowing it, without knowing." The double "without knowing" is deliberate. They came to a kibbutz they had never seen. They also came without knowing that what they were enacting had a hundred-year history. The kibbutz idea, in Period 4, had become recruitable: it could attract young people who had been raised in cities and suburbs, who had no inherited claim on the kibbutz tradition, and who arrived at evacuated communities because the principle of mutual responsibility (transmitted to them through their youth movements, their pre-army programs, the educators' kibbutzim that had helped train them) had become their principle.

Section 3. Land, equality, and the dilemmas of inequality

Equality is the kibbutz's foundational commitment, and yet at every period of the movement's history it has had to negotiate inequalities (between members, between kibbutzim, between kibbutz members and the populations who live alongside them) that the founding commitment could not eliminate and could not honestly ignore. This section traces the migration of that contradiction across the four periods. We treat the political economy of land in detail in Chapter 9; here we hold the question slightly differently. The dilemma we are tracing is not how the kibbutz movement related to the soil it stood on, a question Chapter 9 takes up at length, but how the egalitarian principle survived, faltered, and reactivated as the conditions surrounding it changed. The land question shapes what follows, but it is the equality question that organizes it.

Period 1: The frontier of equals

From its founding the kibbutz movement understood itself as an experiment in equality. The first groups of the Second Aliyah pooled labor, food, and shelter on principles that admitted no individual property and no differential reward. The tower-and-stockade settlements established between 1936 and 1939, fifty-two new kibbutzim raised in a single day each, in defended frontier locations, extended the principle to the most exposed conditions any of these communities would face (Balberg, 2024; Tsuk, 2005). Each kibbutz was, in those years, a community of risk first and a community of production second; equality among members was secured by the simple fact that they shared the same dangers, the same rations, the same agricultural quotas allocated by the Zionist institutions, and the same possibilities of being killed before any of it ripened.

What is significant for the equality dilemma is what land was, in this period, and what it was not. Agricultural land was held under lease from the Jewish National Fund and later from the Israel Land Administration; it was treated, by every party, as a means of production with no separable market value. A kibbutz could not sell its land. Neither could a member, since members did not own kibbutz land in the first place. The result was a form of equality among kibbutzim that was as much a function of the absence of market valuation as of any positive redistributive mechanism. As long as land could not be capitalized, the difference between a kibbutz on rich Jezreel Valley soil and a kibbutz on the dry rim of the Negev was a difference in agricultural possibility but not a difference in wealth (Tsuk, 2005). Each kibbutz was poor in the same currency. Each was the same kind of asset on the same kind of balance sheet.

This is not to say that the period was free of inequality. Internal hierarchies emerged early, particularly around the founders' inner circles, namely the families and individuals whose authority within their own kibbutzim shaped its assignments and its tone. Balberg (2024) records the durable observation, made within Beit HaShita as early as the 1930s, that the founders had "taken up all the positions steering the kibbutz and setting the tone" and that members of later groups felt their input dismissed. Movement-wide hierarchies between veteran kibbutzim and newer ones were also a constant feature. But these were inequalities of authority, biography, and standing rather than of economic position. The land beneath every kibbutz had the same legal value, which was none.

Period 2: Differential salaries inside the kibbutz

The 1985 Stabilization Plan ended Israel's hyperinflation and accelerated the kibbutz movement's slide into a debt crisis whose terms have been documented elsewhere in this book (Chapter 9). What concerns Section 3 is the equality dilemma the crisis produced not between kibbutzim (the center-versus-periphery story Chapter 9 traces in detail) but *within* them. As the kibbutzim moved toward privatization through the 1990s, the operative question moved with them: could equality between members survive the introduction of market signals that the kibbutz had previously held outside its boundaries?

Muki described, in our March 2025 conversation, how this dilemma surfaced through the texture of everyday life. He asked us to picture a kibbutz family in which the wife is a caregiver in the children's house and the husband is a manager in the kibbutz factory. Both are members. Both, on the kibbutz's founding principles, receive the same allowance, live in the same kind of apartment, and exercise the same vote in the general assembly. But the husband's factory begins sending him to professional management trainings at hotels in central Israel, where he sits with executives from companies that pay them market salaries and run them in market-shaped cars. The wife, meanwhile, is sent to a kibbutz movement caregivers' seminar that provides pretzel sticks at the coffee break. He comes home thinking, *next time I rent a luxury car. I don't want to be so small and miserable*. She comes home thinking, *they only gave us pretzel sticks and look what they gave you*. "That's already a lab for changes," Muki concluded.

Chapter 7 takes up the same dilemma through a scene from an earlier period: when the young Amos Oz asked Kibbutz Hulda, in the 1960s, for one day a week to write, the secretariat objected that "we have no way of ranking self-proclaimed artists." Oz himself called the argument "a solid argument" to which he "had no answer." The structural problem the secretariat faced in the 1960s was identical to the one Muki's family vignette captures three decades later: any acknowledgment of differential talent or contribution opens the question of how the kibbutz can adjudicate such differences without abandoning the equality of access that defined it.

The lab produced, through the 1990s, the move to differential salaries: the formal acknowledgment that members would be paid in proportion to the market value of their work outside the kibbutz or their managerial position inside it, with kibbutz-administered redistribution maintaining a floor of mutual guarantee. This was the principle codified in 2003 as the *Kibbutz Mitchadesh* (Renewed Kibbutz) legal classification (Manor, 2004). What it represented, for the equality dilemma, was the kibbutz movement's acceptance that some inequality among members was now structurally necessary to retain members at all, because members who could not earn their market value at home would, eventually, leave to earn it elsewhere. Equality between members ceased to mean equality of outcome and became, in most kibbutzim, equality of access: to the kibbutz's services, its safety net, its shared institutions. The redistributive logic survived. The principle of identical reward did not.

Period 3: Two communities on one map

Period 3 codified what Period 2 had improvised. Israel Land Administration Resolution 737 (1995, replaced by Resolution 959 in 2003) permitted kibbutzim to allocate part of their land for *communal neighborhoods* accommodating people who were not members of the cooperative corporation (Manor, 2004). By the late 2010s more than 150 kibbutzim had initiated such expansion-neighborhood projects (Palgi & Reinharz, 2011). What the Resolutions enabled was the spatial codification of a new form of inequality: the kibbutz member and the non-member neighbor, separated by a few hundred meters of road, sharing the same school and the same swimming pool and the same regional council, but related to the kibbutz's assets in radically different ways.

The case of Kibbutz Galil, documented by Palgi and Reinharz (2011), illustrates the dynamic with unusual sharpness. As the expansion neighborhood filled, parents from the new neighborhood came to outnumber kibbutz parents on the joint educational committee. Educational decisions (budgets, curriculum, facilities) began to be taken by a body in which the non-members held the majority. A kibbutz manager, recalling the period, described the experience from the kibbutz side: "The members of the expansion neighborhood carried on their own communications network, leaving us out" (Palgi & Reinharz, 2011). The economic asymmetry of the arrangement (kibbutz assets owned by the cooperative, expansion-neighborhood houses owned by their occupants, common services managed jointly) had produced a political asymmetry that ran the other direction. In their own community, the kibbutz members were now sometimes the minority partners.

What this represents, for Section 3's argument, is the third migration of the equality dilemma. In Period 1 inequality among kibbutzim had been buffered by the absence of market valuation. In Period 2 inequality among members had been formalized by the differential-salaries reforms. In Period 3 inequality between member and non-member residents had become a feature of the kibbutz settlement's daily life: spatial, demographic, structural. The egalitarian principle had not been abandoned. It had been narrowed, again, to the population it could plausibly govern, while the populations adjacent to that boundary multiplied.

Period 4: "The kibbutzim renewed their mutual responsibility"

By the eve of October 7, 2023, the structural inequality between kibbutzim that the 1990s land reclassification had created had become a settled fact of the movement's economic geography. Kibbutzim near urban centers held land worth hundreds of millions; kibbutzim on the southern and northern frontiers held land that retained its agricultural value alone. The mutual-guarantee mechanisms that had once obtained at the federation level had, as Muki observes in his essay *The Kibbutz After October 7*, largely lapsed:

In the years preceding the war, the difference between the kibbutzim in the periphery and those in the center of the country had deepened. In their beginnings, these kibbutzim had lived on the frontier from a security standpoint. But after the Six-Day War, they lived in greater comfort and in better economic conditions than those in the periphery. The mutual economic responsibility that had existed among the kibbutzim dissipated. With the crisis, however, a dramatic change unfolded. The kibbutzim renewed their mutual responsibility.

What followed in the months after the attack was a movement-wide reactivation of cross-periphery solidarity that the previous decades' economic divergence would not have predicted. Kibbutzim distant from the front absorbed kibbutzim in exile (Tsur, 2024). Sites for evacuees were built on host-kibbutz land. Volunteers from central kibbutzim moved south and north for weeks at a time, on the host kibbutz's payroll, to assist with rehabilitation and rebuilding. The movement's November 2023 status report records the aggregate scale: more than fifty kibbutzim evacuated, around one hundred host kibbutzim, roughly fifty thousand displaced absorbed (Kibbutz Movement, 2023). Chapter 10 develops the empirical record of those months at length; here we hold the same period within the longer arc of the equality dilemma. What the figures do not show, but what Tsur's essay names directly, is that the central kibbutzim mobilizing those resources had not, in their preceding twenty years, been operating in a logic that recognized the frontier kibbutzim as their economic equals. The crisis did not erase the inequality of the previous period. It suspended its consequences.

The most striking moment in this reactivation, for the equality dilemma, was that the wealth of the destroyed kibbutzim could not protect them. Kibbutz Be'eri operated one of the largest commercial printing presses in Israel; Nir Oz had thriving agricultural and industrial ventures; Kfar Aza was, by every conventional measure, prosperous. Their members were, on October 7, displaced into the same dependent position as the members of any peripheral kibbutz with no land windfall to its name. Catastrophe leveled, for a moment, the structural difference that the 1990s had codified. The mutual responsibility that the movement renewed was renewed across an inequality that catastrophe had revealed to be less protective, in the end, than it had appeared to be.

Section 4. Mission and meaning: What is the kibbutz for?

What is the kibbutz for? The question is older than any of the operational answers the movement has given it. Across the four periods, the kibbutz's vocation has been a moving target: first a national instrument of Zionist settlement, then a social experiment whose national tasks had been absorbed by the state, then a form of life desirable for reasons it had not built itself to provide, then, in the months after October 7, a community whose visible competence at facing catastrophe reopened a question many of its own members had stopped asking out loud. None of the four answers has held. Each has produced a different way of failing, or being judged to have failed, the previous one's standard.

Period 1: Mission fatigue

The kibbutz movement of 1948 emerged from the War of Independence carrying the highest national prestige it would ever hold. Kibbutzim provided a third of the new state's government, twenty-six of the 120 of its Knesset, and a disproportionate share of its military commanders (Gavron, 2000). Its founding ambition, namely to settle the land, defend the borders, and build the institutions of the Yishuv, had been visibly accomplished. And the moment of accomplishment was, as Anita Shapira (2010) traces it, the moment of the movement's first crisis of purpose. Kadish Luz, a member of Kibbutz Degania Bet and a leader of the Histadrut labor federation, named what had happened with a phrase that would echo for decades: *mission fatigue*. The fatigue was not a failure of resolve. It was the structural consequence of having succeeded. The pioneering tasks the kibbutz had performed in the pre-state period (settlement, defense, immigrant absorption) were now the responsibilities of state institutions. The army handled defense. The government managed immigration. Settlement of new regions was undertaken increasingly by new immigrants directed by state agencies into *moshavim* and development towns rather than by self-mobilizing kibbutz youth groups. Shlomo Ne'eman, another veteran kibbutz member, captured the implication in a distinction the kibbutz movement was about to spend forty years failing to answer: "There is no limit to the efforts people devote to a national matter. Nowhere does one find such dedication to social goals" (as cited in Shapira, 2010). The kibbutz had been built for the first kind of work and would now have to find its purpose in the second. The transition would prove difficult in ways the founding generation had not anticipated, because national missions and social goals do not call on the same energies and do not reward them at the same scale.

Period 2: "Like everyone else"

If Period 1 ended with a movement looking for a new vocation, Period 2 ended with a movement uncertain whether it required one at all. The combination of the 1985 Stabilization Plan, the debt crisis that overtook most kibbutzim in its wake, and the third generation's departure rates discussed in Section 5 of this chapter produced, by the early 1990s, a self-image at variance with everything the movement had previously claimed to be. The kibbutz secretariats and the kibbutz literature of the period were full of a single sentiment, formulated in different words by different speakers but consistent in its meaning: "our way of life has failed; we need to be like everyone else" (Ben-Rafael & Topel, 2014). The aspiration to be exemplary, which had been the engine of the movement's self-understanding for sixty years, was being abandoned in favor of the aspiration to be ordinary.

Read against Period 1's mission fatigue, the development is striking. The fatigue of 1949 was the fatigue of a movement that had finished its great task and not yet found its next one; the conviction was still that there *would be* a next one. The exhaustion of 1995 was different. It was the conviction that the kibbutz form had been a noble experiment that had failed under the weight of changed conditions and should be honorably wound down toward something resembling a normal Israeli rural settlement. The privatization reforms of the late 1990s and early 2000s, which Chapter 9 documents in detail, were the operational expression of this resolution. The form would be preserved, but its claim to be *for* anything beyond the welfare of its members would not. By the early 2000s, dozens of articles, books, and op-eds carried titles like *A Eulogy for the Kibbutz, The Kibbutz Is Dead, Kibbutz, the End* (Balberg, 2024). What was being eulogized was not the institution but its mission.

Period 3: The kibbutz as desirable address

What followed was a recovery, but a recovery of an unexpected kind. The expansion-neighborhood model, the differential-salaries reforms, and the demographic infusion they together produced rebuilt the kibbutzim as places people wanted to live. By the late 2010s the kibbutz population had stabilized; many kibbutzim held waiting lists; even the agricultural volunteers had returned, now arriving from China, South Korea, and Central America rather than from Western Europe (Balberg, 2024). In 2018 Nir Meir, then secretary of the Kibbutz Movement, gave the recovery its triumphalist formulation: "The state of the kibbutzim has never been better. More members, more children, and much more money" (as cited in Balberg, 2024). The numbers supported him. The dilemma the section is tracing did not.

What new residents came for, when they came, was not what the founders had built the form to be for. They came for a house with a garden, a safe environment for children, community life at a reasonable price, schools that worked, an hour's drive from a Mediterranean beach. These are not the goods of an exemplary social experiment; they are the goods of an attractive rural address. The kibbutz that absorbed them, by accommodating their reasons for arrival, accommodated also a different answer to the question of what the kibbutz was for. It was for them. It was a desirable form of contemporary Israeli middle-class life, organized around enough surviving communal practice to feel distinctive without imposing the sacrifices an exemplary life would have demanded. The form had survived. The question of whether the survival of the form constituted the survival of the idea was the open question of Period 3, and the movement's public voices did not always agree on the answer.

Period 4: The question reopens

October 7 reopened the mission question because catastrophe gave the kibbutz movement, almost overnight, something to do whose meaning a society outside itself could recognize. Within hours of the attack, kibbutzim across the country were absorbing evacuees, opening houses to people they had never met, mobilizing volunteer teams in communities of a few hundred. Within weeks the movement had assembled a coordinated response on a scale that the dominant narrative of the previous twenty years had judged it incapable of producing. As Tsur (2024) writes in his essay *The Kibbutz After October 7*, the response drew on cooperative communal codes that had "seemed to be fading in the years following the kibbutz crisis of the 1990s and the 2000s." The codes were not, it turned out, as faded as the mainstream narrative had thought. The kibbutzim, in his phrase, "renewed their mutual responsibility."

The dilemma this revival presents to Section 4's argument is acute. The renewed mutual responsibility was visible, scaled, and effective. It demonstrated that the kibbutz form had retained capacities the surrounding Israeli society lacked: the ability to mobilize volunteer infrastructure quickly, the practice of dialogue and listening that allowed host and evacuated communities to coordinate without rupture, the organizational memory of how to absorb a stranger into a household for an indefinite period. What it did not yet show, in the months and years after October 7, was whether these capacities would be offered outward as a vocation, as the founders' "religion of labor" and their experiment in collective childrearing had been offered outward as demonstrations to the wider Jewish and Israeli world, or whether they would remain inward, an extraordinary capacity that an Israeli society in fragments could observe but could not draw on. The question is whether the kibbutz movement, having renewed its mutual responsibility for its own, will renew its mission to the larger society it sits inside. Chapter 12 takes this question up directly. Section 4 holds it open as the question of the present, the question to which no one yet knows the answer because the conditions that will determine it are still unfolding.

Section 5. Generations and the question of continuity

Every generation of the kibbutz has decided differently what to keep from the one before and what to break with. The founders broke with the parental world they had left in Europe; the second generation, born into what the founders had built, declined to break with it in any way the founders found legible; the third broke by leaving in droves; the fourth, having been mourned as departed, turned out to be still present in ways only the digital age made possible. Each rupture was experienced, at the time, as a betrayal of the previous generation's project. Each turned out, in retrospect, to be the form in which that project survived. What this section traces is not whether continuity has been preserved but what continuity has actually consisted of.

Period 1: The heretics who were not

The founders' break with their own parents is treated elsewhere in this book; what concerns this section is the next iteration. By the late 1940s a recognizable second-generation type had emerged on the older kibbutzim (tanned, fluent in Hebrew, at ease behind a tractor and a rifle) and he disappointed the founders. S. Yizhar's *The Days of Ziklag* (1958, as cited in Balberg, 2024) gave that disappointment its sharpest voice:

> "They [the founders] needed a pretty word or justification out of some book to get over themselves and work hard, whereas we were born into it, and we need neither words nor a book ... Has someone with a face like mine read A.D. Gordon? I just like working on the tractor all day long in the sun."

A saying attributed variously to several founders captured the paradox: "We wanted to raise heretics, but we raised ignoramuses" (Balberg, 2024). Heresy presupposes orthodoxy; one cannot reject what one does not know. The founders had hoped their children would be the next link in a chain of self-conscious rejections. What they got was a generation that did not need to reject anything because nothing in their inheritance felt like a doctrine that demanded rejection. The kibbutz had become, for them, simply the world. The continuity of the kibbutz from the 1940s through the 1960s rested overwhelmingly on these children's shoulders, but the form of their fidelity was the refusal of the parental gesture. They would not break in the way they had been broken into.

Period 2: The departing children

Three decades later the third generation finally performed the rupture the founders had wanted, but in the wrong direction. They did not stay and break ideologically; they left. Departures rose from roughly four hundred a year before 1985 to over a thousand a year afterwards (Gavron, 2000); Abramitzky's longitudinal data show that more than twenty per cent of his sample left between 1983 and 1995, with the most educated and skilled most likely to leave (Abramitzky, 2018). Sibylle, recalling Kibbutz Barkai in those years: "I do remember in Barkai a departure of very central kibbutz members, from very central families, because there weren't enough changes, there wasn't enough attention to pensions ... if there's a group of four, five, six central, strong people who get up and leave, it's definitely a blow to the community." Muki had spoken to many of the leavers. One gave him a sentence he never forgot: "When the ship sinks, the rats are the first to flee. And that's me. And that's me." The repetition is the hardest part. The third generation's departure coincided with the death of the founders, producing what Muki has described as a community grieving on two fronts at once: "both the departure and the death of the founders had a psychological impact." The continuity of the kibbutz could survive the second generation's complacency; it nearly did not survive the third generation's exit.

Period 3: The returning children

What happened next was not in the script. The children who had left in the 1980s and 1990s began, twenty years on, to come back, not to the dining hall and the children's house, both of which had largely closed, but to expansion neighborhoods and the new-membership tracks carved out by the Public Committee of 2003 (Manor, 2004). As Balberg (2024) records: "Children of kibbutz members who left their home kibbutz as soon as they were able in the 1980s and 1990s now started coming back, renting vacant apartments or building new houses in the expansion neighborhoods." Alongside them came families with no kibbutz biography at all, drawn by the green lawns, the schools, the affordable house with a garden. By the late 2010s only sixty thousand of the approximately 170,000 people living in the two hundred and fifty kibbutzim were members (Balberg, 2024). Muki observes that the educational infrastructure of the present-day kibbutz is now maintained largely by parents who were not themselves raised in it: "they don't come to the kibbutz because of economics; they come to the kibbutz because it seems to them that they'll educate better, more openly, closer to nature." The category of *kibbutz-born* had ceased to predict *kibbutz-resident*; neither predicted *kibbutz-member*. The dilemma of generational continuity ceased to be a question about whether the children would stay and became a question about what they were inheriting when they returned, and how that inheritance related to the inheritance being assembled, alongside them, by people whose families had no part in building it.

Period 4: The dispersed kibbutz

The fourth iteration was prepared by the third but became visible only under catastrophe. The kibbutz that mobilized after October 7, 2023 was not only the residential kibbutz; it was the kibbutz extended through everyone who had ever belonged to it, including those who had been mourned as something close to apostates a generation earlier. As Muki writes in his essay *The Kibbutz After October 7*:

> "In the years preceding the harsh events, the means of communication had developed greatly. Those who had left the kibbutz remained in contact ... With the outbreak of the war, many of those who had left the kibbutz, as well as people who had spent their youth there, rallied to the aid of the kibbutzim in various ways, economically as well as through social services."

The cohort whose departure had once been described in the rats-from-a-sinking-ship vocabulary was the same cohort that organized legal support, lobbied politically, opened apartments to displaced kibbutz children, and flew home from abroad. The estrangement of forty years had been, all along, a relationship maintained at lower bandwidth (sustained by phone calls, then email, then group chats) that turned the diaspora of the kibbutz into a digital extension of the kibbutz itself. Solidarity, Muki notes, "was organized also on the basis of personal conversations ... there was a method in this solidarity. People sat and heard, listened to each other."

Concluding Thoughts: The carrying of the questions

Reading the five sections back as a sociologist, and as a member-observer who has lived inside the institution for over forty years, I find myself drawn to five interpretive observations about what the four-period traces, taken together, reveal. I offer them here in a deliberately analytical register. They are not the joint arguments of this book, which run through the chapters that precede this one and through the conclusion that follows it. They are an attempt to step back, briefly, from the kibbutz as a tradition I belong to and look at it as a sociological phenomenon I am trying to understand.

The first thing that strikes me, when I trace the boundary of belonging across these four moments, is how completely it has migrated from a question of formal membership to a question of practical solidarity. Sociologically, what we are observing is a process of progressive decoupling. The legal category, the residential category, and the practical-community category have come apart, and the operative definition of who is a kibbutz member now varies according to the question one is asking. Each redrawing preserved something that earlier definitions had protected (the legal coherence of the cooperative, the institution's hold on its name, the membership rights of the founders' children, the integrity of a place whose meaning was bound to who slept inside its perimeter), and each lost something earlier definitions had taken for granted. What I take from the four anchors together is that a community sustains itself, in the long run, less by the boundary it draws on paper than by the population willing to act as that community in moments that have nothing to do with the institution's ordinary administration. By that test, the kibbutz of October 2023 was very much larger than its legal membership and very much more concentrated than its physical residence, and the question of who is a kibbutz member has, in my reading, a fifth answer in formation that is unlike any of the previous four.

What strikes me about the four anchor-moments of the second dilemma is how reliably the kibbutz idea has migrated to whichever location had the energy to sustain it. In Period 1 it was carried by the federations themselves, each holding a rival theory of what the idea most was; the dilemma was not adjudicated but institutionalized, and each federation lived inside its own answer while the kibbutz idea, considered as a whole, was held by the difference between them. In Period 2 it was nearly broken on the rock of a national rejection that the mainstream could not survive intact, and what Muki has named the sect-or-assimilation dilemma became the operative question in every kibbutz secretariat. In Period 3 it migrated to a small urban margin that the rural mainstream did not always recognize as kin. In Period 4 it appeared in a population that the mainstream had not produced and the margin had only partly trained: young people drawn to the principle who had never set foot inside a kibbutz before. None of these locations was the answer to the dilemma; each was a place where the dilemma kept being lived. From the standpoint of a sociologist trained to look for the locus of normative energy in a movement, this is a more interesting finding than I would have expected. The kibbutz idea is most alive, in my reading, where the question of what it most is has not been settled, and the institution that sustains it has, repeatedly, been the one that carried the question rather than the one that resolved it.

Equality has been the kibbutz's foundational normative commitment, and yet at every period of the movement's history it has had to negotiate inequalities that the founding commitment could not eliminate and could not, when honestly examined, defend. What I find sociologically striking is that each period has produced a different operative inequality and a different operational answer to it. In Period 1 inequality among kibbutzim was buffered by the absence of market valuation: every kibbutz was poor in the same currency, and equality was as much a function of shared limits as of any positive redistributive mechanism. In Period 2 the introduction of differential salaries acknowledged that equality of outcome could not be sustained if members could not be retained, and the egalitarian principle was narrowed to equality of access: to services, to safety nets, to shared institutions. In Period 3 the expansion-neighborhood model produced a new form of structural inequality, this time spatially codified between member and non-member residents living a few hundred meters apart. In Period 4 a movement-wide mutual responsibility that the previous two decades' divergence had quietly dismantled reactivated within weeks of the catastrophe, in a configuration none of the previous periods had anticipated. None of these was a resolution. None completed the work the founders had begun. What the four periods together demonstrate, in my reading, is something I would phrase deliberately. Equality, in the kibbutz tradition, has been less a destination than a discipline: a commitment that each generation has had to re-narrate to fit conditions the previous one had not anticipated, and that has remained alive in the tradition only because the dilemmas surrounding it have never been allowed to settle.

The kibbutz has been *for* different things at different times, and the sociologist who tracks the changes finds, I think, a rather striking pattern. In Period 1 it was for the building of a state that no longer needed it for that work after 1948. In Period 2 it was, by the consensus of its own secretariats, for a way of life that had failed and needed to be replaced by ordinariness. In Period 3 it was for the production of an attractive form of rural Israeli middle-class life. In Period 4 it has been, briefly and visibly, for the absorption of a society's most exposed communities at the moment of their greatest need. None of these vocations has held. Each was overtaken by conditions the previous one could not have anticipated. What I would draw from this, against the movement's own periodic suspicions of its own decline, is the opposite conclusion: not that the kibbutz has failed to find its purpose but that the question of its purpose has been the form of its continued life. A movement whose vocation could be settled would, by now, be settled. The kibbutz is not. Sociologically, what we are observing is something less dramatic than the recurring crises of meaning the movement has periodically diagnosed, and something more durable. The carrying of an unresolved question of purpose has, in my reading, been one of the kibbutz's distinctive sociological accomplishments, even when the carriers experienced it as failure.

The kibbutz survives, I would argue, in part because of the breaks between generations, not despite them. The founders broke with their parents in Europe. The second generation broke with the first by declining to break, by inheriting the kibbutz as the world rather than as a doctrine that demanded rejection. The third broke by leaving in numbers no one had expected, then partly broke with that break by coming back. The fourth broke with the second's mourning by remaining attached from elsewhere, sustained by communications technologies that had not existed in 1985. Each gesture was, at the time, experienced as a betrayal of what the previous generation thought it had built; each turned out, when the next gesture came, to have been the form in which what was being built actually moved. What strikes me sociologically is the inversion this produces of the standard intergenerational transmission story. What each generation transmitted to the next was not the form of the answer but the form of the question. That, in my reading, is what this book has meant by a living tradition: not a doctrine preserved through time, but a way of organizing a community such that its children inherit the right and the obligation to break with it on terms that the dilemmas themselves dictate.

Read alongside Muki's reflections on these dilemmas elsewhere in the book, these five observations point to a common structure: the kibbutz movement's continuing life has consisted in the carrying of these dilemmas, not in their resolution. What October 7, 2023 and the months that followed have done, across all five, is reactivate questions that had quieted. None of these reactivations is itself a resolution. Each is a reformulation under conditions the previous period had not anticipated.

What remains, at the close of this chapter, is the dilemma it could not address: the relationship between the kibbutz and the populations of post-1948 Israel that the kibbutz did not absorb, and the political project that mobilized their grievances after 1977. That dilemma is not absent because it is unimportant. It is absent because, of all the dilemmas the kibbutz movement has lived, it is the one whose moral and political weight makes it inappropriate as a section among others, and the one whose shape in the present moment makes it the proper subject of the book's concluding chapter. We turn to it there, with the directness it deserves.

What this chapter as a whole has tried to demonstrate is what we have meant, throughout this book, by a movement that is still alive. Not a movement whose answers have proven durable. A movement whose questions have proven to be the form of its life.

12. Is the Room Still Open?

For Avishai Grossman

Avishai Grossman, 1996

Source: Einav Grossman, Avishai's daughter

An Opening Portrait

This book is dedicated to Avishai Grossman, and the conclusion has to begin with him because the book itself, its method, its temperament, its refusal to deliver verdicts, comes closer to him than to anyone else in its pages. Avishai was, in Muki's phrase, "a stubborn pessimist in his hope." He saw difficult things, he discovered difficult things, and he never accepted the verdict of the difficult things he saw. Every concrete decision he had to make contradicted his pessimism, his diagnosis, his analysis of situations and people. He was the man who would say to the boys around him in Ein Shemer who tried to comfort him, who tried to coax him toward optimism, "Dear friends, I am pessimistic." And he would not add the next sentence, the sentence he in fact lived by: "I am pessimistic and I do not give up."

This is not a natural psychological combination. Most people who refuse optimism eventually refuse engagement; most people who refuse to give up eventually buy themselves the consolation of a more optimistic outlook. Avishai did neither. He held both at once, as a discipline, throughout his life. For him faith and truth were a single commandment: how to believe and not lie. He was never willing to be an optimist, because for him the optimist lies. But he never gave up his ideas. He would not allow himself to be protected by hopes he could not honestly hold, and he would not allow himself to be released by despair he could not honestly use. This temperament is what made him a teacher. Muki recalls their first encounter, as boys:

> "Avishai a counselor in *Hashomer Hatzair* with the white shoelace, me a counselor in *Hanoar Ha'oved* with the red shoelace, arguing about whether to celebrate May Day. Avishai said yes, humanism beyond nationalism required the red flag. I said no, the red flag was Soviet Russia, which was not humanistic."

They reached a public conclusion together that the disagreement, examined honestly, was actually agreement: a shared refusal to let the kibbutz movement collapse into nationalism without humanism. From that moment on, what Muki called Avishai's penetrating gaze became, for him, one of the lasting clarifications of his own life.

Avishai's gaze was for people. He wanted to investigate every person, what he believes, what his life project is, how one can stand beside him, how one can also criticize him, how one can give him a hand. There is a small story Muki tells, which strikes us as a parable of the entire kibbutz tradition at its best:

> "At Ein Shemer, Avishai used to take some of the boys to the cemetery, and they would gossip about each of those buried there. Not eulogy. Not whitewash. An act of moral investigation, sustained over a lifetime, refusing both veneration and dismissal, refusing, in the deepest sense, to settle the case of any human being."

When this conclusion talks about hope and its cost, it talks first about that kind of investigation. Hope of this kind is not a forecast. It is an attention.

Avishai's life had two great contradictions. The first was political. He was, all his adult life, pessimistic about the direction of Israeli society, about the kibbutz movement's capacity to hold its ideals, about the political world he had once tried to enter and from which he had withdrawn. He withdrew, Muki insists, from politics, but not from the idea. The distinction is precise. He stopped believing that political institutions could be made to carry the truth. He did not stop believing that the truth had to be carried. The second contradiction was private. When his wife Hagit fell ill with Alzheimer's, Avishai, the man who had never permitted himself optimism in matters of analysis, became an optimistic believer. He stayed. He loved her through it. Muki calls this "the peak of love," optimistic and believing in matters of love, pessimistic and hopeful in matters of ideology. Both were the same fidelity, expressed in two registers. For the late years of his life, Avishai received people. He stopped going out to look for them. He stayed at home, and they came to him, because they had learned that he believed in them. Muki and I were among them. My relationship with Avishai Grossman started in the late 1980s, when I was to become an educator and history teacher at the kibbutz high school, where Avishai was the headmaster. He insisted, over the objections of parents who did not want a non-Jewish German woman as teacher to their children. He insisted, and he insisted again, and he asked me year after year to enter his classroom and tell the children what it had been like to grow up German after the war, how the Holocaust had been spoken of in our schools, how it had marked me. He believed, decades before the writing of this book, that what I had to say belonged in a kibbutz classroom. He believed, in the years before he died, that I should write a book about how I see Israeli society. We are not writing exactly that book here, but it carries his pressure, and this conclusion carries it most directly.

To Avishai Grossman, then, who refused to settle any question, this book is offered as a continuation of his unfinished conversations.

Dilemmas Migrate Rather Than Resolve

The chapters of this book have moved across a wide territory. The founding philosophical motives. The boundaries of belonging. Family, gender, kinship. Education across generations. Work and the meaning of contribution. Art, culture, productivity. Enterprise and industry from the blacksmith's workshop to the global drip-irrigation empire. Land. The kibbutz and the wider Israeli polity. Crisis, transformation, October 7. Each chapter has been organized, by the explicit method we set out at the beginning of the book, around dilemmas the kibbutz has lived rather than resolved. What we want to mark here, in the conclusion, is the structural finding that emerges across the chapters when they are read together. The dilemmas the kibbutz has confronted have not been solved; they have been kept alive. They have migrated from one period to another, taking different operational shapes, generating different practical responses, but not closing.

Take equality, the kibbutz's foundational normative commitment. In the founding decades, equality among kibbutzim was buffered by the absence of market valuation: every kibbutz held land it could not sell, and so every kibbutz was poor in the same currency. In the period of the differential-salaries reforms after 1985, equality among members was renegotiated downward, and the egalitarian principle narrowed to equality of access, to services, to safety nets, to shared institutions, rather than equality of outcome. In the expansion-neighborhood period from the late 1990s onward, a new structural inequality opened between members and non-member residents living a few hundred meters apart. After October 7, mutual responsibility among kibbutzim was re-activated movement-wide, in a configuration none of the previous periods had anticipated. None of these was a resolution. Each was a renewed local answer to a question that the founding generation had not solved and that the present generation has not solved either. What the differential-salaries reforms did not do, however, and Muki insists on this, is to convert economic disparity into an instrument of economic discipline or interpersonal control. Even in privatization the kibbutz declined to use inequality as a lever over its members.

Take ownership. The early Zionist-institutions decision that kibbutz land would never be the kibbutz's own, that the group would be tenants of national institutions rather than private owners, established collective control over the means of production as a constitutive principle. By the time of the privatization reforms, that principle had migrated outward to banks, external investors, multinationals, and individual kibbutzim selling their factories alone, in crisis, for whatever they could get. The dilemma of *shelanu*, what is ours, and what does the word still mean, has not been answered. It has been re-asked, in harder conditions, by every generation.

Take transmission. The founding generation believed that the second generation would inherit a settled life. Muki names this directly as a deep error. The dilemmas proved permanent precisely because they arose from the fundamental structure of the kibbutz experiment, not from contingent failures of design, but from the attempt to reconcile individual authenticity with collective commitment, universal vision with particular identity, ideological purity with pragmatic adaptation. Each generation has had to reinvent kibbutz education under pressure, and each generation has discovered that inherited values cannot simply be transmitted like agricultural techniques.

Take the question of who belongs. The kibbutz's distinctive practice of bounded equality, radical internal equality combined with exclusionary external boundaries, has been the movement's defining characteristic and its defining paradox. The shop without prices still exemplifies radical internal equality. But access to that shop still depends on passing through the admission committee's gates. The boundaries have been widened over time and redrawn in less ideological terms, but the dilemma of how a community can practice radical internal equality while maintaining exclusionary external boundaries has not been solved. It has been kept honest, in the better moments of the movement's history, by being acknowledged.

Take work. The transformation from "economy" to "livelihood," from collective production to individual money-making, was a linguistic revolution that altered how members understood their relationship to labor. It did not resolve the question of what motivates human work. As Muki noted, the literature on motivating workers under livelihood conditions continues to multiply, because the problem has not been solved; it has only been displaced.

This is the architecture of the book and it is, we believe, the architecture of the kibbutz itself. It is a sequence of unresolved dilemmas, each finding a different operational answer in its own period, none of them closing the question. Avishai Grossman would have recognized this immediately. It is the structure he embodied. It is what he meant when he refused to be an optimist and refused to give up.

Where the Idea Lives: The Four Periods and the Unsettled Center

If we step back from any single dilemma and ask where the kibbutz idea itself has lived across the movement's century, the architecture of Chapter 11 gives us our answer: the idea has migrated. It lived in the rivalry of the three federations before the state. It nearly broke on the rock of national repudiation after 1977. It moved to the urban kibbutzim of the 1990s and 2000s and the decades since, now several dozen communities, the most prominent in Beit Shemesh,

Sderot, Nof HaGalil, Tel Aviv, Haifa, and Harish. After October 7 it appeared in a population the mainstream had not produced and the urban margin had only partly trained. None of these locations was the answer to the dilemma of what the kibbutz most is. Each was a place where the dilemma kept being lived.

This is the sociological observation we want to leave with readers: the kibbutz idea is most alive where the question of what it most is has not been settled. The institution that has sustained it has been the one that carried the question rather than the one that resolved it.

Avishai's life is its personal counterpart. He refused to let the question congeal. The cemetery walks at Ein Shemer, gossiping about each of the buried, asking what each had believed and how one could stand beside him while also criticizing him, were a small concentrated practice of the same discipline this book has tried to bring to its chapters. Each life, like each dilemma, deserves both criticism and the offered hand. The movement, in turn, has been weakest when it claimed a settled identity and strongest when it carried its unresolved questions openly.

October 7 and the Limits of Reactivation

Chapter 10 documented what the kibbutz movement did in the eighteen months after October 7. The findings deserve to be brought forward here in summary, because they bear on the disagreement that follows. The kibbutzim absorbed evacuees on a scale the movement had never before been asked to deliver. More than fifty kibbutzim were evacuated; roughly one hundred host kibbutzim absorbed roughly fifty thousand displaced people. Sites for evacuees were built on host-kibbutz land, financed from movement funds whose allocation was renegotiated in real time. Volunteers from central kibbutzim moved south and north for weeks at a time, on the host kibbutz's payroll, to assist with rehabilitation and rebuilding. Mutual responsibility among kibbutzim, which had quietly lapsed across the previous two decades of economic divergence, reactivated within weeks. Walls between kibbutzim, moshavim, and development towns, walls cultivated for decades by political populists trading on resentment, softened, in places, under the weight of shared catastrophe.

This was not a small achievement. Muki's reading of it is that the dialogic, mutual-responsibility instinct of the founding generations proved to be infrastructure rather than memory, proved to be a living capacity rather than a nostalgic story. The architecture of solidarity activated when activation was required. Kibbutzim that had become economically conventional villages over two decades nevertheless mobilized within hours as if the founding ethos had never lapsed. Whatever else October 7 demonstrated about Israeli society, it demonstrated, inside the kibbutz movement, that the tradition still had the capacity to act.

What is striking, however, is also what did not happen.

The kibbutz movement absorbed evacuees, rebuilt, mourned, organized, shared. It did not articulate, in public, a political position commensurate with the moment. It did not name what had happened to the country in the years preceding the attack. It did not name the political project that had spent more than a decade preparing the ground on which the failures of October 7 occurred. It did not claim, in public, the authority that its conduct in the weeks after the attack would have justified. There is no reproach in this observation. The kibbutz movement was, and is, a movement of roughly 193,000people across 271 communities. It has not been a national-scale political actor in any meaningful sense since the early 1970s. It is run by elected secretariats and federation officials whose mandate is the movement's institutional welfare, not its public voice. Its tradition is dialogic, slow, pluralist, suspicious of unified declamations. The instinct of its members in crisis was to act, not to speak, and acting is what they did, at scale and with skill.

And yet a question presses, and it is the question of this conclusion. The question is whether the conduct of the post-October 7 period was the full measure of what the movement could have been, or whether it was, in fact, an incomplete response, a moral and practical mobilization that stopped short of becoming the political and public mobilization the moment required. The question is whether the kibbutz movement, at the moment of greatest national fracture in its lifetime, did everything it could have done. This is the question on which the two authors of this book do not entirely agree.

The Kibbutz and the Israeli "Other"

The relationship between the kibbutz and the populations next to it, Mizrahi immigrants in development towns, Palestinian citizens of Israel, Palestinians under occupation, has been the most consistently evaded question in the movement's history. Chapter 3 traced the long failure to absorb Mizrahi immigrants in the 1950s, the consolidation of Mizrahi political identity against the kibbutz movement in 1977 and 1981, and the reproduction of structural separation, in less ideological terms, in the expansion-neighborhood era. Chapter 9 set out the relationship to the Palestinian question, the land beneath most kibbutzim of the center and the Galilee, and the compartmentalization that allowed a movement so committed to justice to coexist for so long with the history of Palestinian dispossession. We do not rehearse the material here. What we want to mark is the pattern. Bounded solidarity inside and exclusion outside. Mutual responsibility among members; denial of mutual responsibility for those whose presence next door had been made structurally invisible. This is, in our reading, the deepest dilemma of the entire kibbutz experiment, and the one the movement has been least willing to face directly.

The fourth period, which began on October 7, has not produced a resolution. What it has produced is the partial dissolution of the kibbutz-moshav-development-town partition under shared catastrophe; the moral vertigo of Be'eri, Nir Oz, Kfar Aza, Nahal Oz, Re'im, Nirim, and Alumim members, many of them lifelong peace activists murdered on land that was itself contested. The kibbutz members who absorbed evacuees from the south were absorbing not only kibbutz members but moshav residents, development-town families, Bedouin from the Negev. They were absorbing them with skill and at scale. They were not yet articulating a movement-wide understanding of what those weeks had taught them about the country they belonged to. The walls did not fall. They cracked. We register this, here in the conclusion, because if the kibbutz movement has a public future commensurate with its past, the future depends on its willingness to take this dilemma, the dilemma of the other, out of the compartment in which it has been kept for a century, and to bring it into the open. Not as an admission of guilt, which is too cheap and which Avishai would have refused as a comforting closure, but as the next stage of the moral investigation he spent his life conducting.

A Disagreement Between the Authors: In Dialogue We Part

Throughout this book we have written together, about questions on which we either agree or have learned to hold our disagreements lightly. In this section we cannot. The fact at issue is straightforward. For more than a decade, the current government of Israel and the political-media machinery surrounding it have presented the kibbutz movement as a state enemy. The presentation has not been incidental. It has been systematic. The kibbutz has been positioned, in official rhetoric and in the affiliated media ecosystem, as the symbol of an Ashkenazi, secular, leftist, peace-seeking, Arab-loving Israel against which a different Israel is being mobilized.

The mechanisms are familiar to any reader paying attention: the weaponization of ethnic-political grievance into permanent identity; the security-only reframing of Zionism that delegitimizes the kibbutz's humanist tradition as a form of weakness; the systematic naming of judges, journalists, peace activists, reservist organizations, and protest movements as internal enemies; the casting of dialogic, peace-seeking, civic-democratic Israeliness as itself a form of treason. This campaign has been conducted, in the years before October 7, against a kibbutz movement that did not initially understand itself to be at war with the government. After October 7, when the southern kibbutzim of the Gaza envelope were attacked and many of their members, peace activists in lifelong proportion, were murdered, the campaign did not pause. It adjusted. The kibbutzim of the south were mourned in official rhetoric while the kibbutz movement as a whole was kept in the position of internal enemy. The disagreement between Muki and me concerns what the kibbutz movement should have done about it, and what it should do now.

My view is that the kibbutz movement has not reacted strongly enough. It has the standing, the moral capital, and the geographic concentration to position itself publicly as the sane alternative to a reactionary, autocratic, militant, war-seeking government. Not in party-political terms but in civic terms. It is one of the few institutional formations in Israeli civil society with the historical depth, the educational infrastructure, the demographic stability, the organized communities, and the dialogic, secular, humanist, peace-seeking tradition required to play this role. It is, structurally, what is left when the institutions of liberal democracy in Israel have been substantially weakened. It is, structurally, the closest thing the country has to a network of small civic republics. To remain silent in the face of a sustained delegitimization campaign, and worse, to allow the murders of October 7 to be folded into the same delegitimization campaign without sustained public objection, is in my view a form of severe failure. Not because the movement has been complicit. Because it has accepted, by default, a representation of itself as a miserable target of history rather than a possible architect of resistance.

Muki's view is more cautious. He notes that the kibbutz movement is not, and has not been since the 1970s, a national-scale political actor. He notes that its strength has always been the slow, dialogic, educational work of communities, work that does not scale into mass political assertion without becoming the sect-form the movement has resisted. He notes that the moments in the movement's history when it tried to claim a settled political identity, the federations of the 1930s, the labor establishment of the 1950s and 1960s, produced both real achievement and the durable resentment that the current campaign exploits. He notes that the dialogic instinct of the founding generations was exactly the refusal to translate moral seriousness into political assertion, and that the cost of betraying this instinct, even in the name of self-defense, may be greater than the cost of bearing the present attack with a degree of patience. He notes, finally, that Avishai withdrew from politics but not from the idea, and that the distinction matters more now than ever.

Muki also notes the historical record. In 1970 there was no shared organizational framework for the kibbutz movement: it was split among federations, among political parties, divided on the question of settlement after the Six-Day War. He and others of his generation tried to unify the movements and did not succeed. The unified political voice Sibylle's argument assumes the movement could now produce, in his reading, was a voice the movement has never in fact had.

Muki, in correspondence as the chapter took its present shape, put his side this way:

> "In the current situation there is a difficulty, because the struggling democracy is not waging its battle through parties whose ideology is transparent and clear to their leaders. They work more on personal and managerial charisma. The dread of the voter grants them the right not to clarify to themselves ideologically what they actually want. The kibbutz cannot organize itself as a party, since it is a community."

We do not resolve this disagreement here. We cannot, and we like disagreements. The book has been built on the principle that dilemmas are kept alive by being lived, and the present dilemma, the dilemma of how the kibbutz movement should respond to a government apparatus that has named it as enemy, is a dilemma the movement is currently inside. Its members will resolve it, or fail to resolve it, in their own communities, through their own decisions, in their own time. What we want to say, jointly and with both our names, is that the dilemma is real. It cannot be avoided. The public silence of the past decade has had a cost, and the silence of the past two years has had a higher cost; and any future the kibbutz movement carries forward will be shaped, decisively, by what it does or fails to do about this question in the coming years.

We add a small concrete observation. Avishai, for thirty years, conducted in the educational institution in Ein Shemer the practice that this debate has not yet learned to conduct in public. He insisted on my presence in the classroom over the objections of parents who did not want a non-Jewish German teaching their children. He insisted on civic education as a discipline, not a slogan. He insisted that the moral seriousness of the kibbutz tradition meant doing the difficult thing concretely, in the room, with the people in front of you. He withdrew from politics. He did not withdraw from civic life. There may be a model here that the disagreement between us partially conceals: the kibbutz movement does not have to choose between national-scale political assertion and silent endurance. There is a third practice. Civic, educational, neighborhood-by-neighborhood, dialogic, refusing both the sect-form and the silence. It is the practice the movement was built for. It is the practice Avishai conducted. Whether it can be scaled, in the present moment, into a public position commensurate with the threat is the question we leave with the reader.

The Gilead Question

If the present government, or another continuous with it in spirit, continues to rule for another decade, the question that will press itself on the kibbutz movement is no longer whether to position itself politically. It will be whether the conditions for the movement's existence as a distinct civic form persist at all. Margaret Atwood's *The Handmaids Tale* is a novel about a society that did not become Gilead in a single revolution. It became Gilead through the slow narrowing of the spaces in which civic, secular, plural, feminist life could still be conducted. Bank accounts that one day no longer worked for women. Universities that one day no longer taught what they had taught. Newspapers that one day were no longer published. Communities that one day no longer convened. The Republic of Gilead was built less by what it built than by what it allowed to disappear. We invoke Atwood here not as prophecy and not as melodrama. We invoke her as imaginative pressure. The current government has not been shy about its intentions. It has weakened the courts. It has weakened the press. It has weakened the universities. It has weakened the security establishment by replacing professionals with loyalists. It has weakened the educational standards of the public school system. It has weakened the international standing of the country to the point where Israeli passports, in many countries, no longer carry the welcome they once did. It has weakened, in short, exactly the institutional infrastructure on which civic, secular, plural, dialogic Israeliness depends. What it has weakened, the kibbutz movement still possesses, in concentrated and durable form: schools, communities, a secular tradition, a dialogic culture, an educated population, a habit of self-governance, a record of practiced equality among members.

Muki adds an observation on the structure of the threat:

> "The kibbutz cannot exist in a non-democratic society. The tremors in democracy in the West are affecting the State of Israel. Democracies do not vanish; they commit suicide. To live in a direct democracy, in a commune that is not a cult, within a democracy fighting for its existence, this is a great challenge. The difficulty is especially apparent under neoliberalism, which is ostensibly democratic but uses violence and the abdication of responsibility as an organizational and economic instrument. It is not only psychology that is at work, but politics and economics as well."

If the institutional infrastructure of Israeli civil society continues to be weakened, and there is no current evidence that it will not, three trajectories present themselves to the kibbutz movement, and the choice between them will not be made all at once.

The first trajectory is decline by attrition. Land-lease arrangements are quietly altered. Regulatory hostility increases. Demographic pressure compounds. Educational autonomy is narrowed. The kibbutzim become ordinary villages, their distinctive standing eroded, their civic infrastructure absorbed into a more uniformly nationalist landscape. This is the Gilead trajectory in its kibbutz-specific form: not destruction, but normalization downward. It does not require malice. It requires only the slow administrative pressure of a state that no longer believes in the form of life the kibbutzim represent.

The second trajectory is transformation into refuge. The kibbutzim become, in effect, small civic republics, islands of civil sanity and secularity, places where dialogic, peace-seeking, feminist, pluralist, gender-egalitarian Israeliness continues to be practiced because the kibbutz's institutional structure permits it to be. This is not romance. It is what the small monastic communities of late antiquity became, in the centuries of decline that surrounded them. It is what the Quakers became in seventeenth-century England. It is, on a smaller scale and a more secular register, the role intentional communities have repeatedly played when the state around them is closing. The kibbutzim are not monasteries, and they are not religious communities, and the analogy is partial. But the structural function, the preservation of a way of life through a period in which the wider society no longer protects it, is recognizable. In this trajectory, the kibbutz movement does not become the alternative government. It becomes the reservation in which the alternative culture continues to be practiced, while the wider society passes through whatever it passes through.

The third trajectory is reactivation as a moral-political movement. The kibbutz movement returns to a public role it has not played since the early 1970s, this time not as vanguard of the state but as conscience of a society. It uses its institutional concentration, its educational reach, its peripheral and central geographic distribution, to articulate a public alternative to the political project currently underway. It does this through the institutions it already has, such as the schools, the federations, the regional councils, the cultural centers, and through the public voice its members already command. It does this without becoming a political party, because it does not need to. It does this as the collective voice of about a quarter of a million people who have, in their lifetimes, organized their communities around principles incompatible with what the state is currently becoming. These three trajectories are not equally probable. The first is, on present trends, the most likely. The second is already happening informally, in places, without being claimed. The third would require a decision the movement has not yet made. I argue that the second is not enough, that to settle for being a refuge is to accept the loss of everything else. Muki argues that the second may be the only honest possibility, and that the third risks becoming the sect-form the movement was built to refuse.

What we want to leave the reader with is the observation that the question is no longer abstract. It is the question this generation of the kibbutz movement will, in fact, answer by what it does, by what it fails to do, by the cumulative weight of small and large decisions over the next decade. The answer Avishai would have asked of the movement is not "will it work?" That question is too consoling. It is "is it true?" as the discipline he held against every comfort, including the comfort of his own pessimism.

The Room is Yours

We return, in closing, to the formula Avishai's life suggested: pessimistic and hopeful in matters of ideology; optimistic and believing in matters of love. The book's closing claim is that hope, in the kibbutz tradition we have traced, is not optimism. Avishai would not let us call it that. Optimism, for him, was a form of lying, a forecast made against the available evidence, in order to spare oneself the discipline of seeing what is in front of one. Hope is something else. Hope is the refusal to abandon the idea even when honest analysis offers no encouragement. It is the practical decision to keep doing the work, the educational work, the communal work, the dialogic work, the work of mutual responsibility, without first being assured that the work will succeed.

This is what makes hope an act of solidarity rather than a feeling. And this is its cost. Hope of this kind is not consoling. It is laborious, lonely, and unromantic. It is borne unequally, by those who happen to be in the room when the work needs to be done. We close with a small image. In his last years, Avishai stayed at home, and the people he had believed in came to him. Muki was one and I was one. We came to him not because he had answers, and certainly not because he was an optimist. We came because he had, throughout his life, refused to settle the questions, and that refusal had become a kind of room in which questions could continue to be asked.

To Avishai Grossman, who taught us how to keep that room open: this is the book we have been able to write. The room is yours.

Appendix: A Six-panel Visual Timeline of the Kibbutz Movement, 1880–2026

This book has proceeded by dilemma rather than by date. Each chapter takes up a question the kibbutz has never fully settled and follows it across more than a century, which means the chronology has been folded into the argument rather than laid out on its own. The timeline that follows sets that chronology out plainly, for readers who want to see the sequence, the scale, and the institutional shape of the movement in one place.

It runs across six panels. Five cover successive periods: origins (1880–1910), expansion (1911–1939), war and statehood (1940–1967), peak and crisis (1968–1989), and renewal and differentiation (1990–2026). The sixth draws the whole span together. Each panel tracks three things at once: a chronology of events, a set of demographic or economic benchmarks, and the changing architecture of the federations, from a single commune with no umbrella body, through four movements, a rupture, a series of mergers, and back to one.

Read across all six panels, three arcs emerge: growth, from fewer than fifty members at Degania to some 193,000 people in roughly 271 kibbutzim; fragmentation followed by reunification; and the passage from one model to many. The periods marked here are conventional historical divisions and do not coincide with the four periods used in Chapter 11, which follow the life of the dilemmas rather than the life of the institutions. The figures are benchmark approximations; they indicate order of magnitude, not exact counts.

Figure 1 out of 6: Origins, 1880 – 1910. First collective organizations.

PANEL 1 OF 6

Origins

1880 — 1910

First communal crystallization

CHRONOLOGY

1880	Migration from Russia accelerates *migration*
1882	First aliyah begins *settlement*
1896	Herzl publishes The Jewish State *ideology*
1897	First Zionist Congress *ideology*
1904	Second aliyah begins *migration*
1905-09	Worker communes form *labor*
1909	Hashomer established *defense*
1910	Degania founded *settlement · the first kibbutz*

DEMOGRAPHY

<50

members at founding

Degania, 1910

The first permanent commune numbers fewer than fifty members — small enough to organize without a federation.

MOVEMENT DEVELOPMENT

Pre-federation phase — no formal umbrella movement yet

→ 1911

Figure 2 out of 6: Expansion, 1911 – 1939. Institutional differentiation.

PANEL 2 OF 6

Expansion

1911 — 1939

Institutional differentiation

CHRONOLOGY

1913	First child born in a kibbutz *settlement*
1920	Third aliyah · Histadrut · Hagana *institutions*
1921	New kibbutzim in Jezreel Valley *settlement*
1926	Kibbutz Artzi founded *federation · Hashomer Hatzair*
1927	Kibbutz Meuhad founded *federation*
1933	Youth Aliyah · Hever Hakvutzot *federation · immigration*
1934	Kibbutz Dati (Religious) founded *federation · religious*
1936–39	Wall and Tower campaign; WWII begins *settlement · defense · crisis*

DEMOGRAPHY

1921 / 23	1936	1940 (horizon)
1,056	131,000	229,000
members *in 22 kibbutzim*	dunams of land *held by kibbutzim*	dunams of land *held by kibbutzim*

MOVEMENT DEVELOPMENT

1911 — 1939

Kibbutz Artzi · 1926

Kibbutz Meuhad · 1927

Chever HaKvutzot · 1933

Kibbutz Dati (Religious) · 1934

Figure 3 out of 6: War, state foundation and breakup. Maximal historical density.

PANEL 3 OF 6

War, statehood, and rupture

1940 — 1967

Maximum historical density

CHRONOLOGY

1941	Palmach established in kibbutzim	*defense*
1943–45	Holocaust reports; war ends	*crisis*
1946–48	Negev settlement drive; partition	*settlement*
1948	Statehood and war	*statehood · defense*
1950–54	Postwar strain; movement fracture	*crisis*
1951	Meuhad split; Ihud formed	*rupture*
1954–67	Industrialization; consolidation	*economy*
1967	Six-Day War	*defense*

DEMOGRAPHY

1945	1948	1960s
349,000	~54,000	~77,000
dunams of land *held by kibbutzim*	members *at statehood*	members *≈3.5% of Jewish Israel*

MOVEMENT DEVELOPMENT

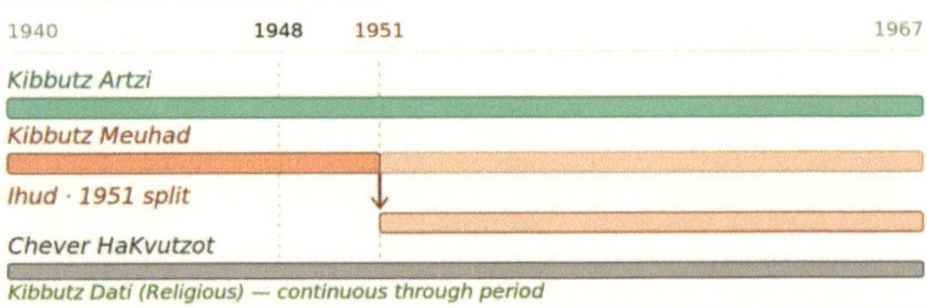

Figure 4 out of 6: Peak and crisis, 1968 – 1898. Social change and economic pressure.

Figure 5 out of 6: Renewal and differentiation, 1990 – 2026. Present structure.

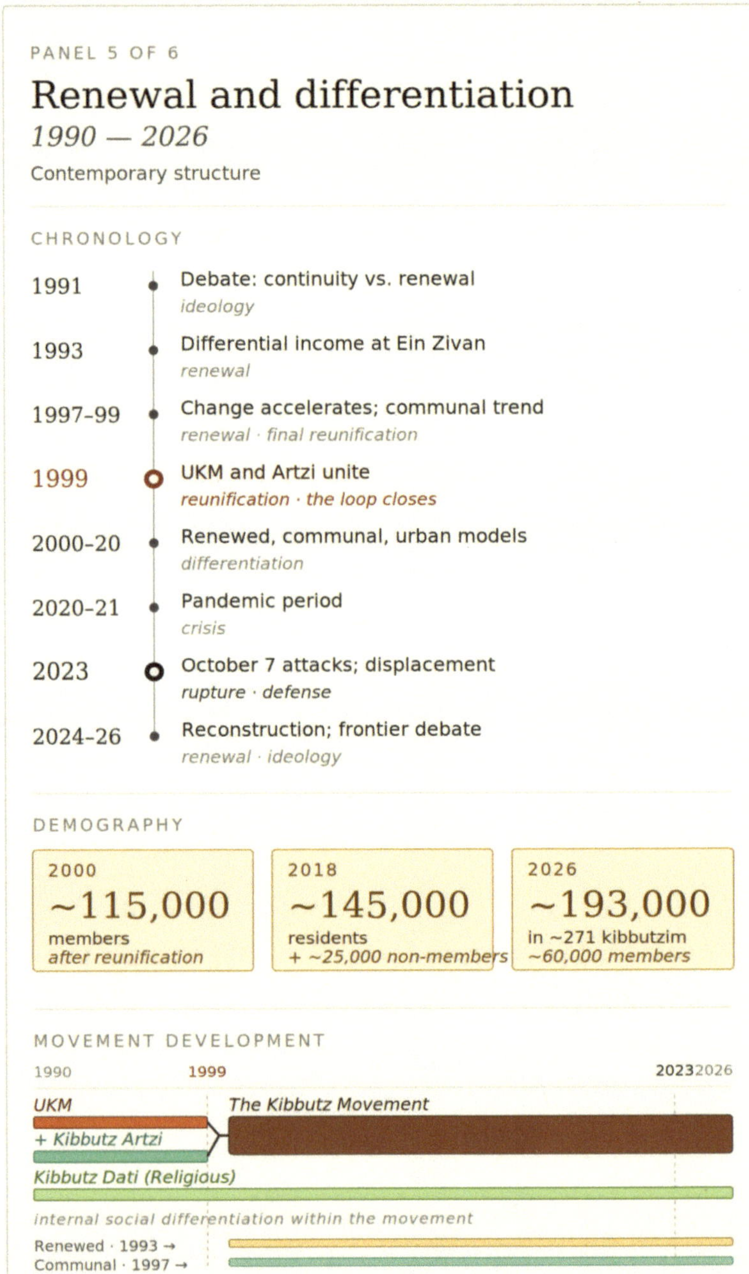

Figure 6 out of 6: The long bow, 1880 – 2026. Three movements over 146 years (synthesis).

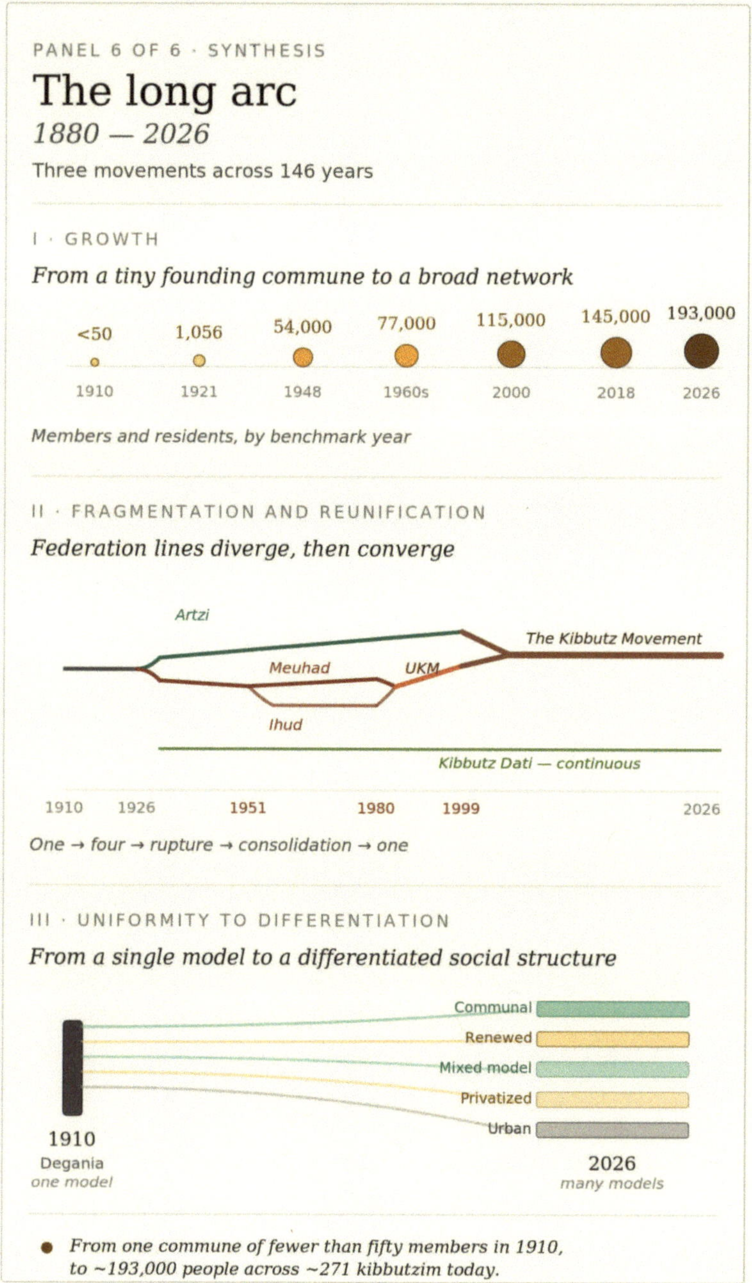

References

Abramitzky, R. (2018). *The mystery of the kibbutz: Egalitarian principles in a capitalist world*. Princeton University Press.

Absentees' Property Law, 5710–1950 (Isr.). https://main.knesset.gov.il/EN/About/History/Documents/kns1_property_eng.pdf

Adorno, T. W. (1998). Education after Auschwitz (H. W. Pickford, Trans.). In *Critical models: Interventions and catchwords* (pp. 191–204). Columbia University Press. (Original work published 1966)

Adorno, T., & Horkheimer, M. (2002). *Dialectic of enlightenment*. Stanford University Press. (Original work published 1944)

Agassi, J. B. (1989). Theories of gender equality: Lessons from the Israeli kibbutz. *Gender & Society, 3*(2), 160–186.

Arendt, H. (1958). *The human condition*. University of Chicago Press.

Arendt, H. (2020). *Vita activa or On the active life*. Piper Verlag.

Avrahami, E. (1996). A kibbutz dilemma: Social movement or self-interested group? *Journal of Rural Cooperation, 24*(1), 31–34.

Balberg, M. (2024). *Here on Earth: A history of the kibbutz*. eScholarship Publishing, University of California.

Bar Or, G. (2016). The founding contexts of kibbutz museums and the case of the Mishkan Museum of Art, Ein Harod. *Images, 9*(1), 105–117.

Ben-Rafael, E., & Shemer, O. (2020). *The metamorphosis of the kibbutz* (Vol. 49). Brill.

Ben-Rafael, E., & Topel, M. (2014). The kibbutz on ebbing waves. In M. Palgi & S. Reinharz (Eds.), *One hundred years of kibbutz life: A century of crises and reinvention*. Transaction Publishers.

Benvenisti, M. (2000). *Sacred landscape: The buried history of the Holy Land since 1948*. University of California Press.

Bröckling, U. (2007). *The entrepreneurial self*. Suhrkamp Verlag.

Brubaker, R. (1992). *Citizenship and nationhood in France and Germany*. Harvard University Press.

Chinski, S. (1994). Debate "The silence of the fish": Theoretical clarifications. *Theory & Criticism, 5*, 187–190. (in Hebrew)

Davidovitch, L., Heilbrunn, S., & Polovin, A. (2009). Impact of change in the kibbutz on risk taking of entrepreneurs. *Journal of Rural Cooperation, 37*(2), 242–260.

De Beer, P., & Koster, F. (2009). *Sticking together or falling apart?: Solidarity in an era of individualization and globalization*. Amsterdam University Press.

Delano, S.F. (2004). Brook Farm: The Dark Side of Utopia. Cambridge: Harvard University Press.

Dichter, S. (2022). *Sharing the promised land*. eBookPro Publishing.

Doubrawa, E. (1998). The politics of the I–Thou: Martin Buber, the anarchist. *The Anarchist Library*. https://theanarchistlibrary.org/library/erhard-doubrawa-the-politics-of-the-i-thou

Epstein, Y. (1907). She'ela ne'elama [The hidden question]. *Ha-Shiloach, 17*.

Fetzer, T., & Ghorashi, H. (2025). *Sociologies in dialogue*. SAGE.

Forman, G., & Kedar, A. (2004). From Arab land to "Israel lands": The legal dispossession of the Palestinians displaced by Israel in the wake of 1948. *Environment and Planning D: Society and Space, 22*(6), 809–830.

Fromm, E. (1976). *Tohave or to be?* Harper & Row.

Fulbrook, M. (1999). *German national identity after the Holocaust*. Polity Press.

Gavron, D. (2000). *The kibbutz: Awakening from utopia*. Rowman & Littlefield.

Gibson, J. L., & Gouws, A. (2003). *Overcoming intolerance in South Africa: Experiments in democratic persuasion*. Cambridge University Press.

Giddens, A. (1984). *The constitution of society: Outline of the theory of structuration*. University of California Press.

Glass, A. (2025). *Nahal Oz: Enduring strength of a multigenerational community*. INSS–Samuel Neaman Institute for National Policy Research.

Gordon, A. D. (1973). *Selected essays by Aaron David Gordon*. Arno Press.

Gordon, A. D. (n.d.). Labour and the natural world. In J. Horrox (Ed.), *Political philosophy*. https://jameshorrox.com/writing/a-d-gordon/

Graeber, D., & Wengrow, D. (2021). *The dawn of everything: A new history of humanity*. Farrar, Straus and Giroux.

Greenberg, Z., & Heilbrunn, S. (2026). Multi-level solidarity in crisis response: Insights from Israeli kibbutz communities following 7 October 2023. *Israel Affairs*, 1–31.

Habib v. Minister of Defense, HCJ 64/51, 5 P.D. 1049 (1951).

Han, B.-C. (2010). *The society of fatigue*. Matthes & Seitz.

Heilbrunn, S. (2005). The impact of organizational change on entrepreneurship in community settings. *Journal of Small Business and Enterprise Development, 12*(3), 422–436.

Heilbrunn, S. (2008). Factors influencing entrepreneurial intensity in communities. Enterprising Communities: People and Places in the Global Economy, 2(1), 37–51.

Heilbrunn, S. (2010). Communities in processes of change: Comparative differences in entrepreneurial motivation. *International Journal of Innovation and Regional Development, 2*(2), 36–49.

Heilbrunn, S., Itzkovitch, Y., & Weinberg, C. (2017). Perceived feasibility and desirability of entrepreneurship in institutional contexts in transition. *Entrepreneurship Research Journal, 7*(4).

Illouz, E., & Sicron, A. (2023). *The emotional life of populism: How fear, disgust, resentment, and love undermine democracy*. Polity Press.

Jiryis, S. (1979). The Arabs in Israel, 1973–79. *Journal of Palestine Studies, 8*(4), 31–56.

Khalidi, W. (Ed.). (1992). *All that remains: The Palestinian villages occupied and depopulated by Israel in 1948*. Institute for Palestine Studies.

Kibbutz Movement. (2023, November). *Cooperative resilience: Kibbutz movement update* [Status report to the ICETT Plenary].

Komlosy, A. (2018). *Work: The last 1000 years* (J. K. Watson with L. Balhorn, Trans.). Verso.

Lamont, M., & Fournier, M. (Eds.). (1992). *Cultivating differences: Symbolic boundaries and the making of inequality*. University of Chicago Press.

Landauer, G. (1919). *Aufruf zum Sozialismus*. Cassirer.

Manor, R. (2004). The "renewed" kibbutz. *Journal of Rural Cooperation, 32*(1), 37–50.

Marx, K., & Engels, F. (2000). *The German ideology* (S. Ryazanskaya, Trans.; Marx/Engels Internet Archive). Marxists.org. https://www.marxists.org/archive/marx/works/1845/german-ideology/ (Original work written 1845–1846)

Mazzucato, M. (2013). *The entrepreneurial state: Debunking public vs. private sector myths*. Anthem Press.

Mazzucato, M. (2021). *Mission economy: A moonshot guide to changing capitalism*. Allen Lane.

Mendes-Flohr, P. (Ed.). (2019). *Where community happens: The kibbutz and the philosophy of communalism*. Academic Studies Press.

Müller, J. W. (2008). A general theory of constitutional patriotism. *International Journal of Constitutional Law, 6*(1), 72–95.

My Jewish Learning. (2017). *A.D. Gordon: The religion of labor*. https://www.myjewishlearning.com/article/a-d-gordon-the-religion-of-labor/

Near, H. (1986). I–Thou–We: Buber's theory of community and the kibbutz. *Economic and Industrial Democracy, 7*(3), 247–274.

Near, H. (1992). *The kibbutz movement: A history* (Vol. 1). Oxford University Press.

Near, H. (1997). *The kibbutz movement: A history* (Vol. 2). Oxford University Press.

Neumann, B. (2024). The gendered outcomes of organizational wage reforms. *Human Relations, 77*(10), 1–26.

Ofrat, G. (1993). *The Israeli Pavilion: Venice Biennale 1993*. La Biennale di Venezia.

Ofrat, G. (1994). Debate "The silence of the fish": Gulag in Ein-Shemer. *Theory & Criticism, 5*, 183–186.

Palgi, M., & Reinharz, S. (Eds.). (2011). *One hundred years of kibbutz life: A century of crises and reinvention*. Transaction Publishers.

Palgi, M., Sofer, M., & Heilbrunn, S. (2020). From work to livelihood: Employment and entrepreneurship in the kibbutz. In E. Ben-Rafael & O. Shemer (Eds.), *The metamorphosis of the kibbutz and after*. Brill.

Perlmutter, A. (1971). A. D. Gordon: A transcendental Zionist. *Middle Eastern Studies, 7*(1), 85–91.

Potok, C. (2015). Martin Buber and the Jews. *Commentary Magazine*. https://www.commentary.org/articles/chaim-potok-2/martin-buber-and-the-jews/

Rabinowitz, D. (1997). *Overlooking Nazareth: The ethnography of exclusion in Galilee* (No. 105). Cambridge University Press.

Ram, U. (2024). Hegemony struggles in Israel: 1920s–2020s. In T. Hermann (Ed.), *The Routledge handbook on Zionism* (pp. 505–519). Routledge.

Rescher, N. (1989). *Moral absolutes: An essay on the nature and rationale of morality*. Peter Lang.

Riemann, F. (2021). *Basic forms of anxiety* (46th ed.). Ernst Reinhard Verlag.

Russell, R., Hanneman, R., & Getz, S. (2013). *The renewal of the kibbutz: From reform to transformation*. Rutgers University Press.

Sandel, M. J. (2021). *The tyranny of merit*. Penguin Books.

Sennett, R. (1998). *The corrosion of character: The personal consequences of work in the new capitalism*. W. W. Norton.

Shafir, G., & Peled, Y. (2002). *Being Israeli: The dynamics of multiple citizenship*. Cambridge University Press.

Shapira, A. (2010, Summer). The kibbutz and the state. *Jewish Review of Books*.

Sharon, A. (2025). *Civil war: How unity is tearing us apart*. Radical Publishing House. (in Hebrew)

Spiro, M. E. (1979). *Gender and culture: Kibbutz women revisited*. Duke University Press.

Talmon-Garber, Y. (2020). The family in a revolutionary movement: The case of the kibbutz in Israel. In *Sociology of the kibbutz* (pp. 251–278). Routledge.

Tamir, T. (2022). *HaMeshutaf kibbutz: Art from the Left 1978–1988*. Yad Yaari; Bialik Institute.

Tiger, L., & Shepher, J. (1975). *Women in the kibbutz*. Harcourt Brace Jovanovich.

Tocqueville, A. de. (2000). *Democracy in America* (H. C. Mansfield & D. Winthrop, Trans.). University of Chicago Press. (Original work published 1835)

Tönnies, F. (1887). Gemeinschaft und gesellschaft. In *Studien zu Gemeinschaft und Gesellschaft: Herausgegeben von Klaus Lichtblau* (pp. 231–255). VS Verlag für Sozialwissenschaften.

Torney-Purta, J., Lehmann, R., Oswald, H., & Schulz, W. (2001). *Citizenship and education in twenty-eight countries: Civic knowledge and engagement at age fourteen*. International Association for the Evaluation of Educational Achievement.

Tsuk, N. (2005). *Community, state and utopia: A study of the Israeli kibbutz and the English garden city* [Doctoral dissertation, University of Cambridge].

Tsur, M. (2024). *The kibbutz after October 7* [Unpublished essay].

Varoufakis, Y. (2017). *Talking to my daughter about the economy: Or, how capitalism works—and how it fails*. Farrar, Straus and Giroux.

Welzer, H., Moller, S., & Tschuggnall, K. (2014). *"Opa war kein Nazi": Nationalsozialismus und Holocaust im Familiengedächtnis*. Fischer Verlag.

Williams, R. (1958). Culture is ordinary. In N. MacKenzie (Ed.), *Conviction*. MacGibbon & Kee.

Yacobi, H. (2009). *The Jewish-Arab city: Spatio-politics in a mixed community*. Routledge.

Yiftachel, O. (2006). *Ethnocracy: Land and identity politics in Israel/Palestine*. University of Pennsylvania Press.

Yizhar, S. (1958). *Yemei Tziklag* [The days of Ziklag]. Am Oved. (in Hebrew)

Zirkler, M. (2019). A blueprint for a life-affirming organisation. In D. Süss & C. Negri (Eds.), *Applied psychology*. Springer. https://doi.org/10.1007/978-3-662-58409-5_5

Glossary

Absentees' Property Law	Israeli Knesset legislation of 1950 (5710–1950) which placed in state custodianship all property whose owners had left or been displaced during the 1948 war. The legal architecture through which depopulated Palestinian land was transferred to the new state and from there leased or sold to existing and new kibbutzim and Jewish settlements.
admission committee	Kibbutz governance body that evaluates candidates for membership and recommends acceptance or rejection to the general assembly. Hebrew: va'ada.
aliyah / Aliyah	Hebrew term for Jewish immigration to the Land of Israel; literally "ascending." The numbered Aliyot (First, Second, and so on) refer to specific waves of immigration in modern Zionist history.
Anschluss	German for "connection" or "annexation." Refers in this book to Nazi Germany's annexation of Austria in March 1938, the formative event in the family history of several of the European-Jewish refugees whose paths led toward Palestine and the kibbutz movement.
Arab house, the	The stone house at the top of the Kibbutz Barkai grounds, and its structural analogues across kibbutzim founded on the land of former Palestinian villages. Ch. 9's recurring leitmotif for the prior inhabitation that kibbutz histories tend to remember and forget at the same time.
Ashkenazi Jews	Jews of Central and Eastern European origin; the dominant cultural group in the founding generations of the kibbutz movement.

batei yeladim Hebrew for children's houses: the dormitory-and-care institutions in which kibbutz children slept and were raised collectively under the communal-sleeping arrangement. Singular: beit yeladim.

Bedarkham Hebrew for "In Their Path." Late-1960s collective memorial volume conceived after the Six-Day War, intended as a movement-wide kibbutz reckoning that ultimately splintered along federation lines.

Bein Tzeirim Hebrew for "Among Youth." Post–Six-Day-War volume edited by Muki Tsur, Yariv Ben-Aharon, and Avishai Grossman, which called for unifying the kibbutz movements and breaking with the pro-Soviet orthodoxy of parts of the movement.

Beit Oren case (1999) High Court petition by eight members of Kibbutz Beit Oren to strip the community of its legal classification as a kibbutz on the grounds that differential salaries, the closed dining hall, and privatized education made the label inapplicable. The case forced a public reckoning that produced the 2002–03 Public Committee's reclassification into Kibbutz Shitufi and Kibbutz Mitchadesh.

Bnei Akiva The religious-Zionist youth movement; counterpart of the secular socialist Hashomer Hatzair. Cited as part of the religious right's continuous chain of formative institutions.

Chever HaKvutzot Federation of kibbutzim founded in 1929 around the Degania tradition. Favoured small, intimate kibbutzim modest in scale, declining the urge to grow into national instruments, and provided general humanistic education in regional schools.

communal sleeping vs. family sleeping Communal sleeping: children spend the night in the children's houses with peer groups and rotating night-watch carers. Family sleeping: children sleep at home with their parents and use the children's houses only for daytime education and care. The shift spread gradually from the 1970s and was completed in 1999.

comprehensive houses Muki Tsur's term for the architectural ensembles built in kibbutzim from the 1950s onward, in which children slept, ate, and studied under one roof. Designed so that the collective, rather than the private home, would be the child's primary world.

Degania The first kibbutz, founded in 1909/1910 on the southern shore of Lake Kinneret. Site of the earliest debates over gender, childcare, and the boundary between family and collective.

Diaspora word	Muki Tsur's analytical phrase for vocabulary that betrays the kibbutz's founding integration of spiritual purpose and productive labor by reverting to the Diaspora separation of livelihood and meaning. "Livelihood" is the paradigm case: a Diaspora word that re-entered kibbutz vocabulary in the mid-1980s.
Erinnerungskultur	German term for "culture of memory": the sustained, deliberate institutional and pedagogical work of remembering the Nazi past in post-war Germany. Introduced in Ch. 5 as the comparative frame for what value transmission across generations actually requires.
expansion neighborhood	Residential neighbourhood built on developed kibbutz land for people who are not members of the cooperative corporation. Non-member residents own their houses, pay community taxes, and share kibbutz facilities, but hold no voting rights and no claim on kibbutz assets. Legal basis: Israel Land Administration Resolution 737 (1995), replaced by Resolution 959 (2003).
Gdud HaAvoda (Work Battalion)	Hebrew for "labor brigade." Founded in 1920; a mobile, semi-militarised workers' unit that took on the heavy infrastructure labor of early Zionist settlement, from road-building to land-clearing. The unit that arrived in the Jezreel Valley after the 1920 Sursock land acquisition.
Gemeinschaft	German for "community." Ferdinand Tönnies's term for the intimate, durable, value-saturated form of social bond associated with village, kin, and shared moral horizon, set against its conceptual opposite, Gesellschaft. Invoked in Ch. 5 as part of the inherited European vocabulary the kibbutz drew on to imagine itself.
general assembly	The plenary decision-making body of a kibbutz, in which all members have a vote. Hebrew: asefa.
Gesellschaft	German for "society." Ferdinand Tönnies's term for the impersonal, contractual, instrumental form of social bond associated with the market and the modern city, set against Gemeinschaft. The pair frames Ch. 5's account of what the kibbutz sought to build and what it was set against.
Gevatron	Iconic singing ensemble from Kibbutz Geva, founded in 1948 and active for decades. Emblematic of the kibbutz movement's investment in choral music as a collective cultural form.

Gilead trajectory	Analytical figure derived from Margaret Atwood's The Handmaid's Tale (1985). Names the slow narrowing of the spaces in which civic, secular, plural, feminist life can be conducted (bank accounts, universities, newspapers, communities), rather than dramatic single-revolution rupture.
HaKibbutz HaArtzi	Federation of kibbutzim founded in 1927 under Meir Ya'ari and Yaakov Hazan. Required ideological collectivity, a shared political-Marxist worldview, as a condition of membership; held the most leftist orientation of the federations; ran educational institutions organized "as another kibbutz."
HaKibbutz HaMeuhad	Federation of kibbutzim founded in 1927 under Yitzhak Tabenkin's leadership. Advocated large kibbutzim open to absorbing newcomers, with diversified agriculture-industry economies, and a pedagogical philosophy of student contact with veteran pioneers. (Also rendered Kibbutz Meuhad.)
halutzim	Hebrew for pioneers. The founding generation of the kibbutz movement, particularly those who arrived during the Second and Third Aliyot and built the early kvutzot.
Hamama	Hebrew for "The Greenhouse." Avital Geva's long-running conceptual-and-agricultural project at Kibbutz Ein Shemer, begun in 1977. A working greenhouse that doubled as an open-ended educational and artistic experiment.
Hand in Hand	Network of bilingual, integrated Jewish–Arab schools in Israel, founded in 1997. Aims to enact institutionally the possibility of a more equal Jewish–Arab civic life by educating children of both communities together in Hebrew and Arabic. Shuli Dichter led the organization in the years following his work at Sikkuy.
Hanita	A kibbutz established in 1938 in northern Palestine, on the Lebanese border. Invoked by Muki Tsur as part of the "Hanita and Madrid" dilemma between building new settlements in Palestine and joining the fight for the Spanish Republic.
Hanoar Ha'oved	Israeli youth movement founded in 1924, associated with the labour-Zionist (Mapai) wing of the kibbutz and labour movement; its members wore a red shoelace. Distinguished from Hashomer Hatzair (white shoelace, Marxist-Zionist orientation).
Hashomer Hatzair	Socialist-Zionist youth movement founded in Eastern Europe, central to the kibbutz movement and to the federation HaKibbutz HaArtzi. Members wore a white shoelace; the parallel labor-Zionist youth movement Hanoar Ha'oved wore a red.

Hesder yeshivot Religious-Zionist yeshivot that combine intensive Torah study with high-commitment military service, typically in combat units. A central institution of the religious-Zionist educational ecosystem discussed in Ch. 5.

Homa u-Migdal Hebrew for "wall and tower." A rapid-settlement technique developed in the mid-1930s during the Arab Revolt and used through the 1939–1948 period: a complete kibbutz core assembled in a single day, often overnight, to establish a fait accompli on the ground.

Kabbalat Shabbat Hebrew Friday-evening ritual welcoming the Sabbath. In Ch. 10, the gatherings held by the Nahal Oz Community Across Generations during the months of displacement function as one of the symbolic forms through which a dispersed community held its ritual life together.

Kibbutz Mitchadesh The "Renewed Kibbutz": a legal classification codified in 2003 (alongside Kibbutz Shitufi) on the recommendation of the Public Committee of 2002–03. The classification explicitly permits differential salaries among members, allocation of apartments, and allocation of production means, provided that mutual guarantee and a basic safety net are preserved.

Kibbutz Shitufi The "Communal Kibbutz": a legal classification codified in 2003 (alongside Kibbutz Mitchadesh) preserving the traditional communal model (no differential salaries among members, no privatized housing) with members holding the kibbutz's assets in common through the cooperative corporation.

koulak Russian for peasant-proprietor. Used by the halutzim to name the consciousness of private ownership they aimed to refuse.

kvutza Early small, intimate communal settlement; precursor to the kibbutz. Plural: kvutzot.

Lebensreform German social and cultural movement (late-nineteenth to early-twentieth century) advocating natural living, vegetarianism, body culture, and reform of everyday life in response to industrialization. An influence on the European intellectual world from which the early halutzim came.

Mechinot Pre-military preparatory programs (literally "preparatory schools") in which Israeli high school graduates spend a year or more before army service. The religious-Zionist mechinot are ideologically intensive; secular versions also exist.

Metzer–Meiser	1972 conceptual-art project staged at the junction between Kibbutz Metzer and the Palestinian village of Meiser. Among the earliest deliberately conceived shared Jewish–Arab artistic spaces in Israel.
Mevo'ot Iron	Regional school in the Wadi Ara area where Avital Geva taught; one of the institutional homes of the Hamama.
mezuzah	A small parchment scroll inscribed with biblical verses, placed in a decorative case affixed to the doorpost of a Jewish home. In Ch. 5, the demand by a Haredi Mizrahi mother for a mezuzah on the children's-house door becomes emblematic of the kibbutz's weakened capacity to define a shared educational horizon.
Mishkan	The Mishkan Museum of Art at Kibbutz Ein Harod, founded by Haim Atar in 1934 and given its permanent building (architect Samuel Bickels) in 1948. The first art museum in any rural settlement in Israel.
mission fatigue	Kadish Luz's phrase (post-1948) for the structural exhaustion experienced by the kibbutz movement after its founding pioneering tasks (settlement, defence, immigrant absorption) had been absorbed by state institutions, and the movement had not yet identified a new vocation.
Mizrahi Jews	Jews of Middle Eastern and North African origin (literally "Eastern").
moshav	A cooperative Israeli agricultural community where families maintain their own households and farms while sharing marketing and other services. Plural: moshavim.
Nahal	Hebrew military framework (founded 1948) combining military service with pioneering settlement. Many kibbutz members served their initial military years in Nahal units.
Nakba	Arabic for "catastrophe." The Palestinian term for the displacement of the 1948 war, in which approximately 700,000 Palestinians fled or were expelled and some 400 villages were depopulated, the same events that the Jewish-Israeli narrative names the War of Independence.
Nomadic Kibbutz	Programme through which agricultural labor was redistributed across the country after October 7: members of evacuated kibbutz communities continued their work (crop tending, fish farming, cattle care) at host sites that absorbed both the people and their professions.

religion of labor Aaron David Gordon's signature concept, elevating physical agricultural work from economic necessity to spiritual imperative. Central to Gordon's vision and to the kibbutz's founding ethos. Introduced in Ch. 2 and fully developed in Ch. 6.

Second Aliyah The wave of Jewish immigration to Ottoman Palestine between roughly 1904 and 1914, whose pioneers established the first kvutzot and laid the ideological foundation of the kibbutz movement.

shelanu Hebrew for "ours" or "what is ours." The kibbutz tradition's term for the collectively held and collectively controlled, the means of production, the assets of the community, the shared life of the place. In Ch. 8 it functions as the keyword for the kibbutz's claim that the factory or enterprise belongs to the community; the post-privatization question of what the word still means recurs in Ch. 12.

shiva The seven-day Jewish mourning period observed after the death of a close relative. In Ch. 5, "parting in shiva" refers to parents who ritually mourned their pioneering children as if they had died upon leaving for Palestine.

Shomria Shared high school of four kibbutzim in the Jezreel Valley (Emek Yizrael). Imagined by its founders as a "republic of youth": a training ground for self-governing socialist citizens, in which adolescents ran committees, debates, and work assignments under minimal adult intervention.

Siach Lohamim Hebrew for "Soldiers' Talk"; published in English as The Seventh Day. The late-1960s volume of open conversations with kibbutz combatants returning from the Six-Day War, edited by Avraham Shapira and a team including Muki Tsur. A defining document of the kibbutz movement's post-1967 self-examination.

Sikkuy Israeli civil society organization, founded in 1991, dedicated to advancing Jewish–Arab equality in citizenship through policy advocacy, municipal cooperation, and public campaigning. Shuli Dichter served as its co-executive director for a decade.

TaKaM Acronym (from Ha-Tnua HaKibbutzit HaMeuhedet, "the United Kibbutz Movement") for the federation formed in 1981 by the merger of HaKibbutz HaMeuhad and Ihud HaKvutzot VeHaKibbutzim. Often read as a defensive consolidation against the kibbutz movement's post-1977 political delegitimization.

urban kibbutzim	Recent form of kibbutz whose principal occupation is education rather than agriculture or industry. Founded in many cases by youth-movement graduates and children of kibbutzim seeking small, liberal, engaged forms of communal life with deep involvement in the surrounding society.
Volcani Institute	Israel's principal agricultural-research institute, founded in 1921. The Hamama's institutional research partner.
Wandervogel	German youth-movement tradition (early twentieth century) associated with hiking, romanticism, and the rejection of industrial modernity. An influence on European intentional-community thinking and on the cultural world from which the early halutzim came.
yeshivot	Jewish religious academies devoted to the study of Talmud and rabbinic literature. In contemporary Israel, the term covers a range of institutions from ultra-Orthodox Lithuanian-style yeshivot to the religious-Zionist Hesder yeshivot. Singular: yeshiva.
Yom Kippur	The Jewish Day of Atonement; a day of fasting and reflection observed annually in autumn. Mentioned in Muki Tsur's recollection of secular kibbutz members keeping a list of those who ate on the day "because of their conscience."
Youth Aliyah	Programme that brought some fifteen thousand Jewish children to Palestine between 1946 and 1948, two-thirds of whom were placed in kibbutzim. For these children, the kibbutz successfully functioned as a substitute for the biological family that had been destroyed.